CRIME AND COMMUNITY IN REFORMATION SCOTLAND: NEGOTIATING POWER IN A BURGH SOCIETY

Perspectives in Economic and Social History

Series Editor: *Andrew August*

Titles in this Series

FORTHCOMING TITLES

Policing Prostitution, 1856–1886: Deviance, Surveillance and Morality
Catherine Lee

Respectability and the London Poor, 1780–1870: The Value of Virtue
Lynn MacKay

Narratives of Drunkenness: Belgium, 1830–1914
An Vleugels

Mercantilism and Economic Underdevelopment in Scotland, 1600–1783
Philipp Robinson Rössner

Residential Institutions in Britain, 1725–1950: Inmates and Environments
Jane Hamlett, Lesley Hoskins and Rebecca Preston (eds)

Conflict, Commerce and Franco–Scottish Relations, 1560–1713
Siobhan Talbott

Consuls and the Institutions of Global Capitalism, 1783–1914
Ferry de Goey

CRIME AND COMMUNITY IN REFORMATION SCOTLAND: NEGOTIATING POWER IN A BURGH SOCIETY

BY

J. R. D. FALCONER

Routledge
Taylor & Francis Group

LONDON AND NEW YORK

First published 2013 by Pickering & Chatto (Publishers) Limited

Published 2016 by Routledge
2 Park Square, Milton Park, Abingdon, Oxfordshire OX14 4RN
711 Third Avenue, New York, NY 10017

First issued in paperback 2015

Routledge is an imprint of the Taylor & Francis Group, an informa business

BRITISH LIBRARY CATALOGUING IN PUBLICATION DATA

Falconer, J. R. D.
Crime and community in Reformation Scotland: negotiating power in a burgh
society. – (Perspectives in economic and social history)
1. Crime – Scotland – History – 16th century. 2. Criminal behaviour – Scotland
– History – 16th century. 3. Scotland – Social conditions – 16th century. 4.
Crime – Scotland – Aberdeen – History – 16th century – Sources. 5. Criminal
Behaviour – Scotland – Aberdeen – History – 16th century – Sources. 6.
Aberdeen (Scotland) – Social conditions – 16th century – Sources.
I. Title II. Series
364.9'411'09031-dc23

ISBN-13: 978-1-138-66463-0 (pbk)
ISBN-13: 978-1-8489-3327-9 (hbk)
Typeset by Pickering & Chatto (Publishers) Limited

CONTENTS

ACKNOWLEDGMENTS

This book, like so many, has its origins in a PhD dissertation. As a doctoral student at the University of Guelph I received generous financial support from the Social Sciences and Humanities Research Council of Canada, the St Andrew's Society of Toronto, Frank and Cecily Watson and the Clan Ferguson. Without this support it would have been impossible to undertake the research in Scottish archives necessary to complete the dissertation. Since 2006 the Grant MacEwan University Research, Scholarly Activity and Creative Achievement Fund has provided a considerable amount of financial support that has helped me undertake research necessary to transform parts of the dissertation into the book. Like the dissertation, this book could only have been completed with the tremendous assistance I received from the archivists at the Aberdeen City Archives and the National Archives of Scotland. In particular, Judith Cripps, formerly head archivist at the Aberdeen City Archives, provided keen insight into the records, generous support and guidance. Thanks must also go to the librarians, archivists and staff at the University of Guelph Archives and Special Collections and the Grant MacEwan University Library who provided a friendly work environment. In Aberdeen, Angela and Terry Mulhern at the Adelphi Guest House provided an excellent place to stay while working in the archives; the Connors family opened their home to me while I was teaching in Ottawa to help support my family and my research; and my uncle, Lawrence Falconer, shared his home and provided much needed distraction during what was a very hectic time in my life. To all of them I am truly thankful!

From the earliest stages of my undergraduate and graduate studies through to the beginnings of my professional academic career I have relied on the kindness and generosity of many colleagues and friends. While the number of scholars who had a role in shaping my development as a historian is quite large, a few went above and beyond, directly and indirectly helping me to become the historian I am today. Ken Munro, John Langdon, Richard Connors, David Marples, Richard Reid, Greg Anderson, Matt Milner, Meg Cameron and Janay Nugent have been solid sources of support. Elizabeth Ewan supervised my PhD dissertation. Since first meeting her over fourteen years ago, Elizabeth has been incredibly generous with her time, knowledge and guidance and I have benefitted greatly from her as both a mentor and friend. Linda Mahood, also at the University of Guelph, has always been there to provide perspective, support and reassurance.

I also owe a great deal of gratitude to my colleagues at the University of Windsor where I first cut my teeth and at Grant MacEwan University where I continue to hone my skills as a university lecturer and historian. At MacEwan the Dean of Arts and Science, David Higgins, and the Associate Dean of Arts, Shahram Manouchehri, have expended a considerable amount of energy assisting me at every turn, while Judith Bode, Lisa Wylie and Valla McLean have provided ample administrative and logistical assistance. Every historian is aware of the great debt we owe to those scholars who came before us and who provide such a wealth of insight and understanding of the period we study. The individuals whose names fill the footnotes of this book are only slightly repaid through the acknowledgement they receive. I continue to be in awe of the amazing research that continues in the field of early modern social history!

Some of the material that appears in this book has benefitted from feedback received from colleagues who have heard snippets of the research delivered at conferences and public papers, or from anonymous reviewers who have offered incredibly useful feedback on the manuscript and on articles I have published. At the *Women and Crime in Britain and North America since 1500* conference held in Lyon, France in September 2008, Anne-Marie Kilday, James Sharpe, Neil Davie, Peter King, Krista Kesselring and John Carter Wood provided words of support and tremendous insights into legal traditions, gender and crime. At the *North American Conference on British Studies* held in Philadelphia (2005) and Baltimore (2010), Keith Wrightson, Steve Hindle, Paul Griffiths, Greg Smith, Susannah Ottaway, Andrea McKenzie and David Cressy shared with me their vast understanding of the early modern period and provided invaluable insights into the history of criminality and social relations. A number of the ideas presented in this book have appeared in articles already in print. In particular, I have explored the area of crime and gender in 'A Family Affair: Households, Misbehaving and the Community in Sixteenth-Century Aberdeen' in *Finding the Family in Medieval and Early Modern Scotland* edited by Janay Nugent and Elizabeth Ewan (Ashgate, 2008), pp. 139–50 and ' "Mony Utheris Divars Odious Crymes": Women, Petty Crime and Power in Later Sixteenth Century Aberdeen', in *Crimes and Misdemeanours: Deviance and the Law in Historical Perspective*, 4:1 (March, 2010), pp. 7–36. While there is some overlap in terms of viewing crime as part of the negotiation of power, the book develops more completely this idea.

My students, first at the University of Windsor, and currently at Grant MacEwan University, have pushed me to think more critically about patriarchy, household formations, criminality and religious influences on social reform. I am often inspired by their desire to learn and their willingness to see, as they should, the early modern world as both unique and yet strangely familiar. I have often joked with friends that the productivity we associate with medieval monks and scholars must surely have been a consequence of their cloistered lives. Yet, without friends and family to support, provoke, and inspire it would all be rather meaningless. To my parents, my sisters and their spouses, and my extended family I owe my continued love and gratitude. To my friends who have stuck by me as I moved from Rock Star to Historian and to those who were closest to me during the writing of the dissertation and start of my career, I will always remember the love and kindness. Ashley Sims helped with the database, constructed the bibliography, and kept me from vice and madness. Her contribution to this book and my life is immeasurable. But as is the case with most of us who labour in areas we love so much, we can often become so absorbed with the work that we become distracted from what matters most. For me, that is my daughter, Hannah, and son, Callum. As a small way of seeking their forgiveness for being too absorbed in my work at times I dedicate this book to them.

LIST OF FIGURES AND TABLES

INTRODUCTION: COMMUNITY, CONFLICT AND CONTROL

In the late evening of 4 October 1549, five sailors from Hamburg conducting trade in Aberdeen attacked a local man, William Portuis, disturbing the Scottish burgh 'under silence of the night'. It is not clear what precipitated the attack, but the court records indicate that the sailors violently assaulted Portuis, bound him, taunted him and carried him off to their ship 'without ony ordour of law or justice'.[1] What's more, the skipper's children stripped Portuis of his sword and bonnet while he was bound and powerless to defend himself. This physical assault combined with the verbal abuse he endured undermined the sense of security Portuis should have felt within the limits of the burgh. As the records make very clear, the attack also posed a direct challenge to the authority of the magistrates whose responsibility it was to insure the safety and welfare of the burgh's inhabitants. Furthermore, the humiliating act committed by the skipper's children underscored the depth of the victim's sense of powerlessness. Although it was likely that Portuis had the means to legally seek restitution for this attack through the burgh court, and that such action would have been welcomed by the magistrates, Portuis chose to act on his own, to right the wrong committed and to regain some of the power that was taken from him. Upon gaining his freedom from the ship, Portuis gathered some of his neighbours together and attacked the ship, throwing stones and assaulting the sailors in an act of retribution that served to restore to him what had been lost.

Although the crimes committed by the sailors (and by Portuis and his neighbours) were not felonies, to classify them as 'petty' trivializes what the contemporary clerk characterized as a violent offence to the Queen, the burgh and well-being of the burgh community.[2] We might also consider the actions of Isobell Gardiner who, in May 1566, destroyed a former provost of Aberdeen's garden. For her actions she was placed in the govis [pillory] with a paper crown on her head bearing an inscription that detailed her offence against her neighbour.[3] In choosing to destroy the garden, an act of retribution, Gardiner used what power she possessed to diminish her neighbour's ability to safeguard his property. Ultimately, the very public punishment Gardiner endured encouraged her neighbours to demonstrate their disapproval of such actions through taunts and jeers. The principle behind such punishments was that it would restore to the victim their honour, reputation and sense of security by making the broader community aware of the affront. However, there was also a restorative aspect to such punishments intended to benefit, in some way, the culprit. Once the punishment had occurred, order was to be restored to the community. In principle, this meant that wrongdoers were to be accepted back into civil society and not to be harmed or incur the lasting enmity of their neighbours. Yet, despite the belief that order was restored once the punishment had been met, many of the burgh's inhabitants regularly proved that their memories were long, and that such prescriptive regulation often failed to reduce conflict within the burgh.

Ten days before Christmas 1582, Helen Allan was convicted for 'mensweiring of hir self befoir the magistrate'.[4] While the immediate charge was for perjury, the account stressed that she had a lengthy history of criminal activities in the burgh. The account states that Allan had been 'accusit of & divers tymes vpon sic crymes as laid to hir charge be the session and ecclesiasticall magistrate' and she:

> being founding getine participant & madnis of ane theifteous buitht and barne in respect quairhof and mony utheris divars odious crymes committit be hir obefoir notefeit and knawin to the consale quhilkis are suppressit for the vilitie & odiousness thairof.[5]

The council determined that because of her criminality Allan should be banished from the town for a year and a day and that if she were found within the burgh limits, she was to be burned on the cheek. While the account of Allan's wrongdoing stands out for the language used to describe the seriousness with which the courts adjudged her actions, her activities provide a demonstrative example of the injurious nature of the petty crimes Aberdonians committed during the period under consideration. Ultimately, criminal activities, like those committed by Portuis, Gardner and Allan, and how they were punished (legally and extra-legally) represented an aspect of the negotiation of social power among those who called Aberdeen their home. Indeed, the court records highlight the fact that early modern societies were in a constant state of negotiation, what Keith Wrightson and others have referred to as the '"the constant jostling and realignments" to be observed in families and communities; the element of negotiation that infused so many relationships of power and authority'.[6]

Early modern concerns over social regulation, misbehaviour, criminal activity, marginalization and power and authority have lengthy historiographical traditions.[7] Increasingly, students of early modern Scottish history can find studies focused on the locales, the people who inhabited the countryside and burghs of the realm, and the issues that affected daily life – poverty, productivity and piety.[8] But while a few historians have examined the impact the Reformation had on social issues, and in particular regulation of behaviour, there have been very few full-length histories of crime in early modern Scotland.[9] This led Julian Goodare to conclude that in order to better understand the role of discipline in early modern Scotland 'what we need, therefore, are better comparative studies of the scope and effectiveness of religious and civil authorities, especially in the localities'.[10] This book aims to fulfill, in some part, this call for a comparative study of authority and power in the localities by examining the role misbehaviour played in defining social space and outlining the boundaries of inclusion and exclusion in the burgh of Aberdeen during the last half of the sixteenth century. It should also provide a starting point for filling the historiographical void suggested by Goodare.

This book examines the crimes tried in the burgh court of Aberdeen between *c.* 1541 and *c.* 1600, and the impact such crimes had on this burgh community during a period of significant religious, economic, social and political change. Over a period of roughly sixty years, the Aberdeen Council Register and Baillie Court Books recorded nearly 2,000 individual convictions for a variety of crimes that included property offences (theft, fraud, trespass, intromission, willful destruction), breaking the peace (physical and verbal assault, riot, 'strublance'), regulatory offences (statute breaking, regrating and forestalling, unlawful practice of crafts and sale of merchandise) and vice (fornication, adultery, breach of sabbath, recusancy, gambling and drunkenness). The accounts left behind shed light on the social interactions of a community at work, play and prayer and the regulatory systems in place that governed proper behaviour and attempted to instill in the inhabitants of the burgh the idea of 'good neighbourliness'.[11] A comparison of the accounts found in the St Nicholas Kirk Session records and Aberdeen's burgh court records reveals that the burgh's secular and spiritual authorities played an interconnected role in regulating behaviour and protecting what contemporaries called the 'common weal of the burgh'.

While the ideals of 'good neighbourliness' and the 'common weal' provided the ideological framework for regulating behaviour, crime challenged such prescriptive ideas enabling individuals, regardless of their social standing, to settle disputes, right wrongs and exercise power in informal, extra-legal ways. Frequently, criminal acts were a means of resolving conflict, asserting control and challenging the boundaries of normative society. The attempts made by individuals to illegally access the exclusive smaller communities within the burgh draws attention to the fact that competing visions of 'order', 'discipline' and 'belonging' drew members of burgh society into conflict. This book contends that through an analysis of criminal activities and enforcement of the burgh's laws and customs we can arrive at a better understanding of the community of the burgh of Aberdeen in the sixteenth century.

Historians who practice 'history from below' have demonstrated that early modern communities were rife with inequality in terms of wealth and formal political power.[12] Recent scholarship building on this perspective has in one way or another argued that inequality could also be measured by other factors such as gender, age, health, occupation, place of abode, religious conformity and adherence to the prescriptions of normative society.[13] While few question the hierarchical nature of early modern societies, it is becoming increasingly clear that binary models, rulers and ruled, superiors and subordinate, are too simplistic to offer any real insight into social relations in this period. As Steve Hindle argued nearly a decade ago, 'while inequalities of *wealth* and *status* are the usual starting points for most discussions of local social relations in early modern England, asymmetries of *power* tend to be implied rather than explored'.[14] Increasingly, historians are adopting the ideas of social theorists who have argued that *power* was more widely distributed and negotiated.[15] As such, 'the disadvantaged in early modern society navigated their way in a world which afforded many sources of influence to their more powerful contemporaries. But in negotiating their way around these potential dangers they did not lack negotiating powers of their own.'[16]

Social theorists, like Michael Mann, have defined 'power' as the 'generalized means' individuals employ for achieving their goals.[17] Historians who have adopted this definition, and apply it in purely political terms, tend to present power as the ability to coerce either through force or sanction.[18] Accordingly, they locate power most often in the state or in some other institution such as the law or the church. Such a definition, however, excludes the means that individuals use to achieve personal goals, goals that may not have far reaching consequences but impact their social structures nonetheless. Even those who have attempted to explore the deeper social meaning behind the exercise of power have employed binary models leaving out any proper discussion of the social relations/power dynamics among individuals of similar socio-economic groupings, gender or occupation. Such understanding of power, and its exercise, raises the question of whether the average sixteenth-century baxter, cordiner, miller's wife or merchant's daughter was able to exercise and negotiate power within their communities. If so, what was the nature of such power and through what means did they attempt to exercise this power to enhance their own social or economic standing in the community or to diminish the power other individuals in their community hoped to exercise?

If we cannot get away entirely from the notion of domination and subordination, especially if we accept Gramsci's ideas of hegemonic power, then, rather than seeing domination and subordination solely in socio-economic terms, it is more fruitful to look at how individuals across their own social groups exercised power as a means of affecting change in their own situation or their neighbour's.[19] To do so power needs to be viewed as something other than a quantifiable object, i.e. something individuals possess, and approach power as a process, or technique.[20] Thus, individuals with similar outlooks, occupying similar places within society worked to establish normative values that defined acceptable behaviour and worked to maintain their position, their networks and their relationships within that community. A clear example of this is the variety of activities magistrates undertook to regulate burgh society. But standing in contrast, or in relation, to this horizontal vision of power, or collective power whereby individuals jointly use the power available to them to control others, is the more vertical, or distributive power system that has one individual seeking to exercise power over another, that often led to competing visions of social space and the jostling for positions within society.[21]

If power is not to be quantified, or even objectified, and we therefore must not see it as something which is attainable, i.e. a goal or a thing to possess, should we continue to discuss power in terms of those who have it and those who do not? More importantly, can we continue to focus solely on power in the political sense of the word, relying on examples which only illustrate rulers and ruled, master and subordinate? Wrongdoing, while frequently caused by malcontents, must certainly have also been a means of affecting change in the community. Such changes may not have been long-lasting and most likely did not affect the entire community, though indeed in some cases they were and did have such consequences. Nonetheless, they impacted upon the lives of individuals as well as on social relations in the community. Collectively, wrongdoing helped to shape normative attitudes and helped to create ideas of what constituted neighbourly behaviour and what did not. Wrongdoing also constituted a direct challenge to the authority vested in the magistrates who governed the burgh or the laws in place to maintain the common weal. Indeed, property crimes, statute breaking, regrating and forestalling and open defiance of burgh officers and public nuisance often brought individuals into a negotiation of power – the power to affect order in the community. Most crimes brought before the burgh court involved multiple levels and participants or were, as Simon Gunn recently demonstrated, 'operative at multiple sites' in a negotiation that while outside the boundaries of formalised political power were actions which sought to bring about a change in the community regardless of how that change may be characterised.[22] In challenging the norms prescribed by the authorities and legitimated by the entire community, those individuals convicted of crimes negotiated the power structures and social space within their social settings.

Crime, Power and the Processes of Exclusion and Inclusion

Three decades ago James Sharpe surveyed what was at that time the burgeoning field of the history of crime and asserted its importance to social historians for understanding past attitudes towards social behaviour, law and order, criminal activity and social control.[23] Largely, such undertakings have been achieved by re-examining the materials used primarily by legal and economic historians. Yet, in so doing, Sharpe argued, historians of crime open themselves up to criticism from both legal and economic historians and other skeptics of social history in general.[24] Over a quarter of a century later, the skepticism has been superseded by the growing interest not only in the history of crime but the firmly entrenched place of social history within the discipline.[25] Perhaps one of the lingering concerns for historians examining crime and social order is the ability to define 'crime' in its contemporary context. Derived from the Latin *cernere* [to judge, discern] the English word 'crime' comes from the same Indo-European root as discriminate, critique and criteria.[26] The ideas these words conjure up make obvious the connection between criminality and the processes of inclusion and exclusion that ordered early modern communities.

Terminology and meaning roots itself in contemporary culture.[27] However, we must not be afraid to accept, when clearly illustrated, that some terms used in the past maintain their meaning across chronological divides constructed by modern commentators. Thus, an important task confronting historians is to remove presentist conceptions of crime and to demonstrate that culturally and temporally constructed attitudes determined whether or not specific activities were considered by contemporaries to be criminal. Failure to do so led Geoffrey Elton to reject on the one hand the equation of adultery and theft as similarly criminal while on the other asserting that theft and treason were 'real crimes'. The key for Elton was whether or not contemporaries placed all such activities in the same category.[28] Unintentionally, this line of thinking builds upon Durkheim's belief that social reality is in essence 'collective representation'.[29] The characteristics attributed to criminal activity may vary from culture to culture and over time. Thus, it is essential to determine contemporary typologies for crime and criminal activity in order to understand their impact on social relationships and structuring social order.

Perhaps the biggest distinction modern commentators make is between those crimes they have labelled 'real' or classified as 'heinous', and those 'misdemeanours', 'misconducts' and 'misbehaviours' that accounted for a larger number of cases brought before local authorities.[30] These latter categories modern historians tend to equate more closely with sin than with 'crime' and frequently situate alongside a concern with preserving social discipline. According to Cynthia Herrup, judges had the discretion to determine whether the accused was guilty of criminal activity or a lapse in judgment. As such, those individuals who possessed the 'attributes of neighbourliness' but temporarily fell from grace benefited from an 'operative definition of criminality', whereas those individuals who demonstrated the deadly sinfulness of sloth, greed and pride were more likely to find themselves on the receiving end of an enforced 'technical definition of criminality'.[31] In other words, magistrates were often in the position to determine whether or not those brought before them in the courts exhibited signs of repentance, signs which differentiated, in Herrup's words, 'criminals from mere offenders'. Such discretion allowed magistrates to determine punishments suitable for the criminal, not just the crime.

By the middle of the sixteenth century, the number of ecclesiastical and lay courts in Scotland numbered in the thousands.[32] Lenman and Parker concluded that each of these courts served a variety of functions and exercised their own jurisdictions but that in all of the courts the primary concern was the maintenance of 'social control'. They argued that felony crimes, murder, aggravated assault, abduction, robbery with violence, and bestiality were 'serious crimes' which were usually tried in the Justiciary courts or the King's High Court. Conversely, less serious offences were under the jurisdiction of the local authorities usually heard in the sheriff, burgh and baron courts.[33] The Aberdeen Council Register, Baillie Court Books and Guildry Accounts suggest that this was also the case for Aberdeen during the sixteenth century.

The accounts found in these records reflect a very pronounced concern that the sorts of crimes brought before the burgh court, what modern commentators would call 'petty crimes', posed a serious threat to the burgh's well-being. This underlying concern, rooted in the need to maintain stability and order within the community, suggests that while contemporaries recognized that there were various degrees of criminal action, *all* criminal actions were seen as serious threats to a well-ordered burgh community. In seeking to preserve the social order and restore individuals 'to the ordor of discipline',[34] burgh authorities acknowledged the fact that individual transgressions had an impact on social interaction, neighbourliness and the various 'dynamics of social relations' within the community. Such transgressions, and the community's involvement in punishing wrongdoing, enabled a greater number of the inhabitants to participate in defining and redefining social boundaries within the burgh. As such, the petty crimes committed within the burgh limits were not considered trivial nor countenanced by the magistrates or broader community.[35] On the contrary, while not the capital offence that murder, rape, arson and larceny were, contemporaries did not qualify the word 'crime' with the word 'petty' when discussing the impact assault, property destruction, statute breaking, regrating and forestalling, theft and reset, guild infractions, civil disobedience and ecclesiastical offences had on the community.

A voluminous historiography exploring the impact that crime and misbehaviour had on local communities in England and on the Continent has shed a great deal of light on both the structures of early modern societies and the nature of power and authority.[36] Susan Amussen has drawn attention to the connection between violence, legitimacy and power. Using Weber as a basis for understanding violence, Amussen highlighted the need to consider 'the ways violence underlies power, on the one hand, and may be a way of claiming power, on the other'.[37] In large part Amussen's argument rests on the idea that acts of violence were an 'area of contested meaning in early modern English society'. More importantly, during the early modern period 'violence was common, a part of the everyday vocabulary of social relations'.[38] In a similar vein Bernard Capp has demonstrated that arson functioned as a 'weapon' for settling disputes 'between neighbours of roughly equal standing, initially at all social levels, and sometimes by the strong against the weak'.[39] Sometimes just threatening to set fire to a home or business in retribution for some wrong or perceived wrong could bring about a resolution to the conflict at hand. According to Capp, such threats acted as a form of 'intimidation and an expression of frustrated rage'.[40] Not only did the act or the threat to act affect social interactions within the communities in which they occurred, the resulting consequences for both victim and perpetrator left an indelible imprint on the society in which they lived. Through such acts, the functions of the courts who tried those accused of committing arson, and the punishment of the perpetrators, there was a recognition that crimes could potentially alter the social structures that bound communities together.[41]

Increasingly historians have argued that crimes were not simply the actions of malcontents and ne'er do wells, but actions undertaken by those who were willing to challenge and redraw the boundaries established by normative values.[42] However, it is clear that it is impossible to make this claim for every criminal action committed in early modern societies. The simple fact that motivations can be difficult to detect in some criminal accounts suggests as much. We must also accept that the 'dark figure of unrecorded crime' often leaves the investigator to puzzle over the social meaning behind crimes committed by anonymous, faceless perpetrators whose victims were left without recourse to reciprocal violence or litigation. Such incidents must remain somewhat on the periphery of the examination of crime and its impact on society; any deductions and analyses of crime and punishment in this period must rely heavily on the available source materials that provide insight into the past. Bearing this in mind, investigations into the deeper social meaning behind criminal actions and the 'subtle ramifications' of social interactions among the members of society under consideration require the examiner to focus on the discernible impact recorded crimes had on the communities in which they were committed.

For example, individual conflict and individual wrongdoing could have a cumulative effect on society. This may be discerned from sudden changes in regulatory processes, a higher frequency of severe penalties being imposed or an overall shift in the political and social structures of the community. The agitation for greater enfranchisement by the town's craftsmen in the 1570s and 1580s provides one of the best examples of this occurring in sixteenth-century Aberdeen. Through extensive and continuous statute breaking and by usurping the

privileges afforded to members of the merchant guildry, the craftsmen sought to
alter the boundaries that excluded them from wider participation in the burgh's
political and economic spheres. The eventual redefinition of burgh politics
outlined in the Common Indenture of 1581 and the collapse of the Menzies'
control over the burgh underscores a negotiation process whereby one group
sought to settle the matter through wrongdoing and another group responded
through litigation and eventually through compromise. The overall cumulative
impact individual transgressions could have within the community is also apparent in the examples of statute breaking committed by the brewsters, baxters and
fleshers in the burgh. Through the contravention of burgh ordinances regulating
the prices and the quality of foodstuffs sold at the markets, these individuals
sought to bring about a change. That their actions resulted in a reinforcement of
burgh authority on the matter and eventually a gradual change in the legislations
reflects the negotiation process.[43]

Another area that underscores such a process is the involvement of cautioners, suretors and lawborrows to ensure the return to proper behaviour of, or the
fulfillment of prescribed penalties by, those convicted of crimes ranging from
adultery to assault. By agreeing to such terms the convicted party (and their guar-
antor) accepted the outcome of a negotiation between the courts and themselves
for the redressing of wrongs committed within the community. Such actions
resemble the oath of binding over that was pervasive in early modern English
society. Steve Hindle has examined the 'quasi-formal processes of dispute settlement' in early modern English society and has argued that:

> binding over....acted as a non-aggression pact, initially precluding any further physical
> self-assertion, and subsequently allowing a cooling off period during which negotia-
> tion, either informally (through mediation) or 'quasi-formally' (through arbitration),
> might restore disputing parties to the condition of charity.[44]

While mediation and arbitration were sites of negotiation, so too were public
punishments. As Peter King has argued for eighteenth-century England, public
punishments used by local authorities to 'reinforce the legitimacy of the law in
the eyes of the poor as well as to demonstrate its power' became a contested site
whereby the 'counter-theatre of the crowd and of the condemned could turn
almost all these points in the judicial process into site of contest and negotiation'.[45] The denial of accusations by the accused, the involvement of witnesses,
the imposition of penalties that individuals may or may not refuse to meet, the
requirement of the community, and the injured party in particular, to accept
the act of forgiveness by the wrongdoer all hint at the way in which crimes *could*
function as part of a negotiation process.

This of course does not mean that all criminal acts or every form of regulation functioned in such a manner. The negotiation of social power model has

limited value for understanding crimes committed by individuals who did not
end up before the courts or who did not enter into a process for settling the
dispute with their victims – either through some form of retribution or restoration.[46] Any limitation, however, stems from the difficulty in determining the
characters involved and the inability to determine the victim's role in the process
in unrecorded crimes or crimes where the transgressor was unknown. Yet, the
transgressors' attempt to exercise power through crime may still be detected.[47]
Inevitably, without litigation, reciprocal violent behaviour, mediation, punishment or restoration, the matter remained unresolved. As such, no negotiation
can have taken place. Nonetheless, in such instances power remains at the heart
of the action and the attempt to restructure normative society through a breach
of proper behaviour reveals the nature of the act committed.

That demonstrations of power through criminal acts represented attempts
at redefining social space and the reallocation of social power should be obvious from the context of the specific conflict under consideration. Chapters 4
and 5 demonstrate that while there were obvious differences between transgressions committed against non-elite inhabitants of the burgh and coordinated
acts of disobedience towards authority figures, the process of diminishing the
victim's social power for the purpose of increasing the transgressor's was similar.
In most instances, the immediate unspecified intention, or at least the immediate impact, behind wronging one's neighbour was to disadvantage them and to
benefit one's self. However, individual transgressions could have a wider effect
on the community. That contemporaries perceived crime in this way is clear in
the accounts mentioned above on p. 7 in which the clerk evoked the threat posed
to the burgh's wellbeing. The same can be said for those accounts in which the
clerk referred to interpersonal disputes that culminated in public acts of verbal
or physical violence as 'strubling [disturbing] the town'. The implicit meaning
behind such designations was that the wider community had been affected by
the individual wrongdoing. In this way, regardless of whether or not a negotiation took place, crimes could have a deeper social meaning in that they
undermined established authority, affected the wider community by potentially
inviting God's wrath into the burgh, contravened accepted codes of conduct and
altered the boundaries that delimited civil society.

An investigation into the impact petty crimes had on a burgh community
reveals that they also played a part in the processes that determined inclusion in,
and exclusion from, burgh society. Through an examination of the way in which
individuals wronged their neighbours, it is possible to see how both their actions,
and the consequences of those actions, put them outwith the community. The
act of exclusion could take many forms. The most basic and obvious of these was
banishment from the burgh. Although frequently used as a deterrent to prevent
recidivism, a number of individuals suffered banishment for a short period of

time, usually a year plus one day. It is difficult to determine the principle behind such a short period of exile. Did magistrates hope such wrongdoers would take up permanent residence elsewhere and thus become the problem of some other community? If so, why not make the banishment of these malcontents permanent? The legislation against vagabonds that appeared in the Acts of Parliament in the sixteenth century suggests that there was broad concern about the behaviour of 'rootless' and idle folk. In cases where the authorities determined that the individual posed a considerable threat, or where they had a lengthy record of wrongdoing, magistrates did order their permanent removal from the burgh. However, for the most part, magistrates rather infrequently imposed either form of banishment in Aberdeen. As I argue in Chapter 2, the magistrates saw banishment as a final option to be employed only in situations where they determined a significant threat to the community's well-being. This, as in many other areas of regulating behaviour and imposing punishments, underscored the distinctions between 'technical' and 'operative' definitions of criminality.[48]

Not every individual with a lengthy conviction record found themselves banished from the town. With the exception of petty theft,[49] crimes committed within the burgh did not determine the penalty the court imposed. Often, the individual convicted of the crime or the circumstances surrounding the events had a greater impact on determining punishment. There was, to a large extent, a very subjective element to establishing the appropriate measure of restorative or regulatory punishment. Some individuals within the community, such as John Duncan, Besse Barcar or James Bannerman, cheated the town, disobeyed the magistrates and verbally and physically assaulted their neighbours on a fairly regular basis, yet managed to live out the rest of their lives within the physical and social boundaries of the burgh.[50] In subsequent chapters I argue that the very infrequent use of banishment as a punishment combined with the relatively moderate approach to treating recidivism suggests that the magistrates were more inclined to restore individuals to proper codes of conduct than to remove them outright from the burgh. Conviction accounts of those banished permanently from the burgh give the impression that the court decided there was no hope for redemption and that as the individual was already outside the accepted boundaries of good neighbourliness, their physical removal from the burgh was a natural progression. In April 1547 the burgh magistrates determined that Alexander Troup, his wife, bairns and servants were to be removed from the burgh 'perpetually'.[51] Interestingly enough, the account is silent on why Troup and his family had incurred such a punishment. The fact that the authorities reserved such penalties for offenders they deemed unredeemable suggests that Troup's offence had been serious.[52] However, as was the case with Duncan, Barcar and Bannerman, there were other means of exclusion within the community.

Chapters 2 and 5 demonstrate that removal from smaller communities within the burgh served such a function. For disobedience, statute breaking or continuous wrongdoing within the community individuals were often banned from practising their craft or exercising their rights as a merchant. The phrase, 'to have tynt [lost] thair fredome', found in many of the extant records for Aberdeen during this period, generally indicates that the court determined this type of exclusionary process to be an appropriate penalty for wronging the community. The potential loss of livelihood, respect in the community, or ability to contribute to the economy of the burgh as well as the removal of the social bonds shared between members of the incorporated crafts or the merchant guildry highlights the sense of exclusion inherent in this form of punishment. Again, loss of freedom could be short term or more permanent. While status may have played a role in making such determinations, the infrequency with which clerks indicated the offender's social standing makes it impossible to come to any definitive conclusion on that matter.

By far the most common process of exclusion and inclusion within the burgh stemmed from public displays of humiliation, often in the form of acts of penance/repentance. This was a rather circular process: individuals who wronged their neighbour or the entire community excluded themselves through their actions, faced further exclusionary measures through some form of penalty, then through the payment of a fine, performance of public penitential acts or through warding began a process where they were re-introduced to the community and, in the words of one contemporary account, 'restored to the ordor of discipline'.[53] In 1541 the burgh court convicted Jonet Paterson for taking Margaret Smyth's cloak. For her offence, the court ordered Paterson to appear before the entire community in the parish kirk and to ask Smyth for forgiveness and 'pay ii poundis vax to the halyblud lycht'.[54] In this way, Paterson was to repair the damage done and to atone for offending the community, the injured party and God. Through this action Paterson would be able to rejoin the community. Interestingly enough, Paterson had been convicted only four days earlier for 'strubling' Katherine Anderson.[55]

Occasionally the records indicate that convicted parties refused to pay their fines, perform their acts of repentance or physically remove themselves from the burgh; however, there are numerous references in the court records to individuals ignoring the sanctions put on their working at their craft or using the rights of the merchant guild. Here, perhaps, we see the clearest examples of individuals continuing to negotiate their social power and redefining their social space. For their efforts, those convicted generally received fines and strict admonitions to respect the boundaries established within the community for maintaining a well ordered and disciplined society. It is fairly safe to presume that a significant number of individuals engaging in this activity escaped notice or somehow managed to avoid being brought before the magistrates. These individuals managed to expand their social space and power by challenging the accepted boundaries that governed inclusion in the smaller communities that made up burgh society.

Likewise, through the contravention of statutes and ordinances passed by the town council, individuals challenged the prices of goods to be sold at the market and the privilege to produce or sell items within the town limits. They also attempted to redefine the boundaries regulating social power and governing burgh politics.[56] As well, property crimes, petty thefts and unruly public behaviour flaunted accepted norms, circumvented individual freedoms and liberties, challenged their victim's own social power and threatened the community's stability. When these acts were committed 'under silence of the night'[57] they underscored the victim's vulnerability and undermined the sense of security that living within the boundaries of the burgh community provided. This certainly was the case when John Fraser struck Margaret Paterson 'in hir awn hous vnder silens of the nycht' stealing a number of her belongings before he made his departure.[58] The notion that such activities disturbed the peace or were committed under the shroud of secrecy also shines through in the account of Andrew Forbes' conviction for disobeying the baillies. Forbes, a local merchant who may have had a previous run-in with the magistrates,[59] was charged with the 'bigging and erecting of ane littill hous on the northsyd of the kirkyard … vnder silens of nicht the samen hous being demolishit obefoir be virtew of ane ordinans of this consell'.[60] The account makes clear the court's concern that Forbes had disregarded their authority, challenged the officers and workmen who had been ordered to oversee the destruction of Forbes' house and contravened burgh statutes. This supports the idea that members of the community perceived their actions as having the potential to challenge the power structures within the community. In these ways, crime and punishment reveal a very real negotiation of social power within the burgh community.[61]

Crimes and the Burgh Court

The burgh court, held in the tolbooth, was the site where the council promulgated statutes and ordinances and where the baillies implemented justice.[62] In the middle ages, courts tended to be held outdoors within the close proximity of a local stronghold or castle. By the fifteenth century, the burgh tolbooth began to house secular courts. In sixteenth-century Aberdeen, the tolbooth was located within the market square to the south-west of the site of the castle, directly across from the market cross. As the principal site of burgh governance, its central location and proximity to the market provided symbolic reference to the authority of the burgh magistrates who regulated the market and presided over the community's activities. The tolbooth also conveniently served as a meeting place for the burgh council – an advisory committee 'representand the

haill town' generally dominated by wealthy merchants 'chosen, together with the
provost and four Baillies' who were to 'treat concerning the common business'
of the burgh.[63] Before proceeding to the next chapter, it is necessary to discuss
briefly the functions of the burgh court whose job it was to uphold the laws
governing civil society.[64]

The burgh court had jurisdiction over all causes raised in the burgh excepting
those reserved to the four pleas of the crown: murder, rape, arson and robbery.[65]
As well, jurisdiction fell to the baillies within the burgh rather than the council
at large.[66] The town's burgesses attended Head Courts held three times a year at
Michaelmas, the Monday after Epiphany (6 January) and the Monday following
Easter, where they heard statutes regulating the community read out to them
and where, at the Michaelmas Head Court, they participated in the election of
burgh officials. In Aberdeen, more frequent sittings of the magistrates occured at
courts known as the *curiae legales* and the *curia tentae per ballivos*. At the *curiae
legales*, burgh officials fixed the price of bread and ale as well as carried out the
regular business of the court – cases of debt, property transactions, guild membership and criminal suits. As Flett and Cripps pointed out in their description
of the Council Register, most of the court's time was occupied with civil actions
concerning property. However, the baillies' court also bore the responsibility of
trying individuals charged with committing non-felonious crimes in the burgh.

According to Balfour, in the sixteenth century criminal jurisdiction in the
burgh maintained the provisions outlined in the *Leges Burgorum*.[67] This meant
that cases of physical and verbal assault, breaking of local statutes, property
crimes, regrating and forestalling, petty thefts, reset, civil disobedience, adultery,
fornication, drunkenness and all other acts contravening proper behaviour within
the burgh fell within the baillies' jurisdiction. Walker has demonstrated that the
procedure of the burgh court followed that of the baron courts: 'attendance of
suitors, fencing the court, summons of the defender executed by the serjeant,
selection of the assize or inquest, and decision announced by the dempster.'[68]
Occasionally, the court records indicate penalties prescribed for transgressions
committed in the burgh. However, many of the accounts indicate that the convicted party was amerced and that modification of their penalties would occur at
a later sitting of the court. The accounts offer no insight into the physical space
that occupied the burgh court in Aberdeen other than references to the tolbooth
or 'counselhous'. For example, the Guildry Accounts record expenses paid for
the upkeep of the tolbooth though none specifically refer to monies spent fur-
nishing the chamber where the court was held.[69]

There were clearly designated areas where persons brought before the court
stood. The 'outer bar' was where individuals called before the magistrates presented their case, responded to questioning, gave testimony and heard the judges'
pronouncements. Both pursuers and defendants alike were not to approach the

outer bar until called and to remove themselves in as reverent a fashion possible once their reason for being in the court was complete. Misbehaving at the bar often resulted in fines, public punishments including being placed in the govis [stocks] and possibly banishment from the burgh. The 'inner bar' was where the provost, baillies, council and court clerk sat; no one except the officers of the court were to 'enter within the inner bar'. Procurators [legal representatives] were to stand at the back of the inner bar and plead their case.

As many of the conviction accounts found in the extant records suggest, the proceedings often included the questioning of the defendant who would then either plead their innocence or admit their guilt. If the defendant denied the charge, often an assise, after hearing the testimony of witnesses called before the court, would determine the accused party's guilt. Once convicted the court would determine the appropriate penalties and act to impose sanctions almost immediately. Occasionally, as was the case with Margaret Blak in May 1581, the court required the convicted party to pay their fine before leaving the tolbooth.[70] More often, the court required the convicted party to set caution for their fines and for their return to good behaviour before they were allowed to leave the courtroom. A number of cases found in the Council Register and Baillie Court Books suggest that the court's pronouncement on individuals convicted of wronging the community could raise the ire of the defendant and their supporters. In cases where the court found individuals 'perturbing' or 'disturbing the court judiciallie' the magistrates imposed fines, acts of repentance or loss of freedoms within the burgh.

The court clerks kept records of the business transacted in the court. For the most part they noted the individuals involved, the matter brought before the court and the court's decision in the case. Occasionally, the clerk provided greater detail especially if the convicted party had previous dealings with the magistrates; for example, it is not uncommon to find references to previous convictions.[71] However, quite often the conviction accounts contain little reference to the social standing of the convicted party or indication of the motives behind their actions. From the court's perspective these factors do not seem to have been important. However, there seems to be some indication that the basic court minutes were to be expanded upon in more specific records held of other burgh officials. The similar accounts found in the Council Register and Baillie Court Books suggest that this was the case. Regardless, the records that have survived paint a clear enough picture of the various crimes committed in the burgh and the regulatory systems employed by the local authorities and the wider community for protecting the common weal of the burgh.

Accounts found in the St Nicholas Kirk Session records attest to the idea that the broader community participated in regulatory activities. For sixteenth-century Aberdeen it is difficult to speak of strictly defined secular and spiritual spheres as concerned power structures and social relations. For although there were processes within the kirk to regulate inclusion in the Christian community, very few Christian inhabitants of any Western European kingdom would have claimed to not belong to the *corpus christianum*.[72] The fact that Scottish burghs did not have multiple parishes until after the Reformation made the corporate identity of burgh communities even stronger. In Aberdeen, the splitting of its sole parish of St Nicholas into two, East and West 'preiching kirks', did not occur until 1596.[73] It is likely that throughout the period under consideration the inhabitants of Aberdeen saw themselves as part of a community associated with St Nicholas parish kirk. Just as the town magistrates attempted to regulate entrance into the smaller communities within the burgh, so too the kirk prescribed proper behaviour that would include inhabitants within the spiritual community and railed against improper behaviour that would exclude inhabitants from receiving her benefits. One of the most important characteristics of sixteenth-century Aberdeen is that the Reformation altered very little of the social structures within the community.[74] Indeed, mass continued to be heard within the burgh and its surrounding areas for at least a decade after the arrival of the first kirk session in 1562. The very Catholic provost, Thomas Menzies of Pitfodels, maintained a Catholic priest in his service until his death in 1576. Yule and other holidays continued to be observed, while a number of craftsmen maintained their traditional observances and welcomed the changing seasons according to ancient rites.[75]

The arrival of the kirk session within the burgh also bears witness to the conservative elements at work in the burgh and the hesitancy with which members of the community embraced the Reformation. The inaugural meeting of the session in 1562 seems to have been in response to the conflict between the Protestant Earl of Moray and the interference in the burgh by the Catholic Earl of Huntly. Moray's arrival in the burgh prompted the magistrates to distance themselves from Huntly. The session disbanded within the year only to materialise again in 1568 in response to another political situation: the deposition of the Queen. It is not until 1573 that the session, led by the new minister in the burgh, John Craig, established more permanent roots in the community.

It is worth noting that from the outset of the first kirk session in 1562 through the rest of the sixteenth century, there was a significant overlap of personnel in positions of secular and spiritual authority. As Michael Graham has argued, 'it is reflective of the peculiar religious *status quo* in Aberdeen that Catholicism was considered no impediment to membership on the session, provided one was of sufficient local importance.'[76] Here again the Menzies family and their supporters played a key role. In 1573 and 1574, the session tried to gently persuade these families to renounce their faith. While sexual matters dominated session business during the course of the sixteenth century, as early as 1568 a small committee had been established to determine the prevalence of Catholic recusancy within the burgh.[77] The Regent Morton's arrival in the burgh in 1574 coincided with the burgh's push to absolve itself of any lasting prejudice associated with their involvement in Huntly's rebellion. Morton pushed the magistrates to adopt Reform practice, to clamp down on the 'superstitious keping of festvall days', remove the organ and choir screens from the kirk and enforce keeping the Sabbath.[78] The fact that the screen was still in place in 1590 and that a number of the town's leading families continued to refuse embracing the new religion underscores the conservatism within the community.

An example taken from the Council Register underscores the important role the wider community played in regulating behaviour within the burgh. In October 1553, the burgh court convicted Molly Abell for defaming and mispersoning Andrew Gray and Margaret Reyth, his wife. For her offence, the provost and baillies ordered her to appear before the entire congregation 'bairfut and bairleg' and on bended knee ask the couple to forgive her for wronging them. As part of the process, Abell revoked the words she spoke as untrue, thus participating in restoring the injured party's reputation. More importantly, the clerk noted in the account of her conviction that Abell was to 'oblist the gud men of the town to caus tham forgif hir'.[79] In this case there are a number of layers to cut through in order to understand the council's vision of the burgh community. The public act of forgiveness included all who witnessed her act of repentance. However, while there was a great deal of openness to this process of bringing Molly Abell back into the community, there seems to have been a competing vision of membership at work.

The idea explicit in this account is that the court required 'the gud men of the town', here characterised as a singular and homogenous group seemingly distinct from the rest of the congregation, to encourage the offended party to accept Molly's repentance and to forgive her. What is not entirely clear is whether the words 'gud men' translates solely to the 'substantious' male inhabitants of the town or can be taken as a contemporary shorthand for those not convicted of crimes, the honest and upstanding protectors of the commonweal. The socio-economic status and the gender of the inhabitants of the burgh are at the heart of this distinction. In the following chapters a closer examination of the varieties of crime and the punishments doled out to perpetrators of these offences helps to shed light on membership within the burgh community and on whose shoulders fell the burden of protecting the commonweal of the burgh. This should also shed light on the various power dynamics within the burgh.

The Sources

Any analysis of specific events, their impact on society and the consequences they produced will focus on individual crimes, enabling the reader to get a broad picture of the social interactions between individuals within Aberdeen in the sixteenth century. The apparent decline in the total number of incidents (petty crimes) brought before the burgh court between 1541 and 1591 raise a number of questions. First, do the records accurately reflect a decline in wrongdoing or were there other hidden reasons, such as expense of court, that obscure the reasons behind this decline? If indeed a decline in such activities can be determined, the next most obvious question to consider is what were the factors that contributed to such a decline? For example, were there specific demographic factors, such as changes in population or economic transitions, or specific regulatory factors such as an increasing role played by the kirk sessions that helped to curb such activities?

Unfortunately, incidents of unproven criminality can only be gleaned through recorded references made to past indiscretions in accounts where crimes have been recorded. Another question the figures presented in Table 3.1 (see below, p. 94) raise that may go unanswered given the paucity of information found in conviction accounts, concerns the steady decline in incidents of physical and verbal violence and strublance brought before the court during this period. While the number of recorded incidents of other petty crimes remained at a relatively constant rate or, as in cases of breaking statutes and disturbing the town, continued to rise, incidents of individual assaults brought before the court declined. Chapter 4 highlights some of the possibilities for this decline. Bearing all of this in mind, the choice of Aberdeen as a site for examining social power during the mid-to-late sixteenth century is obvious. First, as a centre with lasting Catholic sympathies it provides an interesting venue for exploring contemporary ideological conflicts (if indeed there was much) and for detailing the more nuanced shifts in social regulation that would not be as apparent in places such as Dundee or Ayrshire, where the Reformation came swiftly and dug its heels in hard.[80] Second, the Menzies family and their supporters dominated the formal political sphere within the burgh during this period. Increasingly, crime and civil disobedience reflected challenges towards established authority from within and outwith the elite sectors of society. Third, and perhaps most important from a practical perspective, there are extensive surviving records for the royal burgh of Aberdeen.

The Aberdeen Council Register, extant from 1398, offers perhaps the greatest source of information on Aberdeen's social, economic and political landscape. As a window into Aberdeen's past, what it occasionally lacks in clarity it makes up for in the size of the vista it affords. In 1985, Flett and Cripps offered a useful description of the Register's contents:

> Alongside the election of provosts, councillors and office bearers, registrations of property transfer, admission of burgesses, amercements of forestallers, promulgations of statutes to regulate the conduct of the inhabitants and the prices of staple foodstuffs and the proceedings of the chamberlains ayre, clerks of Aberdeen recorded numerous cases of mercantile and property-based debt and law and order offences.[81]

Through an examination of seventeen volumes of the Council Register (vols xvii–xxxiv) I have been able to gather information on local statutes and ordinances, civic elections, guild business and craft injunctions. However, the main evidence taken from this source consists of the conviction accounts for crimes committed in the community and the modifications of penalties prescribed by the burgh court.[82] The content and structure of the conviction accounts vary; frequently they consist only of the names of the convicted party and their victims, the crimes committed and an order to compear. Occasionally, the clerk provides more detail on the nature of the crime, the extent of the damage done and the penalties imposed. In Chapter 4, I examine the meaning behind the shift away from providing fuller details in the accounts to more concise notices of convictions. Unfortunately, despite the strengths of this source, the Register, and many of the other records in the Aberdeen City Archives, frequently fall silent on the personal details of the individuals involved in the cases brought before the courts, both the victims and the accused. In particular, the clerks very infrequently recorded the status and occupation of the parties involved. It is not clear whether or not the officials were unaware of this information or whether this was indicative of an attitude towards certain sectors of Aberdeen society. For example, the records almost always identify the status of those in positions of authority who are on the receiving end of verbal or physical abuse. However, the clerks noted the convicted party's status or occupation, regardless of their place in society, in only about 34 per cent of the records available.[83]

While the Council Register comprises the main source of information for the years 1542 to 1603, other less consistent sources include the Aberdeen Baillie Court Books, St Nicholas Kirk Session Records, the Aberdeen Kirk and Bridge Works Accounts, Aberdeen Guildry Accounts, Mortification Accounts and Treasury Accounts. While each of these sources offers specific insight into community life in sixteenth-century Aberdeen, they do have some limitations. The Register of Mortifications, for example, contains only a few references to the late sixteenth century while the Baillie Court Books contain significant gaps.[84] Likewise, the Guildry Accounts are extant only for the last quarter of this study;[85] they do, however, offer insight into the roles of burgesses and freemen within Aberdonian society during this period and shed light on a number of the concerns, ideas and individuals that are found in the Council Register. The Guildry Accounts also record the unlaws [penalties] paid or performed by craftsmen and merchants convicted for wrongdoing within the burgh. They also record the fees paid for entrance into the exclusive communities within the burgh – the merchant guildry, burgess-ship and the incorporated crafts. The Baillie Court Books bear a striking resemblance to the Council Register and often repeat the information found in that source. However, there are a number of convictions accounts found in the Baillie Court Books that were not recorded in the Register. Through a comparison of the two sources I was able to isolate repetition and highlight cases unique to each. The St Nicholas Kirk Session records, extant from 1562 with gaps,[86] and the Kirk and Bridge Works Accounts provide detailed information on the spiritual concerns within the parish. They also inform us of the ideological thrust behind social interactions, the economics behind poor relief, pastoral care and repentance and the political culture of a town teetering on the side of Protestantism while hanging on to its Catholic sensibilities.

To a large extent the extensive nature of the Council Register counters any limitations these other sources possess. This is not to say that there are no other problems with using these sources to construct an understanding of Aberdeen's past. To depend largely on the conviction accounts as they appear in the Council Register, Baillie Court Books and Guildry Accounts for an accurate picture of the events as they took place, is to overestimate the objectivity of the court officials whose task it was to record these accounts. In large part, conviction accounts lack the transgressor's own words. We hear little to nothing of the explicit motivations behind the acts committed by members of Aberdeen society or of the guilt, remorse or satisfaction they felt in wronging their neighbours. Instead we are left to infer such things from the details provided by court clerks and the context when provided. However, this does not entirely remove the transgressor's voice – the actions they took communicate in a very loud way. In this way, the 'public transcript' as James Scott, Michael Braddick and John Walter have defined it – 'the acceptable public version of relations of domination and subordination' – were negotiated by individual attempts at redrawing the boundaries of normative society through wrongdoing.[87]

Using the information drawn from the sources, I created a simple database. This enabled me to examine rates of convictions over five decades, break down wrongdoing and victimization along gender lines, and compare changes in terms of recording the types of wrongdoing in the burgh records. While the goal is not to present a quantitative analysis of crime and punishment,[88] the database provides a useful tool for distinguishing groups affected by social regulation and crime – groups defined by gender, social status, occupation, guild or burgess membership.[89] Perhaps the greatest danger in entering information drawn from contemporary sources into a computer database is that there is the potential for rendering black and white those areas that do not fit neatly into singular compartments. As such, I used statistical analysis sparingly and only to support the more qualitative analysis of conflict and control in the community.[90]

Regardless, the examination of petty criminal acts committed in Aberdeen provides a fruitful starting point for understanding the multi-layered power dynamics that existed within Scottish urban societies. Clearly, the existence of multiple communities within a single burgh suggests that loyalty to both the smaller and wider communities in which they interacted affected an individual's place in society. In this sense, tensions that arose in the burgh community often reflected disputes not necessarily between superiors and subordinates, though these too occurred, but between individual members seeking to redefine their own sense of place and more importantly to reconstitute their own power within the community. Power in this sense does not equate immediately to formal political influence, but to the means by which individuals or groups, of varying strata of society, influenced their immediate networks of social interaction. We gain a greater understanding of the burgh community in the sixteenth century if we abandon 'binary oppositions' and instead examine the more 'subtle ramifications' of social interactions among the various members of burgh society.[91]

The available sources make it clear that religious reform introduced into Aberdeen in the middle decades of the sixteenth century had limited influence on the concern that crime and sin was detrimental to the town's well-being, and that misbehaviour invited God's wrath into the community was already a well established notion. Undoubtedly, it was such concern that strengthened the burgh magistrates' belief that Thom Moidart had invited unwanted elements into the burgh by housing strangers.[92] The local authorities, both spiritual and secular, worked closely together throughout this period to establish a proper code of conduct and to foster good neighbourliness amongst all the inhabitants of the burgh. However, while the authorities worked to root out unsavoury elements within the community, a number of the burgh's inhabitants challenged such visions of neighbourliness and proper behaviour and through wrongdoing helped to redefine social boundaries and their own individual social space.[93]

In general, committing petty crimes in the burgh was a fairly effective way to instigate such changes. Through individual, and occasionally group, transgressions, members of the burgh community affected shifts in the power dynamics between other individuals or groups within that society. One recent study has argued that violent acts could: 'inform political action or discourse; contribute to the gendering of social behaviour; shape language and textual production; frame and strengthen ... identities.'[94] Many of the transgressions committed in early modern societies were characteristically violent, enabling groups otherwise prohibited from exercising power in any formal capacity within the community to do so in a less conventional manner. In this way, such activities presented opportunities for a wider majority of the community to actively participate in the structuring and restructuring of society.[95] The questions that have been asked of the sources take into account their limitations and address any inconsistencies that emerge.

This book focuses around three basic areas: conflict, community and control. Each of these areas inevitably possesses a myriad of questions and sub categories that need to be addressed. Not only is it important to distinguish what types of crimes were being committed during this period, it is also important to determine who was committing these crimes, what the motives were behind such actions, what impact crime had on society as a whole and what means were employed to curtail such actions. In particular, in what way did violent and non-violent acts perpetrated against individuals within the town indicate a challenge to the boundaries of acceptable behaviour and an attempt to redefine one's social space?[96] The following chapters should go some way to answering these questions.

1 CRIME, COMMUNITY AND BELONGING

At the heart of the regulatory processes at work in Aberdeen was the idea, common in both England and Scotland at the time, of protecting the 'commoun weal'. Paul Slack has argued that for early modern English towns, the common weal 'was not a programme, still less a manifesto for a party, not even a strategy. Well before the 1540s it was a rhetorical slogan conferring legitimacy on almost any public activity; and it was in origin simply a translation of a commonplace aspiration.'[1] While dates associated with historical events and trends tend to also have a specific geographical relationship, Slack's identification of concerns for the common weal existing prior to 1540 in England can be extended to include Scotland as well. Roger Mason has shown that during the early modern period the 'commonweal' roughly equated to the 'community'; this in turn can be taken to mean the 'community of the realm' and the 'community of the burgh'.[2] Accounts found in the Aberdeen Council Register indicate that plague, poverty, idle persons, breakers of local statutes and committers of various other offences occupied the daily business of the baillies and the rest of the town council. In performing their civic duties, these officials equated regulating society and maintaining the established social order with protecting the common weal. Even in instances where the court clerk did not expressly use the words 'commoun weill' or 'guid of the toun' in his accounts, he made it clear that the court perceived such actions as threatening the community. For example, two inhabitants of the burgh convicted for drawing swords and attacking each other found themselves amerced for 'trubling of the town'.[3] While the clerk did not explicitly use the words 'commoun weill', his concern that misbehaviour undermined the community's well-being is apparent. This stands in contrast to attitudes held elsewhere.[4]

The goal of protecting the common weal of the burgh raises a number of questions on the nature of the burgh community. What exactly did the idea of the 'commoun weill' mean to contemporary Aberdonians? Who constituted the community of the burgh and what determined membership within this group? How did criminality affect membership or alter boundaries that included and excluded individuals from participation in the community? Were there competing visions of the community and if so what can the records tell us about alternative

ideas about belonging? Was it only the elites, and those elites in positions of formal power in particular, that were interested in maintaining the common weal
of the burgh? In providing answers to these questions, and the numerous corol-
lary questions they engender, it should be possible to come to some conclusions
on whether or not crimes committed within the burgh constituted an informal
means by which individuals, regardless of their status in society, affected a change
in both their social space and the amount of social power they wielded.

In large part, urban historians of Scotland have focused on the elite sectors
of burgh society - magistrates, burgesses and merchants, and to a somewhat lesser
extent free craftsmen and professionals.[5] A particular area of interest to the relatively few historians exploring Scotland's urban past has been the supposed
tensions between the merchants and craftsmen.[6] Yet, while debate continues over
whether such tensions dominated life in Scottish burghs, very little scholarship has
been undertaken to explore closely the complex nature of specific early modern
Scottish burgh societies. In particular, historians need to look more closely at the
multiple locations of belonging within a single community.[7] For example, a sixteenth-century Aberdonian baxter may naturally have seen himself as a member of
the burgh community. However, his 'sense of place' within the community would
undoubtedly be as different from that of a wealthy guild merchant as it would be
from an unfree day labourer. Of course, wealth and status were not the only factors
determining one's place in the community. One's gender, health, occupation, place
of abode and adherence to the prescriptions of normative society and, after 1562,
religious conformity helped situate individuals within the community. That is not
to say that any one member held a singular place in society. The complex nature of
early-modern burgh social structures, not unlike most modern societies, stemmed
from the basic fact that members of the community could feel a sense of belonging
to a number of different communities that made up burgh society.

Criminality and challenging the boundaries of acceptable behaviour was not
unique to Aberdeen.[8] Indeed, early modern historians have demonstrated that the
changes occurring in the sixteenth century in terms of kin relationships, population growth, plague, famine and dearth, further socio-economic polarization,
growth of commercial activities, the growth of state apparatus, developing legal
practices and shifts in religious practices all influenced contemporary attitudes on
social order, disorder and community.[9] Increasingly, historians have been under-
taking examinations of the localities to shed light on the national experience. In
this respect, studies of early modern Scotland lag behind.[10] The relatively limited
number of studies examining crime and power structures and authority in Scotland during the middle ages and early modern period underscores the real need
to begin exploring such topics.[11] The same can be said for Scottish urban history.

Over the past two decades remarkably few historians have attempted to fill
this relatively large void in Scottish historiography.[12] In the 1980s and 1990s,

E. P. Dennison (formerly Torrie), Michael Lynch, Ian Whyte and Elizabeth
Ewan paved the way for further studies on Scottish burghs.[13] Characteristic of
the work that has been done is a continuous reliance on the notion that social
relations and power structures were dichotomous in nature. Lynch, for example, stressed that the key power dynamic within early modern Scottish burghs
was between 'masters and men, employers and employees, rulers and ruled'.[14]
Indeed, such binary constructions of burgh society are commonplace in most
Scottish urban histories. Dennison has suggested that in Dundee, as crafts
became incorporated in the sixteenth century, an increasingly stratified society
emerged engendering tensions between craftsmen and merchants. However, by
the seventeenth century Dundee had emerged not only as second burgh of the
realm but also a burgh whose 'urban aristocracy embraced both merchants and
craftsmen'.[15] However, Jane Thomas and Elizabeth Ewan have demonstrated
that while such urban aristocracies existed in Scottish burghs, often the power
dynamics within these groups demonstrate a slightly different reality of burgh
life.[16] Ewan underscored the complexities of urban life by arguing that burgh
inhabitants experienced multiple places of belonging given the attachments they
formed to smaller communities within the wider burgh society.[17] Bearing this
idea in mind, this chapter outlines the community of the burgh in sixteenth-
century Aberdeen and highlights the characteristic features of the burgh, its
inhabitants and the mechanisms in place for governing the community.

The Community of the Burgh

The two towns of Old and New Aberdeen lie on the banks of the rivers Don and
Dee respectively and on the coast of what contemporary sixteenth-century Aberdonians referred to as the German Sea. In the twelfth century David I bestowed
upon the inhabitants of New Aberdeen a charter creating the royal burgh of
Aberdeen with all of the attendant privileges and liberties.[18] Throughout the late
middle ages, and well into the modern period, the royal burgh of Aberdeen[19] functioned as an important port with access to European markets, a market town, a
seat of a sheriffdom and one of the four principal burghs of the realm. In 1661 the
Scottish surveyor and cartographer James Gordon of Rothiemay described the
'new burgh' as exceeding 'not onlie the rest of the touns of the north of Scotland,
bot lykewayes any citie quhatsumever of that same latitude, for greatnes, bewtie,
and frequencie of trading'.[20] The capital of north-eastern Scotland, Aberdeen,
according to Rothiemay stood in stark contrast to the surrounding countryside:

> the fields nixt to the gaits of the citie are fruitfull of corns ... and abounds with pas-
> tures; bot any where after yow pas a myll without the toune, the countrey is barran
> lyke, the hills craigy, the plains full of marreshes and mosses....the corne fields mixt
> with thes bot few.[21]

The burgh design resembled that of most other Scottish burghs. Burgage plots lined the town's principal streets running back in a herringbone pattern. These plots, held of the community, provided both the land that housed the town's burgesses as well as areas to grow foodstuffs and keep animals. It was through possession of a burgage that individuals were able to enjoy the rights and liberties associated with burgess-ship – trade, protection, use of merchandise, self-government and freedom to be tried exclusively in the burgh court.[22] Burgesses frequently let out the so-called backlands of their burgages to house workshops for local craftsmen and homes for the poorer sorts.[23] Although a principal port, and an obvious point of disembarkation for invading armies, Aberdeen does not appear to have possessed town walls or other 'protective barriers' during the sixteenth century.[24] Old Aberdeen, as well as the immediate surrounding fishing villages of Nigg and Futty, played a role in the burgh and it is clear from the free movement of the inhabitants of these locales within the town that neither custom and statute nor gated walls could keep them out. Despite frequent references to the fishermen of Futty causing disturbance within the burgh, there is no indication that the burgh was inclined to exclude them from the town. For administrative purposes, the burgh was divided into four quarters – Crooked, Even, Green and Futty – with a Baillie in place to administer to the needs of those living within those boundaries.

As in many urban centres in Northern Europe, Aberdeen possessed a bustling marketplace that in essence defined the burgh's existence.[25] It is likely that the basic design of Aberdeen was in place by the fourteenth century. The Castlegate, in the north-east part of the burgh, was the site of the market; within the market square stood the symbols of civic pride and authority: the market cross, the tolbooth and the tron [the town's weighing device]. Not only did the presence of these symbols underline the town's burgh status with its important mercantile liberties and privileges, they functioned as important sites for regulating behaviour within the community and feature prominently in conviction accounts for the burgh. Indeed, while the tron helped to identify those who tried to cheat the market, the tolbooth housed the burgh court, council meeting hall and occasionally served as a prison.[26] As with the tron and the tolbooth, the market cross functioned in the regulation of behaviour within the community as an important site for public proclamations as well as public punishments.

Rothiemay's depiction of life in the burgh complemented his description of the burgh itself. In his account of the burgh's layout and the surrounding countryside, Rothiemay asserted that the region's 'temperat' climate afforded the townspeople an 'acuteness of wit' and an inclination to be civil not to be found in most northerly parts.[27] Historians since Rothiemay have been inclined to follow his lead in depicting the inhabitants of Aberdeen as a rather civil community. Kennedy, in the nineteenth century, argued that in terms of the unrest and uproar that accompanied the Reformation in other parts of Scotland, 'the mischief done by the reformers at Aberdeen was inconsiderable'.[28] Likewise, Alexander Keith argued that 'the Reformation in Aberdeen involved no victimization by the Reformers ... the picture that presents itself, indeed, is one that might confound those whose conception of the Reformation is based upon highly coloured legends of the religious revolution.'[29] While a rather conservative approach to religion continued in Aberdeen until the early seventeenth century, there were other significant areas that marked a lack of civility within the burgh.[30]

In particular, the political landscape, dominated by the Menzies family for most of the sixteenth century, was frequently bothered by intrigue and unrest. As early as the late 1530s, a Menzies provost of Aberdeen faced internal attacks on his ability to manage the town's funds. While most likely those challenging Menzies rooted their accusation of mismanaging the so-called 'Common Good' funds in typical political opposition, the Privy Council Records describe the individuals involved in putting the matter before the Lords of Council as 'conspirators against the town'.[31] It is interesting that similar accusations appeared in the final days of the Menzies dominance of the provostship of the burgh in the late 1580s. During the 1537 election of Thomas Menzies of Pitfodells (1537–44) the King had to intervene to quell the 'disturbance' that the election engendered. In a letter to the burgh council, James V (r. 1513–42) underlined the prescribed regulations behind the election of town officials, and in particular the need for common consent. However, the King also stressed that the inhabitants of the burgh should 'live in liberty and freedom like burgesmen, but [without] outthrowing of outmen [outsiders] or great persons.'[32] Throughout the sixteenth century the involvement of outsiders, and in particular the Earls of Huntly, caused considerable discontent within the burgh.[33]

By 1535, George, fourth earl of Huntly, had become a member of the Privy Council, Lord Lieutenant of the North and Lord Lieutenant of the Kingdom.[34] His considerable influence in the north almost immediately earned him enmity throughout the kingdom. By 1562 Huntly was in open rebellion. Instigated first by his son's escape from incarceration in Edinburgh for violent behaviour, Huntly's displeasure at the Queen's dispossession of him in the earldom of Moray in favour of James Stewart, her Protestant half-brother, was more likely the cause of his revolt. His marshalling of forces in the north brought the house of Gordon, and those whose support he demanded, into deadly conflict with the Queen and her supporters. While Huntly died shortly after the battle of Corrichie in October 1562 and his lands and title became forfeit, there were serious consequences for the inhabitants of Aberdeen on account of their involvement with this declared rebel.

Within a few years of Corrichie, Mary, Queen of Scots (r. 1542–67) chose to reinstate Huntly's son as the fifth Earl of Huntly. Her motivations may have been directed by her desire to undermine the efforts of Moray who by 1565 had allied himself with other Protestant lords in open rebellion against the Queen on account of her marriage to the Catholic Darnley.[35] George Gordon, now fifth Earl of Huntly, and his supporters actively fought on the Queen's side through-out the remaining civil wars that eventually resulted in her removal from the throne and subsequent imprisonment and execution in England. However, the impact these events had on Aberdeen may be discerned by the actions taken against the burgh community by the King's party (supporters of James VI). As late as 1574 the burgh council complained of the impositions – which included heavy taxation – placed on the burgh for the 'assisting, contributioun, and stent making in tymes bypast, with George Erll of Huntlie'.[36] In letters to Thomas Menzies, the provost of Aberdeen, the Regent Morton indicted the burgh, its magistrates and inhabitants for crimes committed through their involvement with Huntly and his supporters. The list of crimes the burgh community stood accused of committing through this association included:

> the being at the conflictis of Tilleangus and Craibstoune aganis ws and our authori-
> tie, and uthairis crymes of tresonis, murthour, slauchter, mutilatioun, fyre-raising ...
> incest, witchcraft, adulterie, forging, prenting, hame bringing, and outputting of fals
> and adulterat money, sorning [extorting free quarters or provisions], deforcing of our
> officearis, hearing and saying of mes, thift and reset of thift, piracie, and reset thairof.[37]

It is interesting to note that the variety of crimes noted by Morton as being treasonous suggests not only a lack of civility on the parts of the inhabitants of Aberdeen but also underscores the affront to the King's peace within his royal burgh caused by committing crimes within its limits.

It is not entirely clear what role the burgh played in Huntly's 'obstructive activities'.[38] Any involvement the burgh had with Huntly and his supporters was definitely complex and certainly less than completely amicable. This becomes clear in Morton's letter pardoning the burgh for providing aid to Huntly. Here Morton stated that the burgh acted out of 'feir and compulsioun'.[39] It is instructive to note that such 'fear and compulsion' had a lengthy history. In 1463 the burgh had entered into a bond of manrent with the first Earl of Huntly for the purpose of protecting their lucrative fishing and free lands outside the burgh boundaries.[40] While not necessary for the Gordon family to intrude upon burgh politics or the burgh's business, the bond did secure them a prominent position as protector of the burgh. Throughout the period under consideration here, the burgh had to tread carefully in its dealings with Huntly, recognizing the impact his involvement with the burgh could have on the community. Prior to his election as provost of the burgh in 1545, the fourth Earl had already attempted to use his influence in the region to muster recruits from the burgh for an army to pass south to fight the invading English armies.[41] In March 1545, Huntly intervened on behalf of one of his clients, James Manchanis, who the burgh court had convicted of forestalling the market attempting to force the baillies to remit Manchanis' unlaws [fines].[42]

While individual actions, such as the recruitment of soldiers, demonstrate the attempts made by the Gordons to influence the burgh, it is the singular fact that landed interest continued to intrude upon the burgh community throughout the late fifteenth, sixteenth and seventeenth centuries that reveals the community's, and in particular its magistrates', resolve to protect the burgh's liberties from outside influence.[43] When in January 1558, the fourth Earl of Huntly attempted to impose William Leslie, son of the Laird of Balquhaine, on the burgh's merchant guildry, the council refused, citing the burgh's requirement that burgesses make residence within the town limits. However, twenty years later, the council took a different approach by admitting twenty-six Gordons and another fifteen Gordon supporters to the merchant guildry in one day.[44] The taxation imposed on the town by Huntly in 1572 for the removal of his soldiers stationed there to guard against the King's party reveals the uneasy relationship the burgh had with this noble family.[45] Moreover, it speaks clearly to the 'fear and compulsion' highlighted by Morton in his letter of pardon to the burgh in 1574.

If landed interest played a role in cementing the conservative, almost protectionist, outlook of the burgh community in Aberdeen during the sixteenth century, it was largely on account of the clients of local nobles resident within the burgh that such conservatism took root. In particular, the Menzies family and their dominance in Aberdeen politics for nearly a century underscores the fact that change was very slow in coming to the burgh. Despite burgh customs and statutes that dictated the election of a new provost each year, the Menzies family occupied the provostship of the burgh, almost without interruption, for the entire sixteenth century.[46] The staunchly Catholic Thomas Menzies's lengthy reign as Provost, and the succession of his son and their supporters in top administrative roles, meant that a Catholic leaning oligarchy maintained legitimate power within the burgh throughout the period. Following its establishment in 1562 the St Nicholas Kirk Session frequently railed against Menzies and his supporters for maintaining their Catholic faith. In the 1570s, despite their own active participation in the newly formed session, the Menzies maintained their conservative vision of the burgh and continued to balance their Catholic sympathies with the changes brought in by the Reformed kirk. In large part, the ability of the Menzies family and their supporters to hold on to positions of power within the burgh for most of the sixteenth century demonstrates both the strength of their own social power and the community's resistance to change.

The burgh community did, however, experience some change during this period. Using baptismal records to determine population growth, Robert Tyson has argued that by 1574 the population of Aberdeen 'was growing rapidly'.[47] Tyson's figures suggest that between 1574 and 1644 there was a growth rate of nearly 151 per cent and that the population of Aberdeen in 1644 was nearly double its population in 1500.[48] A conservative estimate puts the burgh's entire population during the middle of the sixteenth century period somewhere between 4,000 and 5,000 people.[49] Although it is possible to speak of the wider community of the burgh, there were multiple smaller communities within the burgh that individual inhabitants owed loyalty to and to which they claimed membership. Perhaps the largest group within the community would have been those individuals deemed 'indwellers'. While 'indwell' is a synonym of 'belong', a number of records suggest that the term indweller referred to all inhabitants of a burgh. An entry in the Council Register for 4 January 1560 refers to 'certane strangearis, and sum nichtbours and induellaris of this burght' damaging the property of the Black and White Friars of Aberdeen.[50] Here there seems to be a distinction between neighbours and indwellers. Likewise, in May 1583 the brethren of gild were notified of the harm done by those 'induellaris and burgessis of this burght' who received monies from 'burgessis of uther burghis, and extranearis [strangers]' to purchase goods in Aberdeen. The 'haill brethren of gild' warned to compear that day to hear this accusation agreed to an ordinance that those found guilty of such activities were to be banished from the burgh forever.

These examples provide insight into the multiple affiliations within the burgh community. For example, there was a distinction between burgesses and mere indwellers. Furthermore, this was a gathering of the 'brethren of gild' – those belonging to the exclusive merchant guildry – as a distinct group rather than a convening of the 'haill town'.[51] An entry for December 1589 shows again the clear distinction between burgesses and indwellers. In response to the disorder caused by students at the grammar school around Yule, the council ordered that each scholar was to set caution before they could be received into the school. Unlike most situations that called for a surety, the ordinance stressed that each scholar find two cautioners 'ane burges and ane indweller of the said burght'.[52] While the distinction raises interesting questions, the example demonstrates one of the many processes of inclusion at work. Chapter 2 examines more thoroughly the role cautioners and suretors played in the re-introduction or inclusion of convicted wrongdoers back into the community. I argue that setting caution served the same function for entry into smaller groups within the community such as the grammar school, the gild brethren and even the kirk. The obvious correlation was that those who were unable to find suretors or to meet the criteria were set apart.

Indwellers, then, were those individuals who because of native birth, or who through long-term residency, had access to certain privileges within the town, regardless of wealth, rank or status, that outsiders, 'strangers' or foreigners did not possess. This placed all who fell in the first two categories within the burgh community and those in the latter categories without. Thus, a working definition of the larger burgh community is all who were native born or who through long-term residency secured themselves certain rights and privileges, the most common of which was protection from outside influence.[53] The recognition as an indweller of the burgh was important for the more disadvantaged groups within the town; those seeking poor relief were by statute required to be an indweller possessed of the town's token under threat of expulsion if caught begging without having met these stipulations.[54] However, even those of the upper ranks of burgh society needed to meet certain residency requirements. A perennial problem confronting the burgh authorities was ensuring that those benefiting from the privileges of the burgh in terms of protection, trading rights and access to town resources also contributed to town life by residing within the boundaries of the burgh.

In most European urban settings, merchants and the craftsmen dominated the social, cultural, political and economic spheres. The same can be said for the merchants and craftsmen of Aberdeen. While there is little doubt that in most burghs the former held a controlling interest in the two major sectors of society – local government and trade – in Aberdeen, where the merchants outnumbered craftsmen within the burgh by a ratio of three to one, their influence was significant.[55] In large part, the strong connection between the merchant guildry and the burgh council emphasized the prominent role played by the merchants within the town. As in other parts of society, within the merchant community a hierarchy based on access to foreign trade and wealth meant that minor merchants often found themselves outside the spheres of influence. Alan White has argued that the success in which the craftsmen agitated for extended rights and privileges within the burgh in the 1570s and 1580s owed a great deal to the role minor merchants played in the process.[56]

The relationship between the two 'communities within the community', the merchants and craftsmen, dominates most of the histories of Scottish burghs. The privileges afforded to those who became free of their crafts or who gained the right to use merchandise within the burgh proved enticing to those excluded from these groups. The town council, dominated largely by the guildry, played an active role in making men free; almost without exception gender influenced belonging to either group. Inevitably, tensions emerged over rights of access, determination of inclusion, and the roles played by each group in determining the other's involvement in the community. In the course of the sixteenth century, seven of the crafts within the burgh had become incorporated: the hammermen; baxters; wrights and coopers; tailors; cordiners [shoemakers]; weavers and fleshers.[57] Other crafts such as barbers, litsters, masons and shipmasters belonged to 'societies' that included unfree members of society. This last group made up approximately 60 per cent of the burgh population in the sixteenth century.[58] This group included apprentices, wage-earning labourers, women who may or may not have been engaged in industry and trade, and those poor and indigent individuals who lived below the poverty line. Ian Whyte estimates that in Scottish burghs those considered poor would have made up a significantly lower percentage than the 30 to 40 per cent estimated for England.[59] While unfree, those individuals not belonging to the craft or merchant guilds, but of native birth or long-term residency, qualified for basic rights afforded to members of the community. The right to poor relief, protection from outside forces, the right not to be expelled and the right to a trial within the burgh meant that statute and custom included even the most impoverished indweller in the wider burgh community.

Still, conflicting ideas abound in the historiography surrounding inclusion within the burgh. The idea that the burgh centred on the activities of the market supports the belief that those with the greatest investment in mercantile interests defined the community of the burgh.[60] But as Dennison has argued, far from simply a community gathered around a market, the medieval and early modern burgess would doubtless have viewed the burgh as 'his home; the source of his earning power; of his freedom and obligations; of his sense of oneness and community both with his god and his neighbour'.[61] This view, however, sees the burgh community being made up of burgesses whose only neighbours were those from the same socio-economic status. While contemporaries may have been inclined to socialize with their equals, it is not entirely clear that their vision of the community of the burgh resembles that of modern historians. It is true that the legislation upholding the rights of the merchants to control burgh politics and the tensions between merchants and craftsmen over rights and liberties within the burgh suggest that on a formal political level access or inclusion in the community was limited.[62] That said, must we accept that the community was singular in dimension or is it possible that multiple corporate identities reflected contemporary conceptualizations of membership within that community?[63]

Council, Court and Community

Custom, statutes and ordinances also helped to define burgh power structures, establish and legitimize authority, regulate participation and mediate relationships between the multiple overlapping and intersecting segments of society. The burgh council took an active role in regulating society, prescribing their vision of acceptable behaviour in all matters related to the burgh. The *Leges Burgorum* (Burgh Laws), a compilation of burgh laws of uncertain date, supports this idea. According to the customary oath that provosts swore upon their election to office, they were to 'kepe the customys of the toune and [that] thais sal nocht halde lauch on ony man or woman for wroth na for haterent na for drede or for lufe of ony man, bot thruch ordinans consaile and dome of gude men of the toune'.[64] In his *Practicks*, Balfour recorded a slightly different variation on this oath stating that those individuals chosen to be provost and baillies shall be:

faithfull men, and of gud fame; and thay beand chosin, thay sweir that thay sall be leill and trew to the King, and to the haill communitie of the burgh; that thay sall keip the lawis and consuetudes of the burgh; that thay sall do justice to rich and pure in lyke maner efter thair knawlege; thay sall not hald law on ony man or woman, nor spair ony persoun, for haitred, favour, nor dreid, blind, budde, nor feare of ony man, bot be ordinance, counsall and judgment of gude and wise men of the burgh.[65]

The Reformation did little to alter the established roles of the civil magistrates in Aberdeen. Interestingly enough, the *Confession of Faith* ratified by the Parliament in 1560 linked the requirements for adhering to the 'trew Kirk' with the important role of civil magistrates and the recognition of temporal authority 'to quhome be God is geuin the sworde, to the praise and defence of gude men, and to revenge and punische all opin malefactouris'.[66] Moreover:

> to kings, princes, rulers, and magistrates, we affirm that chiefly and most principally the conservation and purgation of the religion appertains; so that not only they are appointed for civil policy, but also for maintenance of the true religion, and for suppressing of idolatry and superstition whatsoever.[67]

Thus, anyone convicted of transgressing civil statutes was to be deemed an enemy of the state as well as in opposition to 'God's expressed will'.

In this way statute and ordinance outlined the responsibilities of burgh officials for proper governance of the burgh. In the period under consideration, much of the late medieval foundations of burgh government remained intact. According to burgh statutes and parliamentary Acts, at the Head Court held yearly around Michaelmas, the town's burgesses were to elect a provost for the year.[68] In 1503, an Act of James IV ordained that 'all officiars, prowests balzeis & otheris havand office of jurisdiction within burgh be changeit zerlie' and that none were to have office within the burgh except merchants.[69] In accordance with the wisdom of the council members, the provost, whose position in the medieval period was mostly one of prestige rather than actual power, was to maintain the customs of the burgh, dole out justice and defend the kirk.[70] Interestingly enough, the language of the two swords theory of authority so pervasive in medieval political thought carried over into the largely Calvinist influenced Scottish *Confession of Faith*.[71] In the period under consideration, the provost, the baillies, the seargents or officers, Dean of Guild and the kirk's elders and deacons were the authorities who played a key role in formally regulating burgh society. Their powers were legitimated by both statute and consent of the burgesses representing the 'haill community'.

Alan White's work on the political environs of Aberdeen during this period has clearly demonstrated that a very tight-knit oligarchy maintained control of burgh governance from at least the mid-1550s through to the mid-1580s.[72] In particular, White has argued that between 1560 and 1569 twenty-seven men drawn from thirteen Aberdonian families served as burgh councilors. In that same period, only five men acted as baillies; two were sons of the provost and two were his sons-in-law.[73] What makes this more remarkable is that despite the guidelines regulating burgh elections, these positions tended to be passed on hereditarily upon the death of an acting burgh official while in office. In such a manner, the burgh's governance continued to rest in the hands of those most sympathetic to the Menzies family, whose continuous hold on the provostship has already been discussed.

Based on the deep-rooted hold this group had on local government, White argued that 'the idea of the "community of the burgh" was applied in an increasingly narrow sense'.[74] This argument rests, however, on the belief that those in positions of political power – the council, baillies, officers restricted membership in both the smaller communities within burgh society and the wider burgh community.[75] We must also bear in mind that restrictions were in place for determining the eligibility for holding office in the burgh. The Burgh Officers Act of 1535 is quite specific on who was to be chosen an officer of the burgh:

> It is herefore Statute and ordanit that na man in tyme cuming be chosin provest ballies or aldermen in to burt bot thai that ar honest and Substantious burgess merchandise and Induellaris of the said burt vnder the pane of tynsale of thare fredome quha dois in the contrar.[76]

Throughout the sixteenth century merchants controlled burgh politics while craftsmen agitated for extended enfranchisement. In 1534, Perth had at least two craftsmen burgesses sit on the council and by 1538 two craftsmen also sat on the council in Edinburgh.[77] It was not until the 1580s, however, that the craftsmen in Aberdeen somewhat successfully gained the right to sit on the burgh council.[78] As is clear from local and national legislation, attempts were made to prohibit interference in the burgh by local earls, lords and barons and specifically with the officer's liberties.[79] In essence, such Acts strengthened the already established practice within most burghs of limiting outside influence. Although, as the example of Huntly becoming provost in 1545 suggests, statutes were not always the most effective means of regulating communities.

Community, Punishment and Recidivism

There is relative clarity behind the idea that communities are entities with boundaries that both include and exclude.[80] What is rather murky is the extent to which inclusion or exclusion equates to an 'either/or' situation. Much like the problematic notion of identities, there is not always a clear-cut vision of belonging or its negation being set apart.[81] The idea of being apart can be construed as an element of belonging in that burgh communities were frequently set apart from the surrounding rural communities on the basis of the privileges and liberties monarchs bestowed upon them.[82] This implies an intrinsic link between inclusion and exclusion. As such, it should be relatively easy to accept the idea that criteria established to define inclusion will ultimately establish guidelines for exclusion as well, i.e. those who do not meet the criteria. This idea can be employed when examining overarching structures like 'the community' as well as smaller entities within that community.

For the various crimes under consideration the only consistent form of punishment was the banishment of those convicted of petty theft and intromission. In fifty-eight cases occurring between 1540 and 1600, twelve resulted in the banishment of the offending parties, most frequently for a year and a day.[83] Moreover, the court often required the convicted individual to spend time in the govis [pillory] just prior to their banishment. Such was the case for Patre Anderson who the burgh court convicted for the 'wrongous intromission [taking possession of someone else's property without authority] with a kirtill [cloak] and certane salmond fyshe'. The baillies ordered Anderson to be put in the govis:

> thairin to remain be the space of four houris with ane crown of paper on his heid and to be banist out of the town and fredome thairof for ewer and thairefter to be hand to the croce & publicklye the caus of his baneschment to be knawin.[84]

Public humiliation played an important role in the punishing of individuals convicted of wronging his or her neighbour and in shaping those individual's sense of belonging within the community.[85] This is evident in a case where the burgh court convicted two individuals for theft and a third for resetting [keeping] the stolen goods. The court put the thieves, Thomas Durrant and William Forest, in amercement of court, and for her involvement with stolen property, placed Besse Allan (along with Forest) in the govis:

> thair to stand with [a] crown of paper on thair heids fra nyne houris to twelf and thereafter to be present to the mercat croce to stand publickly schewand the caus of thair demerits wherefor they war convikit.[86]

Immediately following this presentation, Forest was scourged and both he and Allan were banished for a year and a day. [87] Contemporaries recognized the didactic as well as the symbolic value of public punishments. They informed the community that public sin required public reform; as Michael Graham has argued, 'humiliation ... would serve as a deterrent to sin'.[88] Public punishments were also, in the words of Foucault, 'a ceremonial by which a momentarily injured sovereignty is reconstituted'.[89] Wrongdoing damaged the integrity of the community, undermined the reputation of the magistrates to maintain order and stability within the burgh, and threatened the right of all members of burgh society to live unscathed within the physical boundaries of the burgh and the social boundaries of the community. Thus, public humiliation impacted the reputation of the wrongdoer by illustrating that the open wounds caused by wrongdoing must be healed in the open. To all involved, wrongdoing put the culprits on the outside of normative society, public punishment helped to (re) introduce those individuals back into the community.

A good example of this comes from a case of verbal assault. In April 1581, Jonet Cruikshank was found guilty of slandering Alex Mollison and ordered to publicly revoke the words she had spoken against him. The entry for 21 May 1581 in volume 2 of the Baillie Court Book records that:

> The said day Jonet Cruikshank quha was convicted obefor for the sklandering and mispersoning or be iniurious wordis of Alex Mollisone and therefore was ordainit to cum this instant at ten hours to the mercat croce of this toune in the presens of the common and pepill p[rese]nt for the tym sall grant and confess the said offens committit be hir....and sall revoke the said iniurious wordis spoken be hir as fals and untrew and ask God and the said Alex forgifness upon hir kneis.[90]

In ordering her to present herself at the market cross and acknowledge her wrongful behaviour, the council forced Cruikshank to open herself up to public scrutiny. This public act also helped restore the good name of the maligned party. In this case, the court required Alex Mollison, the victim of Cruikshank's slanderous and injurious words, to forgive Cruikshank, thus restoring them both within the community.[91] If the community's memory was short, however, and there seems to be no indication that this was the case, additional threats were uttered, and occasionally carried out, to ensure the individual convicted of wronging their good neighbours and the town itself returned to proper behaviour.

The case of the Stewart brothers and their run-in with the authorities between 1566 and 1574 provides some insight into a contemporary attitude towards recidivism. Their experience before the burgh court suggests that the authorities were keen to deliver a strong message that certain types of behaviour had no place in the burgh community. However, how this response played out makes it less clear how willing the magistrates were to enforce the letter of their law. Mentioned for the first time in February 1566, Patrick Stewart was convicted for the striking and blood drawing of Sir William Sunderland, a retired local vicar.[92] The baillies put Stewart in amercement of court but there is no account of his amends being modified, nor is there any statement that should Stewart offend again a more severe punishment would be forthcoming. Three years later, the court convicted Patrick Stewart and his brother George for petty theft. It is important to note that neither Patrick nor George had appeared in the records in the intervening three years. The reason this stands out can be gleaned from the account of the brothers' conviction:

> The said day patrick stewart and george stewart his broder war convikit be ane sworne assise for pykaris [petty thiefs] and for unlawchtful nytboris not worthy to remaine

within this burt & therefore war put in amc of court and the bailleis ordainit the said patrik and george to be scurgit throw the towne & banest of the samyn that is to say the said george for zeir & day and the said patrik perpetuallie for ewer in respeck that he was convikit for siclyk offence ofoir and gif the saidis personis beis found within this burt and fredome thereof to be delyverit in the sherifis handis to sufferit deitht for thair demerits.[93]

It is likely that Patrick's previous conviction influenced the court's decision to banish him from the town. The authorities determined his likeliness to re-offend and chose to remove permanently the threat they believed he posed to the town. However, the account indicated that he was convicted of 'siclyk offence ofoir', suggesting a previous incident of petty thievery. There is no account of such a conviction in the court records.[94] It is possible that the court viewed Stewart's attack on the retired vicar, and his petty thievery, as indicative of a certain life-style. If that is the case then it says a fair bit about how the authorities perceived petty crimes committed within the town. From the perspective of the magis-trates all activities deemed hurtful to the town required appropriate remedy in order to protect the inhabitants and the common weal.

George Stewart, however, had no previous convictions, but his banishment for a year and a day was in line with the punishment given to others who had been convicted of petty theft.[95] The most interesting aspect of the Stewarts' con-victions was the warning that breaching the terms of their banishment would result in the brothers' execution. In a number of other cases where individuals had been banished from the town for their offence, the court threatened that repeat offence would bring about some form of corporal punishment, frequently burning on the cheek.[96] However, such threats posed to prevent recidivism reflected a more 'technical definition of criminality'.[97] In terms of a more 'opera-tive definition', there seems to have been considerable flexibility in doling out punishments to meet the crime. By Feburary 1575 Patrick Stewart had returned to the town, if indeed he had ever left. Seeing that he had clearly disobeyed the terms of his punishment, a sworn assise found Stewart guilty and convicted him:

> for ane common pykar and nytwalkar and an unlautful nytbour and decernit there-fore to be brint on the cheik banist of this town perpetualy in all tym cuming and gif he beis founding eftirward in this town to be hangit.[98]

While there is no mention of him ignoring his banishment, it is likely that the corporal punishment was in response to his being found 'unlawfully' within the burgh. Yet, clearly this was not just a case of three strikes and you were out. Stew-art's previous conviction promised immediate execution if found within the burgh. Instead, his flouting of the earlier conviction led only to corporal punish-ment and further threats.

The Stewart example is not unique. The burgh court convicted an Aberdeen potter, Alexander Burnett, of violent crimes on three separate occasions between 1547 and 1548/9. For his first two offences, the court put Burnett in amercement of court and for his third offence he was ordered to appear before the provost and baillies.[99] Only in the third instance did the authorities indicate that a repeat offence would result in a more severe punishment. Yet, Burnett's second offence had involved the dinging [hitting] of an officer 'in execution of his office', the disobeying of Alexander Rutherford and David Anderson, two of the Baillies of Aberdeen and the 'bosting [threatening] and mannessing [menacing] of the said David Anderson'.[100] For these violent acts of disobedience towards town officials, Burnett was put in the council's will and in amercement of court. However, when a sworn assise convicted Burnett of the 'strubling and blud drawing' of Walter Barron in February 1549, they ordered him to appear before the town magistrate and *'failing'* that he was to appear in St Nicholas Kirk to ask Walter forgiveness for his crimes.

It is difficult to determine whether the order to go before Barron and the congregation to ask forgiveness was a threat to induce him to obey the court or an inevitable punishment for his multiple offences. Nonetheless, by 1562 the burgh authorities had reached the end of their tether with Alexander Burnett. In September of that year, Burnett confessed before the burgh court for the 'strublens, menassing and drawing of ane quhingar [short sword] to patre malysone goldsmyt'. For this crime, the provost and baillies ordered that Burnett 'be baneist of this gud town for ane yeir in respect of the said fault and vther crymes comittit be him obefoir.'[101] Burnett disappears from the Council register until 1570 when an Alexander Burnett potter was physically assaulted by David Robertson, an Aberdeen tailor.[102] The records make it clear that the burgh court held to an established set of conventions for dealing with recidivism. For the most part the court exacted some form of increased penalty on repeat offenders that ranged from pecuniary to penitential forms of punishment, from corporal punishment to banishment from the town. However, this is not entirely clearcut. It is interesting to note that in the recorded accounts of physical violence in Aberdeen the threat or pronouncement of banishment occurs only thirteen times out of 473 cases. Out of these thirteen instances, eight times it was used as a threat to stem repeated offence, the other five times the court banished the individuals from the town. Yet again, a clear pattern does not emerge for incidents where the court actually banished individuals convicted for these crimes. In two of the three instances where the council ordered the transgressor to be banished from the town, the offenders did not have any previous convictions.[103]

In the first of these cases, the burgh court convicted Andrew Lindsay of strubling and dinging [hitting] John Soulis, a baxter, and ordered him banished from the burgh. Lindsay does not appear in the records between 1540, the start of the period under consideration, and 1547 when his banishment occurred.[104]

Nor does Lindsay appear in the records again. Another case involved John Jak, who, like Lindsay before him, had committed no discernible indiscretions in the eyes of the burgh authorities. However, his case stands out from that of Lindsay's in terms of his victim, and the town's response. The record states that the provost and baillies of the town accused Jak of strubling the burgh and hurting and drawing the blood of Alexander King. The record notes that the provost and baillies were acting 'in the name of the kingis majestie', and that the principal victim was the town itself. Jak appeared before the court and confessed to his crime and put himself in the town council's will. Their decision deserves full rehearsal here:

> Efter mature deliberatioun being rytlie advysit vnderstanding the said John to be trowbilsum ordainis him to pay ten poundis penaltie to the thesaurer for the bludement [sic] and ordainis him to be banist this towne & fredome thereof for the space of ane yeir nixt heirefter and gif he beis found within the same and fredome theirof to pay ane hundreyth poundis and to set caution for payment theirof in case he contravene and inhibitions to be put to the inhabitants of this burt not to resave the said john during the said space under the said penaltie of ane hundreyth poundis.[105]

Unlike other cases where the court threatened banished wrongdoers with corporal punishment for not fulfilling the terms of their punishment, in this case the court threatened a fine of 100 pounds Scots. Unlike Burnett's case, but similar to Lindsay's, there is no record of any transgression committed by Jak prior to the one that led to his expulsion from Aberdeen for the hurting of Alexander King; nor does the record of his conviction make reference to past indiscretions. On more than one occasion, the court had convicted Alex Burnett for violent crimes before ordering his banishment. But, as noted earlier, there had been no explicit warning that if Burnett were to commit these crimes in the future it would lead to harsher penalties. Instead, the penalty jumped from a pecuniary fine to banishment. How then do we interpret the application of penalties and their corresponding crimes and the manner in which both reflect attitudes towards crime within the community during this period?

In July 1562 the court convicted John Chalmer for injuring in deed and slandering in word. These actions led the burgh authorities to deem Chalmer an unlawful neighbour. Due to the lack of details in the account, there is some ambiguity surrounding the acts which led to Chalmer's conviction.[106] Yet, in the context of Alex Burnett's and Patrick Stewart's experience with the burgh court, it is easier to understand why the court took the course of action it did in determining that Chalmer was 'not to be sufferit to pas at libertie in this town to commit sic misorder and enormities as he daly committis'.[107] As with Burnett and Stewart, Chalmer too had a history of being brought before the burgh court on a variety of offences. He first appears in the Council Register in September 1543 when the court convicted him, along with Alexander Kempt younger, for the 'strublens' of each other.[108] They were both put in amercement of court and ordered to amend according to the statutes of the town. Chalmer's disregard for the town statutes becomes more apparent in the account of his next conviction.

In December 1553, the court convicted Chalmer, along with six other individuals 'for the braking of the commond ordinance and statutes of this gud town'.[109] Chalmer and the others were amerced. In the intervening ten years, Chalmer's name appears twice in the Council Register; in both instances it is on account of his wife's behaviour.[110] Apart from his convictions, the records are silent on Chalmer's status in Aberdeen society, though we do know his wife was a cake-baker. In November 1555 a dispute arose between Chalmer and David Mar, one of the town's baillies. Seven years later, Mar would be one of Chalmer's accusers in the case that led the court to declare Chalmer an unlawful neighbour. The account of the original dispute in 1555 between Mar and Chalmer raises a few interesting points about the community and the process of regulating behavior:

> The said day John Chalmer was accusit in judgement for the missaying and mispersoning of david mar ane of the Baillies of the said burght with maist wyill and iniurious detractione sayand that he had taken ane hundreith £ of money furth of his bag quhilk wes ane commond theyffe stik and that he had gewin ane fals testimonial on him to the queens grace vnder the town's seall.[111]

The matter was put to a sworn assise which, through Chalmer's own confession, convicted him of slandering Mar. The names of the men on the assise appear above the account of Chalmer's conviction in the court records. Of the seventeen members of the assise, nine members had previous convictions before the burgh court for a number of offences including forestalling, statute breaking, strublens and mispersoning.[112] Two of the members of the assise, John Lawson and Jerome Blak, had been convicted with Chalmer in 1553 for breaking the town statutes. Another member of the assise, Alexander Howeson, appears as the spouse of Elspett Chalmer who was convicted on two occasions for regrating and forestalling and breaking the common ordinances of the town.[113] The sitting on the assise of so many individuals who had previous convictions suggests that once they had paid their fines or performed their repentance the community welcomed them back and deemed them to be 'good [enough] neighbours' to sit on an assise.

If Chalmer's altercation with one of the town's baillies in 1555 did not precipitate his appearance before the court in 1562 it most certainly would have been considered when the magistrates passed judgement. Characterizing Chalmer's actions as the 'misorder and enormities as he daly committis', the court clerk made clear that Chalmer's numerous convictions led to the court banishing him from the burgh. Chalmer does not appear again in the records and we can assume that his twenty years of misdeeds were taken as sufficient cause for banishment. This is telling, for in all of the cases in which banishment was the final outcome for those criminals within the town, the authorities only very reluctantly imposed this sentence. Banishment was a last resort, to be used only in cases that posed a long-term threat to the town's common weal. This suggests that those regulating Aberdonian society during this period perceived the crimes to be serious threats to the community, but most wrongdoers as worthy of redemption.[114]

There are numerous examples of recidivist activities where the court did not impose more severe penalties. In cases of repeated contravention of burgh statutes for baking bread of insufficient weight or selling goods at prices higher than that fixed by the town council, the offending parties continued to fill the town coffers by submitting to an established set of fines. James Bannerman, a local baxter, was convicted nine times over fourteen years for a variety of these types of offences. Alex Joffray, another baxter, appears twelve times in the court records between 1541 and 1564, both as the perpetrator of a number of transgressions within the community and as the victim of one of his 'neighbour's' wrongdoings. In 1541, the council convicted Joffray of breaking town statutes in the baking of bread of insufficient weight and put him in amercement of court.[115] In 1543, Joffray appeared before the burgh court with two other baxters, John Soulis and Duncan Fraser, on the same charge of baking bread of insufficient weight.[116] Once again the baillies put Joffray in amercement of court without comment on his previous transgression and without a change in his penalty.

By 1543 neither Soulis nor Fraser had been convicted of any wrongdoing before the burgh court.[117] While Fraser does not appear again in the Council Register, Soulis's name appears in four other accounts. A John Soulis was also the victim of Andrew Lindsay's violent attack in 1547 which resulted in Lindsay's banishment from the burgh. It is likely that this was the same John Soulis that had been convicted with Alex Joffray and Duncan Fraser in 1543 and the same John Soulis that the court convicted for breaking town ordinances in March 1544 and February 1548.[118] Soulis appears for the last time in the court records in November 1551:

> The said day John sowlis was convikit for the myspersoning of alexander joffray & Wm langton dekyns of the baxtaris craft wherefore he was in amercement of court to forbear in tym cuming & amend as law will and that was gewen for dome.[119]

Despite the fact that this was his third conviction in ten years, Soulis received a fine as his penalty. Unlike his previous convictions for breaking town statutes, this conviction was for a verbal attack on two deacons of his own craft, men who had established some power and authority within the community. It is interesting to note that Soulis' earlier co-defendant, Alex Joffray, had become deacon of their craft. This did not prevent Joffray from breaking town statutes. In 1555, Joffray was convicted for selling goods in great number to strangers. For his wrongdoing, the council ordered Joffray to pay a fine of 10 pounds.[120] Two years later, Joffray appeared before the court again charged with the mispersoning and strublens of Andrew George. For his wrongdoing the magistrates put him in amercement of court.[121]

Despite repeated wrongdoing within the burgh, there is no clear indication that Bannerman, Soulis or Fraser received harsher penalties or were on the receiving end of stern warnings not to commit these crimes in the future. Even in the case of Soulis mispersoning the deacons of his craft, the baillies determined that a fine was suitable restitution. No further modification of the amends appears in the court records. Alexander Joffray's convictions, however, raise a number of points about power dynamics within the burgh. Prior to his elevation to the position of craft deacon, Joffray's convictions had resulted in his being amerced. However, there seems to have been a change in the severity of the penalties he incurred after becoming deacon of the baxter's craft. It is possible that, because Joffray was a recidivist, the court increased his fine to 10 pounds. However, it is just as likely that the higher fine resulted from the court's belief that someone in Joffray's position in the burgh should be held to a higher standard.

Indeed, the account suggests as much. For selling wheat, meal and flour 'in gryt be bell and firlott to strangears dwelling in landwart' Joffray was 'in amercement of court':

> and the counsel modifit his unlaw to tene poundis to be applyit to the commond weill of this guid towne and gyf he beis convikit in doing of siclyk betine this and the feist of michelmas nixt cumis or in *mis using of his office* and craft in serving of the towne or diminissing of the parte of breid devisit be the counsel to be inhibit of his craft for zeir and day thereafter.[122]

Joffray's case is a clear example of a person in a position of some power receiving a serious rebuke for his wrongdoings. Not only was his fine relatively severe, Joffray received a stern warning that to commit such an offence again would result in the loss of his right to practice his occupation for a year and a day. However, when the court convicted Joffray in 1557 for mispersoning Andrew George, the clerk left no indication in the records that he was a repeat offender. This may be because his previous offences were of a different nature although the evidence does not support this idea. As the cases of John Chalmer, Alexander Burnett and Patrick Stewart illustrate, the court tended to punish individuals who had been convicted numerous times before more severely, regardless of the types of crimes committed.[123] It is also possible that the modification of Chalmer's unlaw has not survived.[124]

Threats of additional penalties and punishments were not the only means to deter recidivism in sixteenth-century Aberdeen. However, while they were frequently employed, they were only occasionally acted upon. This suggests that from the perspective of both the town authorities and the entire community there was an established guideline for good behaviour regulated by enforced penalties and stern warnings. Threats to one's freedom, of bodily harm, of removal from the community or for further fines countered the threat posed by the individual, but also by the misdeed for which they had been convicted. This established within the community the activities deemed to be neighbourly and those that threatened the common weal. More importantly, the active role played by the participants in both crime and punishment underscored the power dynamics within the community and helped to define and maintain the social order. In the following chapters, the connection between criminality, the regulation of crime and the maintenance of custom and statute highlights the deeply interconnected social network that characterized burgh communities. More importantly, this connection illustrates the social dynamics in place and the negotiation of social relations that were a continuous part of early modern societies.

2 GODLY DISCIPLINE

Reformation historians frequently argue that the sixteenth century witnessed the introduction of new ideas on how society *should* be regulated.[1] In particular, Professor Collinson has asserted that a certain type of activism emerged from the reform of the Church that resulted in:

> a morally austere and demanding version of Christianity which turned the doctrine of election into a principle of invidious exclusion and stimulated an unrelenting warfare between the elect and the children of perdition, accentuating that mentality of opposites.[2]

A few years earlier Keith Wrightson and David Levine had argued that social regulation in the localities had changed in both degree and scale during the six-teenth century. In their study of the English village of Terling, Wrightson and Levine argued that this change in degree and scale stemmed from the intersection and interconnectedness of 'democratic growth; commercialization; the socio-economic polarization of local societies; the growth of poverty; the expansion of popular literacy; the impact of the Protestant reformation.'[3] In recent years this argument has had its share of detractors. Margaret Spufford challenged the 'Terling thesis' by arguing that 'the attempt to enforce 'godly discipline' was not new to the sixteenth century. For Spufford, it 'is very necessary to separate puri-tan beliefs, or the beliefs of the "hotter sort of protestant" and, indeed, any other type of religious belief, from their moral application to everyday life.'[4] Such an idea, however, stands in stark contrast to the claim made by Michael Graham in his study of 'Godly Discipline' in Reformation-era Scotland that 'the institutions and practice of reformed church discipline was an effort by churches acting on their own to convert reformed doctrine into practice, and to move the religious changes which were taking place from the realm of theology and worship into the realm of everyday life.'[5] The question that emerges from such conflicting visions of the sixteenth century is whether religious change in its own right brought about shifts in regulatory practices and in attitudes towards social order?

In the 'postscript' of the second edition of *Poverty and Piety*, Wrightson responded to Spufford and a number of other critics, arguing that neither he nor Levine made any presumption that regulatory control of social behaviour was absent in the localities prior to the sixteenth century. Wrightson asserts, however, that 'it would be preposterous to ignore the moral urgency of the Reformation era, the evangelical drive of English Protestantism in the provinces, or the growth of popular literacy which could facilitate deeper penetration of the perceptions and ideals of a reformist church and ambitious state.'[6] The most problematic aspect of Spufford's critique of the 'Terling thesis', therefore, is that it assumes a top-down phenomenon in which local elites influenced by this new activism inflicted a more rigid social regulation upon the poorer sorts.[7] This characterization presumes that most members of early modern communities did not allow social, political or economic matters to interfere with their Godly duties or their faith or allow their faith and Godly duties to interfere with their social interactions and business transactions. If, as Spufford – and Marjorie McIntosh – claim, in communities where a Calvinist religious tradition existed, moral regulation was not imposed from above on the humble, a belief ascribed to the Terling thesis, how then do we understand the stipulation by the St Nicholas Kirk Session that penalties for blood drawing and mispersoning were dependent on the degree of the injured party? Even more problematic, is the admonition made in the opening statements of the first Session that the 'minister [not] publeis nor speik of na speciall mater to the rebuking of any notable or particular person' without consent of the assembly.[8]

There seems to be a lack of consensus on the extent to which socio-economic and politico-religious factors brought about a change in scale and degree in social regulation in the localities of early modern England. A few historians have examined the social history of the Reformation in Scotland, and in particular regulation of behaviour. The study of wrongdoing and its impact on social relations and the uses and negotiation of power rests, to some extent, on our understanding of the impact reformation ideas had on social discipline and how deeply these ideas penetrated local communities. Steve Hindle recently suggested, in a slightly different context, that changes in church ritual in the sixteenth century reflected and symbolized changes in the structure of parish community.[9] If this was the case, then the opposite must also be true; no change in ritual would also have a bearing on the structure of the community. It is important for our understanding of social power and the community of the burgh in sixteenth-century Scotland to determine how the types of crimes committed within the burgh affected the social interactions of its inhabitants. Likewise, it is necessary to consider how the community dealt with such activities, what changes in the types of crime took place during the period under consideration, and how contemporaries viewed such behaviour.

This chapter explores the mechanisms for regulating behaviour that were in place in Aberdeen over the course of three generations straddling the period of religious Reformation in Scotland. It argues that on account of the presence of so many of the same individuals in positions of power within both the burgh civil magistracy and the burgh kirk session, a singular vision for establishing/ maintaining proper behaviour and for protecting the town's well-being over-rode any jurisdictional conflict and sublimated any ideological differences among the spiritual and secular authorities within the town. In particular, a variety of statutes and ordinances emanating from local and national authorities, both secular and spiritual, prescribed normative behaviour and established the guidelines for good neighbourliness. This chapter also addresses the ways the wider community participated in regulating such behaviour and how crime and punishment served to both challenge and reinforce power structures within the burgh community. It does so by examining a variety of charges brought before the St Nicholas Kirk Session in Aberdeen and comparing punishments for such activities with punishments for other 'crimes' committed in the burgh. It also examines contemporary beliefs that sin and crime were equally damaging to the well-being of the burgh community.

Crime versus Sin

It is unfortunate that historians examining the impact of criminal activities on Scottish society in the sixteenth century do not have the benefit of a variety of contemporary treatises, sermons and diaries that conceptualize wrongdoing and provide contemporary categorizations of crime and criminal behaviour. While the well-known sixteenth-century Scottish jurists, Balfour (1525–83), Skene (1543–1617) and Craig (1538–1608) all comment on the centrality of positive law in Scottish legal thought, they offer little reflection on criminal responsibility or on characteristics of misbehaving.[10] Instead, historians examining criminal activities in early modern Scotland must rely largely on conviction accounts in extant court records to inform them of whether or not there were distinctions made between certain disreputable acts and other similar activities. Fortunately, it is possible to glean from these accounts contemporary attitudes towards crime, as the court clerks frequently highlighted the dangers such activities posed to a well-ordered society and occasionally reflected the frustrations felt by local magistrates and neighbours alike towards individual wrongdoing within the community.

This is not to say that the sixteenth-century Scottish jurists cannot offer any insights or provide valuable direction on how contemporary Scots thought best to regulate their society. The continued importance of positive law, and in particular the belief in the power of legislation and Parliament's central role in prescribing the statutes for regulating behaviour, stand out in the works of Balfour, Skene and Craig. All three had, at one time or another, worked for the Scottish Parliament to prepare, organize and 'treat upoun the lawes' of the realm.[11] Like most early modern lawyers their perspective on the sources of law was truly 'medieval';

the tripartite division of law into the law of nature, law of God and positive law featured prominently in their respective works. Balfour very clearly argues that statutory law emanating from Parliament 'binds and obliges all the lieges of the realm' who 'must live and be governed under the King's laws and statutes' alone.[12] Craig's own view on positive law stands out in his argument that 'when therefore a controverted question in the Law of Scotland cannot be solved by appealing to the general principles of the Law of Nature or to those of the Law of Nations, recourse must be had to the written law of our own country.'[13]

Similar to Balfour and Craig, Sir John Skene's involvement with parliamentary papers and on commissions for assessing the laws and contemporary legal practices enabled him to acquaint himself with Scotland's legal traditions. Although his treatise *Of Crimes and Judge, in Criminall Causes, conform to the laws of the Realm* (c. 1609) focuses primarily on the jurisdictional concerns for regulating crime, he does offer a brief discussion on the distinctions between types of crimes based on punishments.[14] In large part, the later discussion focuses largely on 'statutory authority' as the guiding principle behind regulating criminal activities. Like Balfour and Craig, Skene also privileged positive law as a key mechanism for regulating crime within the realm.[15] While these Scottish jurists offer limited insights into how they saw various crimes affecting society, we may glean such perspectives from the writings of contemporary English lawyers. Steve Hindle has highlighted the contemporary distinction made by Sir Richard Grosvenor between offences against 'piety', against 'regality' and against 'morality and civility'.[16] The first type of crime, Grosvenor determined, touched closely upon sin or had a 'more neere relation to God and Religion', the second type of crime threatened the king's person or his authority; and the third type 'more properly concerne[s] the politike government of the commonwealth'.[17] Similarly, the English Chief Justice Sir James Whitelocke established a tripartite typology of criminal behaviour that included crimes against the church and the state, but which also illustrated a growing concern with rooting out any threat to the welfare of the commonwealth.[18]

In Scotland it is possible to see the influence of Reform ministers like Knox and John Craig penetrating local communities as their vision of both spiritual and temporal government 'punishing sin in unison' began to take shape. This is most clearly obvious in the hierarchy of offences or 'sins' that the General Assembly established in the *Ordoure of Excommunication and of Public Repentance* in 1569. Murder, witchcraft, adultery, sorcery, abortion and blaspheming were crimes punishable by immediate excommunication whereas fornication, drunkenness, brawling, contempt of kirk and Sabbath breaking were dealt with through acts of public repentance. Michael Graham recently concluded that while such guidelines were straightforward, what was needed was a 'zealous magistrate to act as a nursing mother to the infant kirk'.[19] However, Sharpe warns the reader that crime, 'in its modern usage, was unfamiliar in England throughout our period' and that there was a 'contemporary inability to make a consistently clear distinction between "crime" and "sin".'[20]

Perhaps more suggestive of the importance of collective responsibility, both spiritual and temporal, is the passage taken from the *First Book of Discipline* written in 1560–1:

> As that no Commonwealth can long flourish or long indure without good lawes and sharpe execution of the same, so neither can the kirk of God be brought to purity neither yet be retained in the same without the order of Ecclesiastical discipline, which stands in reproving and correcting of the faults, which the civvill sword either doth neglect or not punish. Blasphemy, adulterie, murder, perjurie and other crimes capitall, worthy of death, ought not properly to fall under censure of the Kirk, because all such open transgressors of Gods lawes ought to be taken away by the civill sword.[21]

The passage goes on to say that where the civil authorities were slow to act, due to the confusion 'Papistry' caused, the new kirk would intervene and punish accordingly. The main tenet behind collective discipline and regulation was that neglect of such responsibilities would invite God's wrath on the entire community.[22]

'To satisfie the magistrate and the kirk'

The constitution laid out in the first kirk session meeting in St Nicholas outlined the parties responsible for regulating acceptable behaviour through the election of elders and deacons and delimited the terms for good neighbourliness. The parallel in terms of language between statutes created by the burgh council and those created by the kirk session is striking. Most noticeably, the reference in council minutes to the 'haill communitie' or 'hail town' present for the time matches closely the language in the kirk session account of the election of elders and deacons who were 'ordainit and providit be the minister underwritten admittit be the *haill congregation* present for the tyme'.[23] The first thirteen pages recording the inaugural kirk session meeting in Aberdeen in 1562 outlined the proper code of behaviour inhabitants of the burgh would have been expected to adhere to. There it was 'statutit and ordainit that upon the Sabbath day all craftsmen and laubourers and all else within this town decist and cease fra all labouring and handework'. Likewise, all within the town were to be in attendance at morning prayers and preaching under pain of 2 shillings.[24] The authorities within the burgh were to levy fines and require public acts of repentance of those individuals who transgressed both burgh and kirk statutes.[25]

The burgh court, as well as the kirk session, had effective ways of dealing with most of these offences and found additional support in Acts of Parliament created for treating specific crimes. For example, in 1551 an Act of Mary Queen of Scots legislated against blasphemers of both great and lesser estates who brought 'the Ire and wraith of God vpone the pepill heirfoir'. According to this Act, rank determined the appropriate penalties; for example the 'puir folk [were] to be put in the stokis or preson'.[26] Michael Graham argued that misbehaviour committed by individuals brought God's displeasure to bear upon the entire community and associated this belief with the introduction of Calvinist social discipline to Scotland after the Reformation.[27] However, it is unclear whether Protestant-minded members of the Three Estates introduced the Act Concerning Blasphemers or whether the concerns inherent in that Act reflected late medieval attitudes towards oaths being sworn. Nonetheless, there is a striking parallel between the Act of Parliament from 1551 and the statute found in the St Nicholas Kirk Session prohibiting the 'taking, speking & using of the name of god in vane all swearing, all bannying and cursing and generaly all aythis'.[28]

Two other Acts of Parliament coming out of the same parliament that legislated against blasphemy proscribed bigamy and adultery. Both stand out for their content, but also for the insight they provide into the type of society that created such acts. According to the legislation, those who committed bigamy were 'of the law periure and infame' and as a consequence were to endure confiscation of their goods, 'warding of their persons for a year and a day and langer induring the Queens will'. More importantly, 'as infame persounis' they were 'neuer habill to bruke office honour dignitie nor benefice in tyme tocum.'[29] According to the statute, more than wealth was prerequisite for being elected a magistrate or burgh official; one's peers must also have considered them good and honourable. Likewise, the statute against adultery bridged secular and ecclesiastical jurisdictions. Those convicted of adultery who did 'not desist for feir of ony spirituall jurisdiction or Censuris of halie kirk' were to be put to the horn and declared a rebel without possibility of intervention from the kirk to suspend the horning.[30]

While the kirk session records document numerous cases of adultery and bigamy, in the locales a more operative definition of the laws was more the norm than the exception. In fact, little distinction is made between the two Acts. For example, in 1562 Gilbert King was brought before St Nicholas Kirk Session and accused of committing adultery. While the account does not name his partner in the act, the clerk noted that King had a 'lawfull wyf as lyf callit Agnes Smyt'.[31] The same session charged Gilbert Anderson and Jonet Mayer of adultery, Anderson's 'wyf being lyf callit Maggie lamb'.[32] In neither case were the individuals declared the Queen's rebel and put to the horn. However, they were ordered to 'conform to the act made against adulterers'. It is not clear whether the act referred to here was the act statuted by the kirk session or the one made at Edinburgh in 1551.[33] Nonetheless, the requirements for repairing the wrong done – public acts of repentance and fines – paralleled those demanded by the provost, baillies and council for a variety of transgressions.[34]

While such statutes delimited the boundaries of acceptable Christian behaviour, they also served as tools that helped regulate inclusion in and exclusion from the benefits of the kirk. In this way, they mirrored those customs, statutes and ordinances that regulated the burgh community. The session not only required individuals convicted of adultery or fornication to pay a fine to the civil magistrates as well as sit in judgment by their peers and betters seeking their forgiveness, they also barred them from receiving any 'benefit' of the kirk until they completed their acts of repentance. In November 1575, the session accused Issobell Matheson of fornication. Before her child could be baptized, Matheson had to pay the pecunial pain [penalty] of 6 shillings to the town magistrate and set caution for her repentance before the kirk.[35] Thomas Fyny and Helen Nicol found themselves in the same situation in February 1576. Accused of fornication, the session prevented them from having their child 'gottin in fornication' baptized until the civil magistrates received their fine of 26s. 8d. Like Matheson, the session required them to set caution for their repentance.

These examples stand out for a number of reasons. First, the session clearly articulated that the children of these offenders would be excluded from the Christian community by means of holding back their baptism until the appropriate measure of repentance occurred. Second, the mechanisms – i.e. statutes and judiciary procedures – regulating exclusion from, and re-introduction into, the kirk community parallel those employed by the civil magistrates. Indeed, fines paid by individuals charged by the session for wrongdoing went into the town coffers while the act of repentance occurred in the parish kirk before the minister and his congregation. Third, the requirement of a cautioner to ensure the offending parties return to good behaviour, not unlike the public acts of repentance, involved members of the community who participated in the process of inclusion. The tandem of magistrate, guildry and kirk, and statutory law and customary practice defined the mechanisms for regulating the community.

In general, statutes and ordinances as well as customary practice also regulated inclusion and exclusion within the community. They regulated behaviour and prescribed the means of being a good neighbour. More importantly, statutes provided the guidelines by which inhabitants delimited power structures. The areas in which authority intersected - the council, the guildry and the kirk - reflect also the areas in which smaller, interconnected communities within burgh society intersected. In large part, responses to regulatory systems within the burgh reflect closely upon such processes of inclusion and exclusion.

In May 1576 the St Nicholas Kirk Session ordained that 'na publict slanderis sik as fornicators, adulteraris or utheris wheresoever resave any benefit of the kirk quhill they first have satisfied the magistrate and nixt to mak their publict repentance before the kirk'.[36] Criminal accounts found in the burgh records do not always indicate that individuals convicted of wrongdoing were

required to satisfy both the civil and spiritual authorities. To counter continued transgressions within the community, the kirk session, with the full force of
the burgh court behind it, used whatever powers it had to punish wrongdoing.
Frequent references in the St Nicholas Kirk Session records reveal that wrongdoers brought before the session were excluded from receiving the benefits of
the kirk.[37] The general procedure for those convicted before the session was to
pay the civil magistrates a fine and to perform public acts of repentance before
the congregation. The overlapping concern with removing unwanted elements
from society and the continued evocation of the civil magistrates suggests that
during the sixteenth century the kirk session and the burgh magistrates coordinated their efforts to enforce discipline and order in the community.[38] Although
conviction accounts in the burgh court records less frequently invoke the kirk's
authority, they do indicate that the kirk played an important role in meting out
justice and maintaining order within Aberdeen society. The use of the word
'slanderis' to describe transgressions other than verbal assaults makes it clear that
contemporaries construed sin and crime as slanderous because it was harmful
and thought to bring shame to the community.[39] For example, the initial records
of the first Kirk Session of St Nicholas in 1562 states that those found guilty of
fornication and adultery for their first fault were to ask 'forgifness at god and
the congregation quhoim they hawe sklanderit'.[40] In similar manner, in March
of 1577 the session ordered that all 'publict slanderis againis Gods word being
convicit hereof salbe upstendit [prohibited] publiclie fray the tabill of the lord
unto the tyme of thair trew repentants.'[41] This could only occur 'be tryall' and
after 'the penaltie to be payit to the magistrat & first repentants on the stoill'.[42]

   Although the continued threat of Catholic recusancy after 1562 plagued
some of the reform-minded members of the community, and in particular the
kirk session, the active participation of the staunchly Catholic Menzies family in
both the civil and spiritual spheres within the burgh ensured a conservative and
traditional approach to regulating Aberdonian society.[43] As was the case in most
early modern communities, in Aberdeen the 'gud men' of the burgh or the 'community' were to be made up of the most upstanding, and honourable men. These
men were called upon to serve as provosts, baillies, kirk session elders, deans of
guild and other public officers. It must have seemed contradictory to some then
that members of the Menzies family were frequently brought before the session
for their own misdeeds. As provosts, baillies and kirk session elders, the Menzies
family was at the heart of the regulatory system in place in Aberdeen. Their own
wrongdoing highlights the tension that existed between the ideals and reality
of burgh life in this period.[44] Nonetheless, the fact that both the burgh court
and kirk session dealt with physical violence, verbal crime, fornication, adultery,
adherence to the Roman church, as well other activities deemed to be harmful to
the community in the same manner, by means of fines, acts of repentance, cor-

poral punishment, incarceration or banishment, suggests that both church and state played a key role in punishing crime and maintaining order.

What links the different types of wrongdoing punished by kirk session and burgh court is the prevailing attitude within the burgh community that all such activities were harmful and detrimental to the common weal. Moreover, the extant records suggest that the burgh authorities, both spiritual and secular, concerned themselves less with making distinctions between crime and sin, and more with maintaining order and ensuring good neighbourliness through regulation of behaviour.[45] In early March 1556 the provost, baillies and council convicted John Forbes for the 'missaying' of Alexander Gray, one of the town's baillies.[46] The Council Register notes that Forbes 'put him self in the bailzeis will for ony faill & offence mad be him to the said bailze'.[47] Although his motivation is unclear, Forbes recognized and acknowledged his fault and obliged himself to return to good behaviour and abide by the baillies' command. Similarly, in May 1574 Robert Nicholson became cautioner for his son Thomas that he would 'satisfy the kirk' for the fornication committed between Thomas and Maly Mair 'and restoir thaim to the ordor of discipline'.[48] In both cases, the authorities who pronounced judgment, the guilty parties themselves and members of the community participated in the proper restoration of 'order'.

This also comes across in a number of other cases found in the St Nicholas Kirk Session records and in the Council Register. On 14 September 1575, James Anderson, the son of an Aberdeen litster, confessed before the session that he had fornicated with Issobell Vylberson. For his offence Anderson was to compear the next day and to 'bring with hym ane cautionar to satisfie the magistrate & the kirk'.[49] Appearing before the session again the next day along with his cautioner Robert Mullan, Anderson received a fine of 40 shillings that was to be paid 'to the magistrate for his pecunial pane' and an order 'to satisfy the kirk' by making 'his repentans on the stull in front of the haill kirk'.[50] Anderson's act of repentance bears a striking similarity to the acts of repentance required in two separate cases recorded in the Council Register. In both of these cases, however, the type of offence committed stands in contrast to the one the kirk session convicted James Anderson of committing.

In April 1571 the burgh court convicted John Sanders and his son Robert for troubling and the 'blud drawing' of Alexander Robertson and also for attacking Robertson's dog. For their offence, the court ordered the Sanders to set lawborrow [legal security to keep the peace] that Robertson would not suffer any further attack in the future from either father or son.[51] On 18 May 1571, the baillies modified the amends of the crime committed by John and Robert Sanders.[52] For their transgression they were ordered to appear in the tolbooth the following Monday and 'thair in presens of the haill communitie present for the tyme sit downe upoune his [sic] kneis & ask first god and syn the said Alexander forgifnes'. The court also ordered them to pay Robertson 20 shillings.[53] Likewise, in 1572 the burgh court convicted James Huntar for troubling and striking Robert Ross. Having put Huntar in amercement of court, the baillies modified his amends and ordered him:

> to sit downe vpon his kneis in the tollbuith and thair to ask first God forgiveness and Syn the said Robert and to pay him xx S for the trubling & blood drawing of him and aucht s for the Baillies unlaw and to abstane in tyme cuming under the pane of five merks.[54]

The public acts of repentance performed by the Sanders men and Huntar took the same form used by other penitents required to seek forgiveness from God, the town and their victims within the parish kirk. However, in these cases the act of repentance took place in the tolbooth, the centre of civic justice within the burgh. This may suggest that crime and sin fell under the purview of both spiritual and secular authorities and the distinction between the two, at least in terms of regulating unwanted behaviour, was not as crucial as historians have been prone to believe.[55] Although the stool of repentance was missing, the Sanders' and Huntar's pecuniary and penitential punishment bears a striking parallel with that required of James Anderson in satisfying the magistrate and the kirk. Both suggest a concern to protect the community from behaviour deemed unneighbourly and which posed the danger of bringing God's wrath down upon the town. The types of activities described represent some of the main threats posed to the common weal of the burgh and to both godly discipline, as it was invoked from the 1560s on, and to good neighbourliness throughout the period.

In Chapter 3, I examine the town council's use of statutes and ordinances to regulate life within the community.[56] From fixing the prices of goods to banning pigs from the town streets, these statutes sought to establish regulatory processes to maintain order within society and establish behaviour deemed to be neighbourly. During the meeting of the Head Court, and in subsequent sittings of the council, those present set guidelines for punishing faults and for controlling crime. The very public nature of publishing these guidelines - often by open proclamation at the market cross - corresponded neatly with the public displays of repentance for wrongdoers.[57] In such manner the importance of the tolbooth, as the centre of justice within the town; the market cross, as the public site for doling out corporal punishments and acts of ritual repentance; and the kirk or pulpit, as a combination of the two, stand out.

While the kirk session records provide us with insight into the mechanisms in place after the Reformation began to permeate Aberdonian society from about 1562, we should not assume that prior to the Reformation the old kirk did not hold similar symbolic importance as a site of acknowledging fault within the community. It is fairly clear that the only major change in practice in the post-Reformation kirk in terms of public forgiveness was the loss of the highly ritualized aspects of the long procession and offering of gifts of wax to the altar of the 'holy blud'.[58] That said, explicit statements left in the kirk session records underscore the very important role the kirk, and in particular the pulpit, played in regulating society. Of particular interest is the way in which it clearly functioned as part of the same processes of inclusion and exclusion in which the burgh court also participated. For example, a statute made by the session in 1576 outlines the interconnected role of both spiritual and secular authorities in Aberdeen and underscores the intrinsic importance of the pulpit as a means of including and excluding members of the community:

> The said day it is statutit and ordainit with consent of the elderis and deaconis of the session of the last yeir and be the minister and session electit and acceptand this day that the haill personis electit this day called by the minister in pulpit and not compearand to accept that they be warnit be the officers to compear and accept.[59]

The threat for not appearing was the loss of any benefit of the kirk - i.e. communion, baptism, marriage and funeral rites. Strangely similar is the statute made a few months earlier outlining that 'all fornicators and adulterers in this burgh be warned be the minister on Sunday nixt to compear before the session on Thursday nixt and failzing of compearand to express the names of thaim not compearand in pulpit be thair names on Sunday nixt.'[60] Members of the community 'outed' in the pulpit were to appear before the session for their crime irrespective of the nature of their offence. Such public exposure served as a process of exclusion. These same individuals, when brought before the session and forced to pay their fine to the civil magistrate and to make their repentance before the community, participated in the subsequent process of inclusion that reintroduced the offender back into the community.[61]

As both statutes suggest, failure to appear meant that the individuals, and often their family members, were not to receive any benefit of the kirk, thus excluding them from the community and important aspects of membership - in particular marriage and baptism. This is best exemplified in the statute made in March 1576 outlining that children begotten of fornicators were not to be baptized until the parents satisfied the magistrate and the kirk for their offence.[62] These processes mirror those already established by the town council and the burgh court for regulating behaviour within the community: the threat of banishment from the town, the loss of the right to practise one's craft within the burgh limits, and the exclusion from the social benefits of belonging to the guild, merchant or craft 'and the freedoms thereof', parallel the exclusion from the benefits of the kirk that the kirk session used to prompt individuals to return to godly discipline.

If it is true that the reformed Kirk in Scotland had a keenly articulated sense of order and discipline, as outlined in the *First Book of Discipline* and the *Book of Common Order*, the Kirk Session in Aberdeen and the town council sought hard to ensure that for the 'guid of the town and the inhabitants thereof' order and discipline reigned. This is evident in the accounts that reveal the manner in which the leading men of the burgh systematically regulated the boundaries of good behaviour. That members of the town council and town officials made up a significant portion of the kirk session as elders and deacons demonstrates the interconnected relationship between ecclesiastical and civic justice within the burgh. This is best exemplified in the ordinances recorded in the opening pages of the St Nicholas Kirk Session records for 1562 which outline the penalties to be incurred for any wrongdoing within the community. There is no doubting the non-secular nature of the ordinances as they appear in the Kirk Session records. As Michael Graham has referred to them they took the form of 'the Ten Commandments, with explanations and punishments'.[63] That said, transgressions, usually within the purview of the burgh court, and the penalties attached to such wrongdoing found within these ordinances, indicate that there was some overlap in concern for the community between the spiritual and secular authorities. This is abundantly clear in cases of slander, mispersoning, blood drawing and other forms of strublance.[64] It is equally clear in cases involving nightwalkers and vagabonds, theft, beggary and the 'idyll puir'.[65] As concerned the 'gryte plague of poverty regnand within this town and scarcite of vittuals', the St Nicholas Kirk Session ordered that:

> where ar many sundry beggaris pykaris & pylleris of utheris menis guids and geir and gryte theyft committit thro[ughou]t.... it is statutit and ordainit that all strangearis beggaris not beand of this town be removit thairfra & nain to be tholit to remane heir above 24 hours and those harbouring the laug to be punist for breaking this charge.[66]

Moreover, all 'decayit & purell natywe born within this town to be billet',[67] so that the minister could discern the deserving poor from those unworthy of receiving the benefits of the kirk and congregation.[68]

This bears a striking resemblance to the statute issued by the town council in 1546 indicating that the native beggars were to receive the 'tounis takyn' and all 'wther begaris to be chargit to dewoid the towne within twenty four hours.'[69] All nightwalkers, drunkards and various other breakers of the king's peace were to be admonished from the pulpit in a manner similar to those convicted of fornication, adultery and slander. In such manner, crime and sin found similar response from the kirk. Moreover, the similarities in pecuniary, penitential and corporal punishment executed by the kirk and magistrate underscore the close connection between spiritual and secular regulation of behaviour within the burgh community.

In October 1575, the Kirk Session ordered William Robson to 'satisfy the magistrate and kirk for the crym of adulterie committed be him with Katherine Symson.'[70] This case clearly indicates that from the perspective of the session, at least, both the secular and spiritual authorities required 'satisfaction' for William's wrongdoing.[71] Of perhaps greater interest is the lengthy process involving both the kirk and the civil magistrates in curbing the wrongdoings perpetrated by Robson. Robson first appears in the Kirk Session records in September 1575 as being 'examined by the session for committing adultery with Katherine Symson.'[72] At the end of October that year, Robson was ordered to pay 5 merks for his offence and to find caution 'within fourteen days for relief of the Baillies and haill session.'[73] This reinforces the earlier discussion on the important role the entire community played in regulating society. In this instance, the magistrate, the Kirk Session and the cautioner, representing the neighbour within the community, participated in the process of bringing about Robson's redemption. Robson's next appearance before the kirk was in February 1576. Here, the public nature of regulating social order shines through.

The Kirk Session records indicate that 'the session ordainit the minister to mak publict charged on Sunday nixt in pulpit to maister Wm Robson to enter his repentance for the filthe crym of adultery committit be him with Katherin Symson'.[74] What the records do not make clear is whether Robson and Symson continuously engaged in the 'filthe crym of adultery' after first being brought before the Kirk Session or whether the process of dealing with their crimes was simply a lengthy one. This is made more unclear by the fact that the Kirk Session records make mention of Robson and Symson again for 26 September 1576. On that date, the session ordered Robson to appear before the synod 'to resave his inhibitions of repentance of the adultery committed with Katherine Symson'.[75] These individuals appear in the Kirk Session records for the last time in December 1576, fourteen months after Robson first appeared before the Kirk Session for his crime. Neither Katherine Symson's nor William Robson's name appear again in the Kirk Session, or burgh court, records for any other wrongdoing. Unfortunately, their names vanish from the records without any indication of whether or not the session required Symson to perform the same acts of repentance or to pay similar fines to the magistrates. We also learn nothing of their status within Aberdeen society or whether the absence of their names from the records after December 1576 is truly indicative of their return to Godly discipline and good neighbourliness.[76]

The disciplinary actions taken by the burgh council and baillies and the elders and deacons of the kirk session to curb a variety of offences accentuates the perception that petty crimes posed a very real threat to the entire community. As I have suggested, it is not altogether accurate to argue that in Aberdeen this was an entirely new process dependent on a reformed theology based on godly discipline. Indeed, the history of the Reformation in Aberdeen makes it clear that the burgh very hesitantly moved towards establishing a Reform Kirk but was entirely cognizant of the political necessity of doing so.[77] That is not say that there were not any reform-minded individuals within the town, only that reform followed closely the conservative character of the burgh.[78] As a number of historians examining the Reformation in Aberdeen have suggested, the establishment of the Reform Kirk in Aberdeen was predicated on the impact it would have on the politics of the burgh and the entire region. By and large, the involvement of the leading men of the town - Menzies, Forbes, Mar, Chalmer, Gray- in both the burgh council and St Nicholas Kirk Session meant that formal power to regulate society continued to rest in the hands of the same individuals.

Restorative Justice

The burgh court records, Council Register and St Nicholas Kirk Session records contain numerous examples of wrongdoers being required to restore things to their proper order after their actions had caused change within the burgh. Clerks frequently recorded the magistrates demanding the convicted party to 'abstan in tym cuming' or 'desist' from their wrongdoing with an accompanying order to cease the activities deemed hurtful to the town. For example, John Lame and William Sym, convicted in 1550 for the strublens of each other, had to appear during high mass to make amends 'and to abstain in tym cuming fra siclyk faltis under the pane of banishing thaim the town'.[79] Similarly, the court ordered John Cowper's wife, who had been convicted for the regrating of victuals, to abstain in the future from such activities 'vnder the pane of banesing the town' and 'wes remittit of hir unlaw vnder this condition'.[80]

Examples of the restorative aspect of punishment can also be found in instances of theft or property crime where the burgh court ordered the convicted party to return, repair, restore or mend the damaged goods. This was the case for Steven Allan and John Gunther, who the provost and baillies accused in 1562 of 'intromission with the leid [baptismal font] quhilk was stollin of thair pariche kirk vpoun the font stuil of the same extending to thirty stane.'[81] Allan and Gunther argued that they were not aware the item had been stolen 'nor quhair of it wes takin' and as such had the right to buy the item from whoever had sold it to them. In response, the provost, baillies and council ordered that the two set surety 'to put on the said leid vpoun the said kirk be ane sufficient craftisman quhair ... and mak the same als gud and sufficient as the same wes obefoir vpoun thair awne expens.'[82] Indicative of how serious the baillies perceived their crime, the pair was warned that if convicted again for any offence, they would be banished 'perpetuallie of the town'. Similarly, John Deuchar, a local cordwainer, was brought before the baillies for stealing stones out of Alexander Menzies' dyke.[83] For his wrongdoing, the baillies ordered him 'to restoir and repone the saidis stanes an repair the said dyik als guid as is was at the way taking thereof.'[84] In both cases, the penalty for their transgressions was the restoration of the items that were taken from their original owners and the repair of any damage caused by their actions.

This is also reminiscent of the act of revoking injurious language spoken by an individual against one of their neighbours, a common punishment for those convicted of verbal assaults. In October 1581, the burgh court convicted Jonet Troup for the mispersoning of Elizabeth Irving. For her crime, the baillies ordered Troup to appear at the market cross:

> with ane crown of paper on hir hede and on sunday thereftir to cum to the kirk and thair in presens of the peple and provost revoik and agane call the wordis that she hes spokin upon Elizabeth Irwing and to ask God and the said forgiveness.[85]

Six months earlier, for his slandering of Andrew Dun, Andrew Gow had been ordered to pay '£5 of penaltie before he depart the tollbuyth and ask the said ado forgiveness and revoke the words as fals'.[86] The magistrates believed that publicly humiliating Troup and Gow and ordering them to revoke their slanderous words was an effective deterrent against this type of crime and a suitable punishment for those convicted of such offences. The experience of the two was not unique; over a fifty-year period (1542–92) the provost and baillies ordered nearly 18 per cent, or 54 out of 309, of all those convicted of some form of verbal assault to ask the injured party forgiveness before the whole community at the tolbooth, the market cross, and most often within the parish kirk.[87] Through the act of forgiveness and the revocation of the injurious words, the wrongdoer restored the injured party's good name and reputation.[88]

Nowhere is this more clear than in the example made of Henry Pantown. In February 1564/5, the baillies convicted Pantown for breaking the common ordinances of the town in baking of 'quhyt breid being forbiddyne be the Baillies obefoir'.[89] In a fit of anger over the court's decision, Pantown launched into a verbal assault against the magistrates, calling the provost and baillies 'common oppressors', 'dyors' [debtors] and 'bystors [bastards]'. A sworn assise determined that Pantown's defamation of the provost and baillies warranted his being put in the govis for three hours and his banishment from the town 'induring the counsellis will'.[90] The severity of his punishment stemmed from the damage Pantown inflicted on the magistrates' reputation, the challenges he made to their authority and the threat he posed to the order and discipline within the town. For his wrongdoing the baillies also 'dischargit the said henry of his fremanschip' and prohibited him from baking in the future. Thus, while his banishment may have been short term, the magistrates determined that Pantown's punishment should have lasting consequences. The revocation of his right to practise his craft freely in the town was a significant loss in terms of his belonging to the community, his social status and potential for earning an income.

There is no indication that Pantown had repeatedly broken the statutes and ordinances in the past nor committed any other transgression within the community. It is also not immediately discernible why the town had forbidden the baking of wheat bread at this time, although most of the realm was experiencing dearth as a result of famine.[91][92] Dearth across Scotland between 1550 and 1600 led to proclamations from Edinburgh against hoarding and new legislation that targeted forestallers.[93] Acts against forestallers were passed or renewed in parliament in 1540, 1551, 1563, 1567, 1579, 1587 and 1592. It is not surprising then that Aberdeen's magistrates remained concerned that famine, dearth and poverty in the realm would breed idleness, vagrancy and petty crime and ultimately threaten the social fabric established by hardworking, god-fearing neighbours. What is crucial to understand is that the town's officials were willing and able to enforce their full authority when members of the community challenged their power and reputation. Thus, while Pantown did not have to revoke the words he spoke or ask the provost and baillies forgiveness, his penalty underscored both the threat his actions posed to the order and discipline within the town and the need to restore the magistrate's reputation.

The Kirk Session also worked to restore an injured party's reputation if it had been diminished by some form of assault. For example, in May 1574 Esse Leslie brought a bill of complaint before the session alleging that Besse Nandy had slandered her 'saying that she wes participant of the theftis away taking of' a brewing cauldron from Thomas Redland's brew house.'[94] The session ordered her to present witnesses to corroborate the slander allegedly commited by Nandy. Leslie presented Elspet Kyntoir and Jonett Douglas who both substantiated Leslie's claim that Nandy had slandered her in saying that she had participated in the theft from the brewhouse. The session ordered that the case be put to further consideration. Similarly, in May 1576 Gilbert Anderson was called before the session to answer to the charge of slandering Margaret Perkins, the relict of umquhil Richard Listair. The session found Anderson guilty of the offence and ordered him to pay the magistrate 10*s* 'to be giwen to the puir' and to ask Margaret for forgiveness before the session.[95] In both instances, restoration of the injured party's reputation was an important part of the punishment. Moreover, while the outcome of Leslie's case is not recorded in the Session records, the involvement of Kyntoir and Douglas to bear witness, and the advisement of the elders and deacons in determining fault, suggests that the community played a role in bringing about conflict resolution and restoring the town to good order and discipline.

As stated earlier, banishment was not the only threat the burgh court used to compel a wrongdoer to abstain from hurtful activities and return to good behaviour. Equally compelling was the threat of a substantial fine. In a number of cases, the fine levied on the individual at the time of their conviction was far less than that which was used as a threat against future offence. For example, in 1580 David Kelly's conviction for 'forestalling and regrating this burt' resulted in an order to set caution for his unlaw and 'to abstane in tym cuming vnder the pane of fourtie poundis his vnlaw modefeid to xl s'.[96] In cases where individuals had been convicted of regrating and forestalling, and the court ordered the convicted party to cease and desist from such activities in the future, the additional penalties for failing to abstain ranged from 5 merks to 40 pounds to banishment from the town. Of these cases, less than 15 per cent can be explained by concerns of recidivism.[97] In all of these cases the baillies explicitly ordered the wrongdoer to abstain or desist from committing similar crimes in the future. In large part then, the burgh court, as well as the transgressor, participated in restorative discipline: one through the process of levying a penalty and delimiting the parameters for the return to good behaviour and the other through the fulfillment of the required punishment and the abstention from similar wrongdoing in the future.

Community Involvement in Regulating Misbehaviour

While the burgh authorities, both secular and spiritual, played a primary role in regulating behaviour, the wider community actively participated in the processes to root out wrongdoing. In such manner, the inhabitants of the burgh, to some extent, governed the power structures and social relations that defined the burgh community. When in April 1574 the Kirk Session accused Andrew Philipson of drunk and disorderly behaviour, the local magistrates ordered him 'to present himself in the place of repentance and there to ask God and *his kirkmen* [forgiveness] and als desyrid the magistrate to promis him civilly.'[98] Thus, the community as a whole participated in Philipson's rehabilitation. This is apparent in the frequent requirement of one's neighbours to accept the convicted person's act of atonement and grant them forgiveness. Many of the unlaws [penalties] recorded in the Guildry Accounts, Council Register and Baillie Court Books specify that convicted parties were to set caution or lawborrow, and sometimes both, to vouch for their continued good behaviour.[99] Such requirements made certain individual actions, consequences and responses the concern of the entire community and as such should be seen as a mechanism for inclusion and exclusion within the community. By making the wider community aware of the crimes committed by certain individuals, the town authorities asserted that the 'common weil' of the burgh, the town's well-being, was the responsibility of all of its inhabitants.

The burgh community filled a role carved out for them by a local magistracy dependent on their assistance through acting as cautioners for convicted neighbours, bearing witness to the faults of their fellow inhabitants through public acts of repentance, and by ensuring that those individuals banished from the town or banned from practicing their crafts did not attempt to challenge these injunctions. In a period where formal policing of the community was haphazard at best, the involvement of the burgh's inhabitants was necessary for maintaining the common weal.[100] To a large extent, the various crimes brought before the burgh court and the kirk session, and how authorities viewed/categorized/ dealt with such wrongdoing, informs us of the type of society contemporaries were keen to establish and maintain. Although there is little definitive proof that all sixteenth-century Aberdonians, regardless of their status, concerned themselves with maintaining the 'common weill of the burgh', this was not simply a top-down process. The frequency with which individual members of the community brought their 'neighbours' before the courts on account of some wrong being done to them or another member of the community, or to vouch for their return to 'good neighbourliness', suggests that establishing proper behaviour and working towards a stable social order was not solely within the purview of town officials.[101] Here it is perhaps instructive to note the seventeenth-century Scots jurist Viscount Stair's argument that the burgh itself was 'a cautioner' to protect the 'liberties' and maintain the 'safety and security of the people'.[102] While the liberties afforded to the burgh and the institutions that helped to define it served to protect its inhabitants, the community itself played a crucial role in regulating behaviour and maintaining social stability. This it accomplished primarily through acting as individual cautioners and lawborrows to convicted members of the community and participating in public punishments.

In his study of the 'remedy of Lawborrows' in Scotland, George Clark argued that by the sixteenth century 'the remedy of Lawburrows, either as an end in itself, or as a means of keeping the peace between parties until the dispute was then resolved was very commonly used throughout Scotland.'[103] Thus, we find that Robert Galloway, who the burgh court convicted of the 'strublens, striking and mispersoning' of Jonet Castell, was ordered to pay the 20*d.* expense of court and 'take caution and lawborrowis that the said Jonett salbe harmless and skaythless of him'.[104] Nearly twenty years later, in January 1575, the baillies put Gilbert Skarlit in amercement of court for physically assaulting Besse Gray 'with ane quhingar' and ordered him to 'sett lawborrowis'.[105] It should be noted that it was not only the case that upstanding 'citizens' vouched for those who tended to fall from grace and commit acts against their neighbours, the community and the local authorities, although occasionally this was the case.[106] In some instances it was possible for individuals convicted themselves of upsetting the social order to vouch for another's return to good behaviour. Thus, in August 1551, the council determined that William Lyon and Robert Mar should 'becom suretie and Lawborrowis the ane for the uther that James Kailinar salbe harmless & skaythless for thai'.[107] Lawborrows, cautioners and sureties risked staking their name and reputation on the convicted party's ability and willingness to follow through with the orders of the court or kirk and possibly incurring a fine if they failed to do so.[108] From the perspective of the burgh authorities, those individuals who became cautioners were 'good neighbours' and proper members of the community who demonstrated a commitment to ensuring the maintenance of stability and order in the burgh. This is clear in a strublance case brought before the burgh court on 31 July 1566. On that day the burgh court found Thomas Mar and William Gardner guilty of strubling each other and put them both in amercement of court. While there is little unique in this example, the baillies also convicted David Mar 'as he quha becom sourtie for Thomas Mar that the town should be skaythless'. While the scribe did not record the penalty that David Mar incurred, his actions provide a clear example of the potential risk of not fulfilling the duties of a cautioner.

While setting caution and surety differed subtly from finding lawborrows, frequently the court required offenders to take out all three.[109] For example, 'Alex Haverson becam cautioner and Suretie and lawborrow for Symon Burnett that William Casse wobster salbe harmless and skaythless of the said Symon.'[110] The records of the Kirk Session of St Nicholas indicate that this was not solely a secular practice. Despite its tenuous existence in Aberdeen before the seventeenth century,[111] once in place, the Kirk Session frequently required that offenders find members of the community to vouch for their return to good behaviour. In the opening accounts of the minutes of the first Kirk Session of St Nicholas in 1562, the session noted that first-time offenders convicted of adultery and fornication were to set caution for their return to proper discipline.[112] The session ordered William Robson, the Aberdeen man brought before the Kirk Session for his adulterous relationship with Katherine Symson, 'to find ane sufficient cautionar actit and obligit within 8 days.'[113] Although we do not know who became cautioner for Robson's misdeeds, we do know that the session required him to 'releiff the Baillies and haill session at the kingis grace & his right hands of all that may be laid to thair charge in tym cuming and alsua that he sall satisfy the kirk in repentans as he beis comandit'.[114] Moreover, it is clear that Robson's behaviour had an impact on the wider community; the inclusion of a member of burgh society to vouch for his return to proper discipline and the requirement of satisfying both the kirk and the civil magistrates suggest as much. Interestingly, the idea that the adulterous behaviour breached the king's peace indicates that such activities were a threat to the common weal of the burgh.

Frequently, the town's authorities, secular and religious, required that caution, surety or lawborrow be in place before the convicted party was able to leave the tolbooth. At the beginning of March 1549/50, the baillies modified the unlaws of Jonet Stevinson and Margaret Innes, ordering them to appear before the congregation the following Sunday and to set caution for 'fulfilling of the same before they depart the tolbooth'.[115] Conversely, Besse Watson was ordered to sett caution 'on Thursday nixt for the kirk and magistrate for the crym of fornication committit by her with master Arthur adamson'.[116]

In early September 1566, Gilbert Menzies and John Lyons became involved in an argument that led to each of them striking the other and causing a commotion within the burgh. Apparently, though the details are missing from the account, Gilbert's brother Patrick joined in and became involved in a war of words with John Lyons. There is no indication of what precipitated the initial conflict nor does the clerk note what motivated Patrick Menzies to involve himself in the dispute. However, the records do indicate that the town and its inhabitants were the real victims of this crime. The baillies, recognizing the disorder such disputes cause within the town 'chargit the saidis persons that the townschipe and the inhabitants thairof salbe skaithless of ilkane [each of them].'[117] It is worth bearing in mind the telling example of David Lyndsay, his wife Jonet Paterson, George Duncan and Vill Nicholl who a sworn assise found guilty of being 'insufficient neighbours, common resaittaris and pykaris not vorthy to be haldin within this guid town'.[118] Interestingly, the clerk considered the four to be 'neighbours' of the town, albeit of a poor quality. However, what is most striking about the account of their conviction and subsequent punishment is the admonishment to the entire town not to harbour these individuals. It deserves full rehearsal:

> Wherefore the ballies and consell ordainit thai all four to be banyst of this town for ever mair & gyf on any of thai beis fundin in this town be nycht or day to be brynt on the cheik with an Iron and deliverit in the sheriffs hands to be condemned to the deid and gyf any neighbour of this guid town giffs thai harbery and rassaytts thai to be accusit and reput participant of their crymes, this given for dome and proclaimit openly at the mercat croce.[119]

While the word neighbour may seem as ambiguous as community, the fact that the clerk used this word to designate both the accused parties and the rest of the inhabitants of the town suggests that from a rhetorical standpoint, at the very least, all inhabitants of the burgh were perceived as neighbours.

The account of the four 'insufficient neighbours' offers insight into the processes at work for excluding and including individuals within the community on the basis of their crimes and punishments. In terms of exclusion, the most obvious aspect taken from this example is the fact that the four individuals were expelled from the burgh with all that such expulsions entailed, loss of protection and any other rights they may have held of the town, as well as a sense of belonging they may have felt. In terms of inclusion, I have already suggested that all individuals involved in the case (those convicted of the offence as well as those implicated in possibly harbouring the wrongdoers) were considered part of the same group – neighbours of the burgh. The elements that denote wider participation in the inclusionary process regulating membership in burgh society included the public proclamation that identified the wrongdoers, the witnessing of their punishments and the order to essentially police the burgh by ensuring that no neighbour offered protection to the banished individuals. The explicit statement that those caught harbouring convicts banned from the town would 'be accusit and reput participant of their crymes', supports this argument. In such a manner, processes of inclusion and exclusion were inherent in criminal activities and the mechanisms that regulated crime within the burgh. As suggested earlier, one of the most effective tools employed in such processes was the open proclamation often made at the market cross. This tool makes the offence, the punishment and the regulation known to all members of the community, establishing the boundaries of inclusion and exclusion within the burgh.[120]

Public acts of repentance and public punishments, including the govis, brought greater community involvement in regulating behaviour. Numerous accounts detail the public acts of forgiveness demanded of individuals convicted of wronging other members of the community. In January 1553 the town council ordered Alex Ferguson to appear before the congregation of St Nicholas and to go 'befoir the procession barheid with ane new candil of tua pound of wax in his hand and thair efter ask God & the toun forgifness of his offens'.[121] In September of that year, the baillies put Richard Mytt and Duncan Colle in amercement of court for disturbing the town by verbally and physically assaulting each other.[122] For committing these offences, the pair were to present themselves within the parish kirk during high mass and on bended knee ask each other's forgiveness.[123] The baillies warned Ferguson that if convicted in the future for any further wrongdoing he would be banished permanently from the burgh.

Incidents such as the ones that brought Mytt, Colle and Ferguson before the burgh court and the parish congregation abound in the burgh records. But it was not only acts of physical and verbal violence that town officials saw as disruptive and hurtful to the town's well-being. Indeed, the same records document numerous cases of individuals brought before the courts for regrating and forestalling, resetting [the act or practice of receiving stolen property], deforcement [the crime of forcibly preventing an officer of the law from discharging his duty], statute breaking, labouring when they were not supposed to and not labouring when they should, theft, property destruction and general wrongdoing. For each example it is possible to note in the clerk's account of the offence that the magistrates perceived such activities, regardless of whether they had been initially perpetrated against another member of the community, as hurtful to the entire town. A corporate identity was built upon the idea of good behaviour, being a good neighbour and protecting the common weal. Individuals recognized that the power behind/inherent in wrongdoing could challenge the established identity of the community. As such, the town's authorities sought to mitigate such activities and instill a sense of proper neighbourly behaviour amongst all inhabitants within the town.

In terms of regulating crime, the burgh authorities' primary concern was for the maintenance of the common weal of the burgh and the restoration of order and discipline. The involvement of the same persons in both the spiritual and secular spheres ensured a consistent application of the prescribed values and a consistent approach to wrongful behaviour. As such, it would be fruitless to attempt to separate the motivations, or the mechanisms, for dealing with crime and sin in sixteenth-century Aberdeen. Later chapters reveal that, in large part, the burgh court and the kirk session used similar methods for punishing wrongdoing while the fear of God's wrath visiting the community served as an ideological underpinning for maintaining the social order. Punishment that helped to regulate behaviour and restore order also enabled the redemption of those convicted for wronging the community. As such, banishment from the burgh occurred very infrequently and the threat of exclusion from the burgh served as a deterrent against continuous misbehaviour. Through public proclamations at the market cross and from the pulpit the authorities included the entire community in the process of regulating misbehaviour. In a similar manner, acts of revocation and acts of repairing damage and restoring stolen goods helped to shape the form of discipline within burgh society. The wider community involvement meant that more than the authorities and the individual transgressor participated in restoring order to the burgh. Furthermore, the point at which crime and punishment intersected served as an area of tension between collective and distributive power models within the burgh.

The following chapters look more closely at the individual types of petty crimes committed in the burgh between 1540 and 1600. Through an analysis of the types of crime committed, the individuals who committed such crimes and those affected, both directly and indirectly, by such activities, it is possible to develop a better understanding of the burgh community. Moreover, it becomes increasingly clear that misbehaviour was not simply a reckless disregard for one's neighbours or the community in which they lived. Rather, misbehaviour served the important function of enabling individuals with limited access to established institutions of power to exercise power illegally or extra-legally. Rather than simple attempts to subvert the authority of the magistrates within the burgh, their actions represented attempts to negotiate social power between themselves and other individual neighbours of the community. In this way crime acted as an important mechanism for redefining the boundaries of the burgh community.

3 PROPERTY

The orthodox assessment of the pre-modern Scottish burgh is that it was a community 'organised around a market'.[1] But while there is no questioning that the market played a significant role in the lives of the inhabitants of early modern Scottish burghs, burghs were so much more than centres for the exchange of goods. They were also the social space where individuals lived, worked, played and prayed. As such, these centres of social interaction also witnessed their fair share of conflict. Earlier chapters have shown that local magistrates, keen to promote the 'social virtue of good neighbourliness', were determined to maintain the customs (both of the burgh and the realm) and patrol the morals of the burghs' inhabitants. Thus, in their attempts to protect what contemporaries called the 'common weal of the burgh', local magistrates strove to curb wrongdoing, maintain the social structures that enabled burgh society to function, and construct the boundaries that reinforced a sense of place in the minds of the burgh's inhabitants.[2] It was here that the ideals and actualities of sixteenth-century burgh life frequently intersected.

Because the market was such a central part of burgh life, a not inconsiderable portion of the petty crimes committed in Aberdeen were, in some way, connected with property and the exchange of goods. Some of these crimes were perceived as vandalic, physical acts that violated the social space occupied by neighbours within the burgh or actions that threatened the security the burgh was supposed to provide its inhabitants. Occasionally, as in the case of 'breaking statutes', they were acts of protest against ordinances that fixed prices and determined the quality of goods for sale at the market. However, the most frequently committed crimes related to the exchange of goods were regrating [buying goods in high numbers for the purpose of re-selling at a profit] and forestalling the market [buying goods before they arrived at the market]. Through such acts wrongdoers actively defrauded their neighbours. Many of the individuals convicted of these crimes were also guilty of usurping the rights to 'use merchandise' and to practise certain crafts guaranteed to the free craftsmen and guild merchants. While Aberdeen's court clerks very infrequently recorded, and most likely rarely knew, the specific motivations behind such activities, it is reasonable to believe that the potential for increased profits, an assumed change in social status, and an improved livelihood inspired individuals to commit property crimes. As such, petty theft, property destruction, regrating and forestalling and usurping the status of craftsmen and merchants caused discord and disorder within the burgh. Through such actions, individuals attempted to exercise their social power over their neighbours and the magistrates who regulated the community. The crimes under consideration in this chapter share this trait with other crimes examined in Chapters 4 and 5.

Through wrongdoing and the responses to such activities, the inhabitants of the burgh, both elites and non-elites, helped to shape the boundaries of burgh society. While it is difficult to argue that every criminal act contributed to a wholesale shift in social attitudes or social control, it is relatively clear that they had an impact on 'neighbourliness' and on the common weal of the burgh. Although the previous chapters focused on how burgh magistrates and the broader community responded to such behaviour and examined the processes of inclusion and exclusion inherent in crime and punishment, the main purpose of this chapter (as well as the next two) is to examine the types of petty crimes committed in Aberdeen and the perpetrators of such acts. While focusing on the variety of ways in which individuals sought to challenge the prescribed forms of acceptable behaviour, this chapter examines the impact non-violent petty crimes had on the burgh community.

'A Sense of Place': Illegal Attempts to gain Inclusion in Exclusive Communities

A number of cases brought before the burgh court concerned individuals who usurped the liberties and privileges associated with the merchant guild and incorporated crafts. These cases reflect attempts to negotiate the regulations in place to safeguard entry into the smaller, more exclusive, communities within the burgh. On 20 March 1552 two wrights, Henry Kindness and Andrew Lyon, stood before the baillies accused of using their craft without having been made free. The two asked the court for a day to ready their defence. Unfortunately for Kindness, whatever line of reasoning he used fell on deaf ears because on 23 March 1552 a sworn assise convicted him 'for the wrangous josing [possessing] and using of the privilege of ane freman of this burght lauborand & usand his craft'.[3] As will become apparent, a significant number of Aberdonians of both high and low status attempted to enjoy privileges associated with either the merchant guild or the free crafts that they were barred from enjoying. Occasionally, this action took the form of using both the privileges of a guild merchant and those of a free craftsman. In other examples, the individual convicted of usurping liberties and privileges attempted to enter only one of these restricted communities. In either

situation, the usurpation exemplifies one of the ways in which Aberdonians challenged the boundaries of established communities within the burgh.

Examples of unfree craftsmen brought before the baillies or Dean of Guild
on account of their labouring without having attained their freedom abound
in the extant records from this period. An interesting example illustrating the
process of inclusion and exclusion based on access to the freedom of specific
crafts comes at the start of the period under consideration. In October 1541
the court convicted three cordiners [cordwainers] of using their craft having not
attained the freedom to do so. All three were put in amercement of court and the
council ordered the burgh officers 'to clos oup the durris qll thai be made fre'.[4]
The records are silent on why the council determined these cordiners should
be made free of their craft at this point. Moreover, the council's involvement in
making craftsmen free was a continuous thorn in the side of the incorporated
crafts, their deacons and the numerous craftsmen who saw this as undue interference.[5] By attempting to enter communities barred from them and enjoy the
associated privileges and liberties, members of Aberdeen society tried, albeit not
always successfully, to negotiate inclusion in the smaller communities within the
burgh. The fact that these craftsmen were successful illustrates that such behaviour could be key to a successful negotiation of social space.

Negotiation, in this sense, centred on the steps taken by individuals within the
wider burgh society to expand their sense of inclusion to smaller communities normally closed to them. By illegally using the liberties and privileges not afforded to
them, members of the community sought to challenge the well-protected boundaries that excluded them from full participation in certain sectors of burgh life. That
this was not a process that sought to turn hierarchical structures on their head can
be discerned from the fact that members of the more prestigious merchant guild
attempted to usurp the rights of free craftsmen. The negotiation factor, or settling
of the boundaries, took the form of one party seeking to restructure guidelines for
inclusion in certain communities and the other party, those who sought to protect
the established terms of inclusion and exclusion, responding through acceptance
of the individual's claim, a violent physical or verbal response or through prosecution in the courts. As stated, this was not only attempted by individuals of the
lower ranks of society. A number of the brethren of guild were brought before the
baillies for usurping the privileges of the craftsmen. In August 1583, Alexander
Litster was accused by the Dean of Guild

> for labouring and using of the litster occupation beand a free burgess of gild and inhi-
> beit [warned] obefoir be Alexander Forbes dene of gild at command of the counsel to
> work at the said craft or ellis revoke his aith of gilderie & burgesship.[6]

Litster confessed to having ignored the inhibition and found himself convicted
and placed in amercement of court for disregarding the council's orders.[7] Lit-

ster's case is interesting for a number of reasons. It demonstrates that despite the privileges associated with being a part of the merchant guild - status, trading rights and use of merchandise - there were other elements within burgh society that could entice a guild brother to jeopardize his inclusion in the guildry. It is unclear whether Litster was originally a craftsman who, through a fee and the intervention of someone on the town council, gained entrance to the guildry.[8] There is also no indication of whether or not following his conviction the council forced Litster to remain within the guild and give up using the litster craft or caused him to forgo his membership in the Guildry, with all of its attendant liberties, and continue labouring as a litster. What is certain is that Litster attempted to circumvent custom and statute in order to enjoy the benefits of belonging to both communities.

Loss of the liberties associated with the guild was substantial. The *Statuta Gilde* states that:

> giff ony our brether pass avay fra the gyld neclygentlye, nan of the brether sall minister till hym consall na help in vord nor in deyde vythin the burgh nor vtuth [outwith]. All thocht he be impedyt and in perall of lyff and membryce or in ony ther erdly charge, he sall haue na help of thaim.[9]

Apart from losing counsel and aid from other brethren of guild, Litster put at risk the right to buy goods for sale again, the right to participate in election of town officials, the benefit of guild assistance should he have fallen into poverty and all of the social and convivial aspects of the guildry.[10]

It is interesting to note that in a number of other Scottish burghs, craftsmen were admitted to the merchant guild. In Aberdeen, the trend, prior to the mid-sixteenth century, was to exclude craftsmen in order to maintain the purity of mercantile interests. Thus, in February 1584 John Walker 'burgess of gild was convikit be the sworne assise abowe written for the using of the walker craft aganis the ordour and honor of ane free burgess of gild and statutes of this burt maid thair.'[11] In Aberdeen, statute and custom singled out in particular litsters, fleshers, walkers and weavers for exclusion from the merchant guild.[12] Elizabeth Ewan has argued that a number of walkers and weavers within the realm were part of the Flemish population and thus traditionally set apart from the rest of the community. This may have been the primary reason for their exclusion from the guild. However, she also notes that by the fifteenth century guilds in Dunfermline and Perth had begun to accept these groups.[13] Walker's offence was the usurpation of privileges not afforded to him and his attempt to challenge the boundaries of two exclusive communities within the burgh. For continuing to use the walker craft after becoming a burgess of guild, John Walker was put in amercement of court and subjected to a fine.

A month prior to Walker's conviction, three other Aberdonian burgesses of guild, Andrew Kelly, Thomas Moreis and James Robertson, were brought before the burgh Court for using the goldsmith and walker crafts. Their case highlights the activities of the burgesses of Aberdeen and the processes at work for regulating the community. Robertson confessed before the court to 'working at the said goldsmyt craft in his father buyt and thairanent put him in the provost bailleis and consale will to be *corectit* be thame'.[14] The court convicted Robertson and put him in amercement of court. Moreis and Kelly, however, denied working as walkers. An assise made up of both craftsmen and guild brethren, including a former Dean of Guild, David Anderson, convicted the pair for 'working at the walker craft thay beand fre burgess of gild *joning the said craft with the office of the gild brethren*'.[15] While on some level this seems to have been the norm within most Scottish burghs, there is some reason to believe that the guild and free crafts were not as exclusive as statutes and court cases suggest.

Although there is some reason to believe that both the guildry and various crafts could be 'virtual closed shops' for those seeking to understand better the mechanisms in place for regulating entry into the merchant and craft guilds in Scotland, the explicit guidelines Guildries recorded in their accounts have not served as accurate markers for who was actually included or excluded from such communities.[16] Based on David McNiven's study of Aberdeen, Michael Lynch has concluded that by 1590 the Aberdeen guild brethren perceived the guildry to have fallen into 'poverty' on account of its lack of exclusivity. For the accounts of the composition of burgesses of guild that are extant for Aberdeen in this period, roughly 1583–1603, there is a dramatic increase in the monies that flowed into the burgh's coffers from depositions and the obligatory guild wine. The average sum paid in 1582 by those seeking entry to the guildry who did not have access through their father or their wife's father was around 10 merks.[17] By the mid-1580s the deposition had risen to 10 pounds and by the 1590s some individuals were paying 20 to 22 pounds for their entry into the guildry.[18] Interestingly enough the same day that John Kaden and John Strathauchin paid 22 pounds and 20 pounds respectively to enter the guildry, two baxters, John Duncan and William Pratt, each paid 10 merks. The lack of a fixed rate for entry into the guild by non-hereditary means makes it difficult to fully ascertain the motivations behind such regulations in place for safeguarding entry into the guild. This is seen in the fact that the burgh's total intake for creating freemen in 1584 was less than half the £58.13*s*.4*d*. brought in for compositions in 1585. What this suggests is that by the last decades of the sixteenth century, the guildry's finances had become a major factor in determining entrance to the guildry.[19] Even more revealing is that within ten years the total amount recorded in the accounts given by John Tullideff, Dean of Guild from Michaelmas 1593 to Michaelmas 1594, was listed at £246.4s.4d.[20] If indeed the guild court complained of the merchant guildry's apparent poverty, it was not on account of entrance fees.

The Guildry Accounts for this period present a number of challenges for determining how closely members regulated entry into the brethren. For instance, most of the accounts combine the composition of free burgesses of guild with accounts of those individuals made burgesses or free of their crafts.[21] The umbrella heading 'composition of freemen made in our time' speaks to the financial concerns of the Dean in recording his accounts. While there are indicators pointing to who was entering certain sectors of Aberdeen society, such as the guild wine required by burgesses of guild or the reference to specific crafts, the accounts show many craftsmen also becoming free burgesses of guild. The lack of a fully extant account of all freemen made before the 1580s makes it difficult to determine where individuals fit in terms of their access to the multiple smaller communities that comprised the wider burgh community. In the case of Alexander Litster, it would be interesting to note when, or if, he became free of his craft. It is safe to assume that he had become a burgess sometime before entry to the guild, as his court record refers to the oath he had taken.

Oaths served to reinforce the bonds established between those members of the community who uttered them and to outline the responsibilities and rights of entering a privileged group.[22] Burgess-ship meant exemption from tolls within the burgh, though burgesses were responsible for paying taxes. Likewise, burgess-ship was largely dependent on landholding, thus requiring a certain amount of capital. Much of what made up the oath individuals swore when becoming a burgess reflected the responsibilities they took on. In particular, they swore to be true to the monarch and the community in which they became burgess.[23] They also swore to provide council and aid to the community and to defend 'the liberties, lawis and customis of the burgh'.[24] It should not seem coincidental that the responsibilities associated with guild membership were similar to those taken on by burgesses. The overlap is suggestive of one of the ways the many communities intersected within the burgh.

There are further examples of individuals attempting to move within different spheres of burgh life. In May 1576, the Dean of Guild charged Wilson Burley, a local merchant, with using the tailor craft. Burley's fine for this transgression was 40 shillings.[25] Unfortunately, the records do not provide evidence of Burley continuing to practise the tailor craft, nor do they indicate that he abstained from using his hands to labour as the Guildry and baillies would have demanded of him. While it is only possible to speak to the records left behind, we must also accept the possibility that in at least some instances individuals would have continued to push the limits of the boundaries established either by using a craft they were not sanctioned to use or usurping the privileges of a guild brother they had not attained. While some individuals may have moved from one sphere to another, not always were they willing to give up the sector of the burgh community they originally came from. In the example of Kelly, Moreis and Robertson, we witnessed three burgesses of gild convicted for enjoying the benefits of the free crafts. Twenty years earlier, a sworn assise had convicted Moreis, along with four other craftsmen, for 'using of merchandyce as brether of gild thai not beand fre bot of thair craft'.[26] It might be easy to see this as a 'grass is always greener' scenario but it is perhaps more fruitful to see examples like this as representing attempts by members of the community to negotiate the power structures within the burgh that were defined by statute.

One of the craftsmen convicted with Moreis in 1561 was Gavin Wishert, a cordiner with a lengthy conviction record spanning twenty-six years.[27] Wishert appeared before the burgh courts at least eight times between 1556 and 1582, and with the exception of one act of violence,[28] a breaking of an arrestment,[29] and a quarrel with a Dean of Guild that the courts viewed as 'strubling the town',[30] the reason he found himself in trouble was his inability, or unwillingness, to accept his place in the community as a free craftsmen. In five of his eight appearances before the court, Wishert was convicted of breaking town ordinances in barking of raw hides and leather; in at least one of the five instances, the court specifically referred to his 'braking and contravening the statutis and ordinances of this gud town and using and usurping of the libertie and privilege of ane free burges of gild.'[31]

However, by the early 1580s Wishart's standing with the Guildry may have changed. A dispute with David Indeaucht, Dean of Guild, brought Wishert before the court in 1583. The dispute resulted from disparaging comments Wishert made about Indeaucht in front of the baillies and Indeaucht's reciprocating with a cuff to Wishert's head. The baillies found 'the prouocation in the said Gavin'.[32] The court's finding in favour of Indeaucht and the clerk's purposeful recording of the Dean's status in society underscores the idea that prominence within the burgh accorded Indeaucht the right to expect respect from other burgh inhabitants. Interestingly enough, when the baillies ordered each of the individuals to set caution, Wishert was able to find caution from Alexander Forbes who, according to the Guildry Accounts, was the Dean of Guild between Michaelmas 1582 and Michaelmas 1586, not Indeaucht as the Council Register states.[33] This entire event may reflect a disputed election result, though neither the Council Register nor the Guildry accounts leave any notice that this was the case. Regardless, the fact that Wishert was able to call on someone of Forbes' stature as a cautioner suggests that his 'credit' was still good and that his activities in the community had not entirely strained his relationship with other members.

The examples given here were not unique. While a number of craftsmen and merchants tried to stretch the boundaries of inclusion and exclusion in different parts of the community, others, more typically unfreemen, made similar attempts. Frequent entries in the Council Register record the activities of unfree individuals labouring at crafts or buying and selling goods. The accounts record that most of the individuals who were convicted were put in amercement of court and ordered to pay a fine. While such penalties suggest that these trespasses were seen as minor irritants, the language used to describe their activities hint at the attitudes held towards breaching boundaries of accepted social structures. In February 1559 John Crukshank 'flesher was convikit for the using of the said craft using the prevlege of ane freman of this burght he being unfre'.[34] Similarly, in April of that same year the baillies convicted George Skynner for buying 'merchand gud aganis the statutes of this town & prevelege thairof'.[35] While statutes were a tool employed to regulate the community, attitudes towards privilege and liberty were the customs that helped to shape power structures within the larger community. Such attitudes surrounded the crafts, the guildry, the council and magistracy, as well as the larger burgh community.

In July 1571 the burgh court convicted William Robertson of purchasing a cow and 'using the privilege of the flesher craft he being ane free burges of gild & not to use the privilege of a craftsman'.[36] In 1572, the court convicted four coopers, Jerome Blak, John Couper, Nichol Chalmer and Andrew Darg 'in jugement in passing to the red' and buying goods 'contrair the libertie of thair craft'.[37] An even clearer example of the articulation of such ideas of privilege and liberty comes from an entry in the Council Register for 19 October 1576.

> The said day William Brwn being accusit be the Baillies for braking and abrogating of the statutes and actis of this gud town in selling of schene [shoes] in grait in commond marcattis aganis the privilege of ane frie burges of gild usurpand thairby the occupation of ane cordinar.[38]

The court convicted Brown and put him in amercement of court, and the baillies ordained that 'giff ewer the said williame beis convict for the lyk cryme and offens in ony tyme hereafter his unlaw to be ten pundis unforgiven.'[39] Brown's case reveals that from a technical or explicit definition of statutes and ordinances – the key regulating mechanisms within the community – challenges to the established boundaries of certain sectors of burgh society were to be met with the full execution of the law.[40] That is not to say that most members of burgh society did not in some manner attempt to negotiate the boundaries of the power and social structures defined by statute. Rather, regulation and reaction worked together to define, delimit and describe life in late medieval early modern Aberdeen.

Statute Breaking and Cheating the Market

In late April 1544, the provost and baillies of Aberdeen gathered in the townhouse to hear the petition of Gilbert Menzies resigning a tack of fishing on the Dee in favour of his heir George Sherar.[41] For the town council, whose main responsibilities centered on preserving the customs of the town, the trade monopolies, the rights of its burgesses and the peace of the community, this was not an unusual occurrence. Also not unusual was the language employed to record the transfer of the fishing rights to Sherar:

> The said day gilbert menzies comperit in jugement befor the provost & Baillies in presence of the town being convenit for the maist part *representand the haill body of the towne* and resignyit remittit and regaif in the hands of Thomas menzies provost forsaid ane halferme fishing of the pott vpoune the watter of dee.[42]

While it is not exactly clear just who was in attendance on that day, those who were there firmly believed that they 'represented' the entire burgh community. This was also the case later that month when the council required ratification of the statutes and ordinances made for the upcoming year. 'The haill town being warnyt be the hand bell passand throwis all the rowis of this towne comperit for the maist part within the tollbuyth assentit all in ane voce to the ordinans of consell and the inibitions to be maid for defens of this gud town.'[43] In this case, concerns surrounding the activities of the English armies were the focus of the town's 'inhibitions'.

In terms of delineating the boundaries of a burgh community, statutory law and customary practice functioned in a comparable manner to city walls, town gates or ports of entry. They served as markers of inclusion and exclusion as well as regulatory systems which could mitigate changes or conserve traditional social space. This is most obviously noted in the practice of electing town officials, fixing prices, delineating entry into the guild brethren or free burgesship, providing for the poor, removing unwanted elements such as vagrants from the burgh, taxation, controlling access to privileges and mediating behaviour. This of course is not an exhaustive list. Yet, it does hint at the way in which abstractions can provide a tangible measure of the processes which regulated membership in an early modern Scottish burgh.[44]

Often originating in local customary practice, burgh statutes regulated burgh activities while defining the limits of inclusion and exclusion within the community. The organic nature of such practices is evident in the very origins of Scottish burghs which arose out of local settlements that developed commercial or administrative functions, established trading monopolies later enshrined by Acts of Scottish monarchs, and evolved into recognizable urban *communitas*.[45] It also characterizes the privileges and freedoms granted to the community and its members that were defined by both statute and custom and occasionally mediated by individual attempts at circumventing such liberties. In this way, incidents of misbehaviour and criminality reveal both the flexibility with which local authorities interpreted and executed the laws they adopted and the manner in which members from various sectors of society negotiated social power and

redefined their social space.[46] Two things stand out when examining the statutes
and ordinances found in the Aberdeen Council Register: first, for the most part
the provost, baillies and council were inclined to maintain the laws and customs
established by their predecessors, introducing changes very slowly unless neces-
sitated by some direct cause, such as war, dearth or plague that had an immediate
impact on the common weal;[47] second, in terms of regulating behaviour within
the town, the local authorities frequently relied on Acts of Parliament for introducing changes to earlier burgh laws. For example, Acts of Parliament concerning
the treatment of forestallers and regrators increasingly required the burghs to
share the convicted party's escheated goods with the Crown. This often influenced burgh magistrates in Aberdeen to impose fines that went directly into the
burgh coffers rather than force the escheatment of goods that would leave the
burgh with only half of the intake. This leaves the impression that magistrates
were flexible in the treatment of individuals convicted of abrogating statutes
and other petty crimes. However, it was just as likely that the magistrates were
inclined to keep the monies brought in through fines from leaving the burgh.

Apart from direct physical or verbal attacks on the magistrates, acts of regrating and forestalling or acts contravening the rights and privileges of freemen
directly challenged the authority vested in the local magistracy. This was the case
largely because such acts posed a direct threat to the mercantile interests which
underpinned the power of the magistracy and threatened the welfare of the community the officials represented. This was particularly the case with actions that
defied the fixed price of goods within the town. Each Michaelmas at the Guild
Court, the burgh council passed statutes that fixed the prices of bread, ale, beef
and mutton and delimited the activities of the craftsmen responsible for such
goods. In large part, the burgh's magistrates dealt with poverty by keeping the
prices of foodstuffs low; it was relatively clear to them that low prices benefited
everyone in the community. Activities that contravened such statutes reveal the
interests of those craftsmen who sought to increase their earnings and to challenge the power structures established by the merchants and the town council
and, to some extent, their neighbours. Thus, the burgh court's attempts to punish those who sold goods at prices dearer than had been legislated were part of
the process of regulating the market for the benefit of the community and the
protection of the native poor.[48]

Gibson and Smout have raised concerns over reading statute prices too
closely given the difficulties with ascertaining the extent to which the authorities
enforced the prices they fixed.[49] Still, out of 1881 cases of misbehaviour brought
before the courts between 1542 and 1591, 648 were for regrating and forestalling and for contravening such statutes. Thus, roughly 35 per cent of the business
brought before the burgh courts dealt with matters surrounding the market and
the liberties associated with the production and sale of goods. The bulk of the

offences that I have categorized as contravening statutes were for selling goods at prices above, or of a quality less than, those fixed by statute. The rest reflected growing concerns over movement between the free and unfree, and the craft and merchant, communities.

By far the most frequent offenders contravening statutes in mid-sixteenth century Aberdeen were the baxters who the court often convicted of baking 'breid of less weght' or of 'insufficient stuff' or occasionally fined for baking bread on Sundays.[50] Prices for bread were dictated by the cost of materials plus an appropriate allowance for the baker's labour. This was, in principle, the same for all 'food-processing crafts'.[51] Much of the scholarship examining costs and standards of living in early modern Scotland has shown that regulations were in place to ensure fair prices, safe-guard against dearth and therefore protect the consumer.[52] This can be detected in the conviction of six women in May 1543 for the 'braking of common ordinans'. Besse Walker, Katherine Joffray, Janet Branch, Issobell Flesher, Christine Lorimer and the wife of Thom Germand confessed before the court for breaking the statutes of the town in 'spilling of the mercat & taking mair vittall' than necessary to sustain themselves and 'housing thairof or the price wes maid thairvpoun'. The court perceived this as being harmful to the entire community. They were ordered to abstain until the next Michaelmas when 'the Baillies will chois & admytt to mak pryce of the malt & in the mercat & latt the same to the nytbors of the same pryce.'[53] Like baxters, fleshers were often brought before the court for selling their goods at high prices. Gilbert Falconer and John Murray, for example, were convicted by the baillies of 'braking of the statutes of this gud town in selling mutton and beiff darrar and of graitar prycis weirs cotenit in the said statutes.' They were ordered to pay a fine of 8 shillings, approximately one day's wages, before they were allowed to leave the tolbooth.[54]

In large part what was at work here was the intersection of rights and privileges of the smaller communities within the burgh. As Gibson and Smout argued, 'the burgh was a restricted trading community founded upon a monopolistic control of trade, but its privileges were to be enjoyed in common by all who had a right to them.'[55] Moreover, the officials elected to regulate the community were part of the privileged elite responsible for the maintenance of the entire community and protection of the various rights accorded to the different inhabitants of the burgh. Safeguarding the Guild Brethren and their rights to exclusivity and trade monopolies was as important as protecting the rights of free craftsmen from incursions into their crafts by unfree practitioners. Protecting access to goods for all inhabitants meant ensuring that prices were set at such a level that even the indigent could afford the basic necessities of life while maintaining the quality of the product and the right of craftsmen to earn a reasonable profit for their labour. On account of this, regrating and forestalling posed one of the greatest threats to the community; most of the inhabitants saw such activities as threatening the entire burgh economy.[56] It was also one of the crimes that had the largest number of recidivists.

Between 1535 and 1592, Parliament acted six times to curb the activities of regraters described so eloquently in one Aberdeen account as 'contagious enemies to this common weill, devoraris and suckeris of the blude and substance of the pure'.[57] In 1535 an Act of James V forbade regrating of the burgh markets 'vnder the pane of prisoning of thare personis and escheting of all sik gudis cost or Erlit be thame'. The escheated goods were to be distributed 'two parts to go to the King, a third to the sheriff or provost and Baillies of the burgh'.[58] The ratification of older Acts concerning regrating and forestalling in 1567 and 1579 suggest a rise in such activities. This is made abundantly clear in 1587 when the Acts were 'to be newly presented at the mercat crosses'.[59] In 1592, an Act of James VI altered the penalty structure for convicted regrators and forestallers. For their first offence they were to be fined 40 shillings and ordered to abstain under threat of 100 merks. For their second fault the fine increased to 100 merks. If convicted a third time, the offender was then to 'tyne [forfeit] all his guids'.[60] Clearly, those active within parliament - and this included elite members of Aberdeen society - saw such activities as harmful to the community.

The court records leave the impression that when it came to punishing regrators and forestallers Aberdeen's authorities were flexible with their application of the strict penalties spelled out in national legislation. Out of 257 cases of regrating and forestalling brought before Aberdeen's burgh court during this period, in only two instances the authorities used banishment as a threat against recidivism and only three times were goods escheated to the burgh.[61] In all other instances the court levied fines against the convicted party ranging from 8 shillings to 10 pounds. This suggests that the burgh's levy of fines for forestallers was a means of preventing the Crown from getting the lion's share, or at least half, prescribed by statute. What is clear is that despite the severity with which this crime was regarded, burgh magistrates chose a more operative definition of the law in handling regrators and forestallers. As will become apparent, for most cases of petty crime brought before the burgh court, the magistrates chose to be more flexible than statute required.

Statute breaking ranged from baking bread of lower quality to selling goods at prices higher than what the town's officials decreed. It could also include housing individuals suspected of the plague or banished from the burgh or using merchandise when the ordinances forbade doing so. All such actions challenged the established laws governing the burgh, but also sought to place individuals committing such acts above those who respected the laws and abided by their regulations. More than the tangible effects felt in the market stemming from actions which reduced the available goods for sale, lowered the quality of foodstuffs or interfered with the prices established for the benefit of the entire community, the act of statute breaking attempted to redefine social power within the community.[62] The concern magistrates had for maintaining their authority in the burgh can be discerned in the various accounts of individuals breaking statutes and flouting accepted practices within the burgh.

In 1566, the burgh court convicted Andrew Ray, a sadler, for 'barking and selling of ledder'.[63] His behaviour raised two areas of concern. First, he wrongfully engaged in activities that were 'nocht of his craft to do'. Ray had also sold the 'barkit [tanned] ledder' to John Deuchar and John Maison against the ordinances governing his craft. For breaking these statutes, the court ordered Ray to pay a fine. Five years later, Ray and another sadler, Lawrens Masar, confessed to the burgh court that they had barked hides 'contrar the statutes and ordinance of the towne and privilege thereof'.[64] The baillies ordered both of them to pay a fine of 40 shillings and to abstain from such activities under threat of a further fine of 10 pounds. John Deuchar's conviction for establishing a bark pot [a pot used for tanning leather] in an area the council had forbidden him from establishing one before is perhaps a more explicit example of challenging the council's authority.[65] In determining his guilt, the baillies cited his 'braking of the command and ordinance giffen him be the bailleis and consale' as well as 'his manifest contempt' for the court.[66] These activities undermined the structures that governed the inhabitants of the burgh and the privileges they possessed. Having been convicted twice in five years, Ray either did not learn his lesson from the experience he had before the court magistrates or determined that the prescribed penalty did not outweigh the potential for gain through committing such acts in the future. James Arclay, another Aberdeen cordiner not afraid to openly challenge the authority of the burgh magistrates or impose his will on his neighbours, was convicted in October 1571 for 'bying of hydis fra the fleshers, and als for selling of barkit hydis to owtland folkis or [before] the towne was staikit.'[provided][67] While the court convicted Arclay for breaking statutes, his true offence was that he put his own interests, and the interests of outsiders, before those of his neighbours within the burgh by selling goods to strangers that should have been destined for the burgh's market. Such disregard for the community could not have endeared him to the burgh magistrates or his neighbours. As a result of his actions Arclay incurred a fine of 5 pounds.

Not all statute breaking was the same. While contravening statutes that regulated the prices or quality of goods to be sold at the market compares with other fraudulent acts including regrating or forestalling, housing strangers or those suspected of being infected with the plague posed significantly different threats to the community.[68] The burgh council quarantined Hew Munro's entire household after it was suspected that a member of his house had contracted the plague.[69] The council likewise ordered Alexander Scott to have his house 'clengit' [cleansed] and to 'remaine closise in quhil it be clengit; and his broderis sone

to be sene be the officiaris nakit, gif he hes or hed the pest.'[70] The baillies determined that if Scott's nephew was infected he was to be expelled from the town
while the unnamed women who gave him shelter were to be 'put in the links'.
David Spilyelaucht was not as lucky. For 'braking the commond ordinance and
statutis' of the town in not revealing his child's condition to the baillies, Spilyelaucht was to have his left hand burned with a hot iron.[71] In the mid-1540s,
and again in the mid-1580s, the town passed a number of statutes for protecting
the community from the plague.[72] Many of the ordinances indicated that those
found guilty of contravening the statutes would suffer banishment or execution.
In May 1585, the baillies convicted Margaret Nune and Marzeon Young for
lodging strangers contravening the 'law anent the pest'. Further indication of the
burgh magistrates being more flexible with the law's prescriptions, the provost
and baillies commuted their death sentence to banishment from the burgh.[73]

When taken together, incidents of statute breaking and regrating the market
account for more than a third of the total number of offences brought before the
court between 1541 and 1591 as recorded in the Council Register and Baillie
Court Books. Despite how such activities affected the community, and occupied so much of the magistrates' time, with the exception of plague infractions
or housing strangers, penalties for such offences usually took the form of a fine.
Very rarely do we find individuals convicted for such offences being put in ward,
enduring corporal punishment or public humiliation. Thus, Caline Leithe's experience before the burgh court for 'braking of the commond ordinance of this
guid town kempt for the weil of the same' that led to her feet being put in the
govis for six hours stands out as exceptional.[74] What is more, the baillies ordered
that a conviction for a similar offence in the future would result in her execution. Unfortunately it cannot be determined how this story played out, as Leithe's
name vanishes from the records for the rest of the period under consideration.

According to the extant records, the burgh court did not banish a single individual convicted of statute breaking between 1541 and 1595. Only once did the
authorities use banishment as a threat against future transgressions.[75] In 1595
Nicol Chalmer and William Best, two unfreemen, were found to be working
as tailors within the burgh. For this transgression against the town statutes and
against free craftsmen, the baillies ordered both men to remain in ward within
the tolbooth until they could set sufficient caution that they would return to
good behaviour and pay the fine they incurred.[76] In 1546, the court convicted
Charles Davidson of baking and selling bread of considerably less weight than
stipulated by the town's ordinances. This led the court to confiscate all the bread
he possessed and distribute it to the poor within the burgh limits.[77] The fact that
the court had convicted Davidson of this same charge twice in the previous two
years, led the baillies to ban him from baking within the burgh in the future.[78] In
1569, James Wilson's greed led him to commit the fraudulent crime of tampering

with the town's weigh scales. For cheating the community, the baillies ordered Wilson to put himself in their will and determined that the 'boll of maill quhikis he mesurit thairowt to be eschet for his unlaw.'[79] When it came to protecting the common weal of the burgh, the magistrates could enforce the statutes and customs that protected the community's liberties. Thus, when Alexander Williamson, a servant of an Edinburgh burgess, attempted to transport raw cloth and plaid out of the burgh limits against the town's privileges, the town authorities intervened, convicted Williamson and took possession of the goods in question.[80] Fines and goods escheated to the burgh went towards the 'Common Good', the funds earmarked for maintaining the town's physical and social structures. Thus, in some sense, convicted parties helped alleviate the plight of the town's poor, sick and indigent as well as contributed to the maintenance of the town's buildings, streets and harbour front. While the use of monies brought into the town coffers through fines was an appropriate means of giving back to the burgh what wrongdoers had taken away, it would be inaccurate to suggest that because an individual wronged their neighbours through their criminal action they lacked any sense of neighbourliness.[81] No doubt criminals were unwanted elements in burgh society, but it is not the case that those convicted of crimes earned the lasting enmity of their neighbours. John Deuchar may be a case in point.

John Deuchar was a local cordiner who spent a significant amount of time before the burgh magistrates in the 1560s and 1570s. The majority of his offences against the community came in the form of breaking statutes that governed the burgh's market. Although convicted six times for breaking statutes and for regrating and forestalling, Deuchar continued to live within the community relatively unscathed. In May 1567 the baillies convicted John Mannis for strubling and mispersoning Deuchar and ordered him to be put in the branks [an iron bridle and gag used for public punishment].[82] The records do not make clear whether Mannis and Deuchar had been involved in a personal dispute or whether Mannis' injurious language had included references to Deuchar's past offences. Regardless, the authorities determined that Mannis had undermined Deuchar's credit and standing in the community and therefore should be punished. There are a number of things to consider about this case: first, was Mannis attempting to undermine or challenge Deuchar's place in the community because he perceived him to be outside the boundaries of respectable society? Second, despite Deuchar's flouting of burgh laws and the authority of the baillies to enforce them, the court determined that he still possessed the right to be protected from attacks from other members of the community.

In response to the first point, if it was the case that Mannis had attempted to undermine or challenge Deuchar's place in the community then such an attack may be construed as an attempt to negotiate Deuchar's social space. Deuchar had been convicted of the crime that accounted for nearly 35 per cent of the total number of crimes brought before the burgh court. If Mannis' attack was in response to these activities, then it is clear that the community did not dismiss such crimes as unpleasant consequences of burgh life. As indicated earlier, the authorities, both national and local, consistently attempted to root out such behaviour. However, the regularity with which members of the community committed these acts underscores the value some burgh inhabitants placed in attempting to redefine the rules that governed civil society through misbehaving. It also demonstrates the interest individuals held in exercising whatever power they might possess to elevate their status or enhance their livelihood.[83] That the authorities protected individuals who engaged in such behaviour informs us of contemporary attitudes towards crime. It also points to the constant jostling for power and the negotiation of social space that Keith Wrightson, Steve Hindle and Craig Muldrew have written about extensively. In large part, such incidents also reflect Herrup's idea that magistrates considered whether individuals brought before them had temporarily fallen from grace or were generally inclined towards criminal behaviour.[84]

That members of the community perceived regrating as fraudulent behaviour is apparent in an account of Tibbe Davidson's conviction for 'bying and topping of meyll not putit in the mercat defrauding alexander menzies of his duety of the toll'.[85] Davidson was put in amercement of court. Similarly, the court clerk depicted George Burnett's regrating and forestalling of the market as causing 'hurt and skayth of the gud town and the neighbours theirof'.[86] For causing such hurt in the community, Burnett paid a fine of 5 pounds. Alex Murray and William Anderson faced possible escheat of their goods for being convicted of regrating and forestalling the market.[87] The baillies likewise convicted Philip Foular for regrating the market in buying a great number of fish. They warned him that if ever he committed this offence again he would escheat all of the fish he was in possession of and they would be given to the poor for their sustenance.[88] As stated earlier, the actual escheat of goods was rare within the burgh. Most individuals convicted faced a fine and a warning.

Despite the lenient penalties prescribed for such activities, and the fact that of all petty crimes committed within the burgh regrating and forestalling had the highest number of recidivists, recidivism was still relatively low in this area. Thirteen per cent (34 : 271) of all incidents or regrating and forestalling can be attributed to recidivists. While this may be a conservative estimate given that a number of these individuals may have been convicted prior to the period under consideration, the figure is somewhat revealing. Some of these individuals, like Andrew Chalmer, had little compunction in continuing his wrongdoing despite the court's admonitions to abstain. Chalmer and his wife, Marjorie Forbes, were brought before the baillies on a number of occasions facing charges of statute breaking and regrating and forestalling. The court convicted Chalmer in 1576 for statute breaking and in 1578 for regrating. Forbes's conviction for regrating and forestalling came in 1577 while Chalmer was twice convicted in 1581 for this crime. In 1582, Chalmer appeared twice before the magistrates, once for statute breaking and once for regrating and forestalling.[89] For each of these offences Chalmer, or his wife, incurred a fine. Only the account for Chalmer's conviction for regrating in 1578 specifies the amount of his fine; both Chalmer, and John Duncan, a local tailor convicted for regrating on the same day, were ordered to pay the baillies 10 pounds within forty-eight hours for their transgression.[90] We may presume that Chalmer paid his fine because his name is absent from the subsequent entry in the Council Register, indicating that Duncan had lost his liberty within the burgh for failure to comply.[91] It is not entirely clear if the 10 pound fine in 1578 was higher than earlier fines Chalmer had incurred. Nor is there any real indication that the court sought to restrain Chalmer through any action other than pecuniary measures. For his last two convictions the accounts simply state that Chalmer put himself in the provost's, baillies' and council's will.

This should not imply that the court was little bothered by such activities. Although fines seem to have been unsuccessful deterrents, they could prove costly. For Chalmer, a fairly successful cooper in the burgh who probably earned 11 shillings a day, a fine of 10 pounds was steep. Andrew Riddell, who appeared four times before the burgh court between 1577 and 1578 on charges of regrating and forestalling, was an unfreeman labouring in the burgh. For 'regrating of this gud town and forestalling of the samyn in bying of skins being an unfreeman' Riddell incurred fines of 5 pounds and was ordered to set caution.[92] In this period most labourers earned 6 to 7 shillings per day working on average 220 days in a year.[93] Thus, Riddell's fine amounted to nearly one month's wages. He was also ordered to set caution and warned to abstain under the threat of incurring a fine of 100 pounds.[94] The baillies ordered Robert Williamson, a tailor, to pay the same amount for his frequent usurpation of the liberties of a free burgess of guild and his regrating of the market.[95] Likewise, Matthew Guild, a local armourer who joined forces with John Duncan in the 1580s in the craftsmen's protest of the local government and merchant supremacy within the burgh, paid fines of 20 merks for his convictions for regrating and forestalling in 1575 and 1576.[96] John Deuchar's convictions for forestalling in 1567 and regrating in 1576 earned him fines of 40 shillings, or roughly one week's wages. In comparison to the fines given to Chalmer and Riddle, Deuchar received a relatively low fine. This, however, should not be taken as an indication of his wealth and status in the burgh. Deuchar was wealthy enough to prosecute a case against the burgh before the Privy Council, travelling to Edinburgh and appearing personally before the higher court in 1565.[97]

Regardless, the court regularly used fines to deal with incidents of regrating and forestalling. This brought monies into the town coffers that would have been lost to the burgh on account of tolls individuals should have paid by bringing goods to market for sale. It also proved more beneficial to the burgh to impose fines than to enforce the legislation governing forestalling coming from Edinburgh. By 1592 Parliament had determined that previous legislation was ineffective and recidivism had become a problem. As a result, Parliament passed new laws defining regrating and forestalling and stipulating the penalties that convicted individuals would incur.

Vandalic Property Crimes and 'Wrongous Away Taking'

The court records suggest that many of the property crimes committed between 1542 and 1591 had a vandalic quality to them. While the records tend to leave out the details of the initial disputes that contributed to such crimes, there is a clear impression that, for the most part, destruction of property was an alternative method of prosecuting an ongoing argument.[98] This is clear in a case involving Thomas Hay younger. In February 1542, a conflict emerged between Hay younger and David Rolland. The baillies initially convicted Hay younger for strubling and drawing Rolland's blood 'under silence of the night' and acquitted Rolland of any wrongdoing.[99] The baillies, interestingly enough, also convicted Hay younger for the 'strublance and perturbation' of Alexander Nicholson's house 'vnder sylens of nycht he being absent'. In the subsequent account, the baillies warned all three men 'to stand at the deliverans of the provest, balzeis & consale anent the said strublens & blud drawing'.[100] Although Nicholson did not figure in the violence that erupted between Rolland and Hay younger, it is clear from Hay's attack on Nicholson's house and Nicholson's inclusion in the warning to appear before the magistrates that the original dispute included all three men.[101]

Occasionally, as in the example of the baillies destroying the house built by Andrew Forbes[102] or in the younger Hay's attack on Andrew Nicholson's house, damage or destruction of property was a means of settling a dispute or prosecuting a conflict. The accounts make it clear that such attacks were part of an ongoing process. By diminishing or destroying the material goods of one of their neighbours, individuals exercised their power over their victim and attempted to increase their victim's sense of vulnerability. Through responses to such actions, such as reciprocal violent acts, prosecution in the courts and eventual acceptance of the terms of restorative justice, the victim participated in a negotiation process that attempted to restore the power taken away from them by the transgressor. In June 1574 the burgh court convicted John Sanders and put him in amercement of court for scaling the backside of the tolbooth and 'braken of the top of the knok [clock]'.[103] The following February James Ewyn was brought before the court for the 'wrongous uppluking in presens of gilbert collision balzie of certane stakis & proppis set up be Andrew thornton for safetie of the said androwis young heage [hedge] in his contempt of the said balzie.'[104] Charles Theilgriene found himself in trouble with the baillies for 'siking [seeking] and slaying betwixt the rowes in the kingis geit of ane sow pertening to alexander chalmer fleshear'.[105] Theilgrene, for his wrongdoing, had to pay Chalmer 13 shillings for the sow as well as an unspecified amount to cover the baillies's fine.

Clearly it was not beyond the imagination of sixteenth-century Aberdonians to disturb the burgh's peace through acts of property destruction. However, the actual number of individuals brought before the court on such charges was relatively low when compared with other forms of petty crime. If you exclude instances of petty theft, statute breaking and regrating and forestalling from 'property crimes', vandalic crimes accounted for only 1.4 per cent of the total number of petty crimes brought before the burgh court between 1542 and 1591. Yet, despite the relatively low occurrence, such crimes had an impact on the inhabitants of the burgh as well as the burgh authorities. At some point in August 1553, Jonet Kane became involved in a dispute with William Gray. Although the details are lacking, we do know that as the argument reached its crescendo Kane verbally assaulted Gray and destroyed his 'corn' field. For this action, the baillies put Kane in amercement of court and ordered her amends to be modified by the council.[106] In June 1554, Alexander Hayt went to the trouble of digging a hole under, and removing the sand used to help support, a stone dyke built by the Black Friars. John Blak, representing the friars, took an act of court against Hayt arguing that on account of Hayt's activities the wall had become unstable and had fallen down. The act of court asked that Hayt 'be indettit to upset the skaith sustenit be thaim and for remeid of law quhen tyme & place requires'.[107] There is no indication that religious unrest motivated Hayt's actions nor is it apparent that his own property bordered the Black Friars.[108] In handling such cases, the burgh court frequently ordered the convicted parties to repair or replace the items they damaged.[109] However, the court could also impose more severe penalties on those convicted of such crimes.

We recall that in May 1566 Isobel Gardner suffered the indignity of being placed in the govis and was subjected to the ridicule of her neighbours after the court convicted her of willfully destroying the garden of a former Baillie. Gardner did not have a history of run-ins with the law; in fact, she had never been brought before the court on any charge prior to May 1566. However, she was considerably less connected to the burgh magistracy than her victim. While it is possible that Gardner was unable to pay the fine that the baillies would have typically imposed on culprits of comparable crimes, it is also possible that the victim's status influenced the court's decision to make a spectacle out of Gardner.[110] Nonetheless, the entire incident, from the moment Gardner destroyed the garden to the moment the she stood in the govis, represented a negotiation of social space and power. Both parties imposed their will on one another (one through wrongdoing, the other through prosecution), ultimately resulting in a newly defined relationship between the accused, her neighbours and her victim. Here, the victim's ability to harness a majority of the power through his social status, political networks or economic wherewithal enabled him to settle the dispute in his favour.[111] What is important to note is that both parties participated in this exercise and negotiation of power through the actions they took. Moreover, the very public exercise of the magistrate's power helped to reinforce a sense of place for all who were involved.

Occasionally, these acts had a more tangible impact on the wider community. Such was the case in August 1548 when Andrew Low let out the waters from a loch that serviced the local mills within the burgh.[112] Without a more complete account of the incident, and indeed of Low's penalty, it is difficult to determine whether this was an act of sabotage intending to impede the town's millers' work, whether Low was directing his protest at either one of the burgh millers or against the town magistrates, or whether the entire incident was accidental. Although the account does not provide the details of the type of mills affected by this incident, by slowing down or halting the production from the mills we may assume that Low's actions affected the labourers employed at the mill, the craftsmen who depended on the materials to produce their wares, the inhabitants who benefited from the goods and the town officials concerned to receive the tolls yielded from such goods brought to the market.[113] The baillies's decision to convict Low suggests that from the court's perspective, at least, they did not view the incident as accidental. Low's conviction resulted in his being put in amercement of court; unfortunately, there is no record of any modification to his unlaw.

Robert Cassidy made apparent his awareness of the community and the regulations governing the burgh when he brought a bill of complaint against John and Robert Forbes in May 1575. According to the complaint, the Forbes had cut down sod used for roofing that belonged to Cassidy, who sought restitution for their wrongdoing. The Forbes claimed that they had done 'na wrang' having cut the sod down from the town commons. According to the court records, Cassidy produced 'certane statutes ordinances and aiths of the provost, balleis & consale of this burgh,' to support his claim that the Forbes had wronged him.[114] After great deliberation, the council resolved the matter by reaffirming the original statutes governing usage of the common land and by finding the Forbes guilty of cutting down and taking away sod belonging to Cassidy.

Not all actions involving the destruction or removal of property had an immediate or lasting impact on the entire burgh. Nonetheless, individual disputes that resulted in the damage or destruction of property influenced the interpersonal relationships that defined 'neighbourliness' within the community. An argument between Ambrose Littlejohn, a tailor, and James Walker, a fuller, resulted in Littlejohn breaking Walker's windows. The court determined that Littlejohn should repair them and 'mak them as guid as were' within forty-eight hours and pay the baillies 8 shillings for his destructive behaviour.[115] Walker, however, was not beyond reproach. In October 1558 the court convicted him for the 'wrangous cutting of ane wob of yarn furth of Maltman Henderson wobsteris wark he being a worker thereupon'.[116] For his transgression against his employer, the baillies ordered Walker to pay Henderson 36 shillings. Henderson does not appear in any other account of wrongdoing during this period. On the other hand, the court had previously convicted Walker of breaking statutes and regrating.[117] While we do not know the reasons behind Walker's activities, we can be relatively certain that his behaviour left an impression on members of the community with whom he had close contact. Regardless of whether Robert Mane and Adam Mair held a working relationship, or any other standing connection, a dispute between them led to violent consequences. The details of the initial argument are absent from the records, but at some point Mane cut down a pole used by Mair to hang his clothes. In response, Mair drew a short sword and attacked Mane.[118] Both men incurred fines for their actions. Likewise, the burgh court convicted Ritchie Anderson for breaking an iron pole belonging to David Anderson and ordered him to set sufficient caution that he would restore the item before he left the tolbooth. The magistrates made it clear to Ritchie that failure to comply with their orders would result in his banishment from the burgh for a year and a day.[119]

On 29 June 1575 John Couper appeared before the Baillie court accused of 'braking in of ane sheall in towne' [shelter used by salmon fishermen] and the 'wrangous away taking of ane gryt numer of salmond fishe'. Although two separate accounts of Couper's conviction still exist, neither provide any information on whose dwelling Couper broke into, the motivations behind his actions or whether the consequences he faced actually came to pass. The Baillie Court Book accounts state that for his actions, Couper was to be scourged, ritually paraded through the streets and banished from the town. Seven years later, a John Couper stood convicted for regrating the market. It is possible that this was the same man who the baillies had ordered to be publicly humiliated and banished from the town. For the most part the records are generally silent on whether or not punishments were carried out. However, there are a number of occasions where individuals who had been either ordered out of the town or warned against committing future crimes at the risk of incurring more serious penalties suffered neither. Couper's presence in the community seven years after having been banished illustrates an area where ideals and actualities clashed. Exemplified in their use of statutes as well as discretionary powers, the authorities employed both 'technical' and 'operative' definitions of the law to regulate the community.[120] Bearing this in mind, Couper's wrongdoing and refusal to remove himself permanently from the burgh, not unlike the magistrates' use of discretion, demonstrated an ability to exercise power within the burgh and suggests a negotiation of the social relations between all of the parties involved including the wider community.

John Couper's experience was not unique for Aberdeen. As I have already noted, John Deuchar was convicted in 1576 for stealing the stones from Alexander Menzies' dyke.[121] Deuchar's lengthy history with the burgh court, and the increasing tension in the burgh between craftsmen and merchants, may have inspired Deuchar to act out in this manner against a member of the most prominent family in the burgh. On 13 August 1587 the court convicted Andrew Maine and Alex Lasone fleshers for the 'wrongous intromission and away taking of the lead and netts of Alex Knowles elder and George Troup'.[122] Like Couper, Maine and Lasone exercised their will by interfering with Knowles' and Troup's goods and livelihood. The court demanded that Maine and Lasone find a cautioner, that they would pay their fines and never offend again within the burgh limits. Alexander Mollison, a local baxter who later became a deacon of his craft, became cautioner for Maine and Lasone, guaranteeing their return to good behaviour as well as their ability and willingness to pay the baillies' fine. Although there is no record of the penalties Maine and Lasone incurred, the baillies convicted Mollison three days later of 'strubling the court'. It is likely that this stemmed from some displeasure Mollison felt towards the decision in the Maine and Lasone case or from his failure to keep the guarantee.

In previous chapters I argued that incidents of petty theft or intromission (often referred to in the court records as 'wrongous away taking' or 'wrongous intromission') consistently resulted in banishment from the town. While there is little doubt that that this type of crime resulted in banishment more frequently than any other 'petty' criminal act committed within the burgh, it was not a hard and fast rule. For example, in May 1550 the baillies put Margaret Skynner and her daughter in amercement of court for taking a 'creill full of elding' [basket full of fuels] from one of Duncan Fraser's servants. The court ordered the pair to return to Fraser's servant the 'creil and elding again als guid as thai intromitit' within twenty-four hours under the threat of incurring a fine.[123] Alexander Litster's initiative to begin dismantling the property belonging to the Carmelite Friars in 1559 may have had to do with some hostility he felt towards the Catholic Church and even more to do with coveting the materials used for their stone fence. Regardless, the magistrates ordered Litster to return the stones to the friars within twenty-four hours.[124] Almost exactly one year later, Adam Mair stood accused 'be the bailleis in jugement in name of the town' for taking stones belonging to the Black Friars 'to his awn vtilitie and particular use'.[125] Mair denied the charges and the baillies gave him five days to prove his innocence. The records fall silent on the matter and we may assume that either Mair returned the stones or proved his innocence.

The intromission [assumption of ownership without proper authority] or theft of property belonging to one's neighbour from their dwellings or lands certainly disrupted community relations and went against the ideas of good neighbourliness. However, the taking away of goods from an individual after violently assaulting or 'strubling' them was a clear attempt to overpower their victim. In December 1541 the baillies convicted Jonet Paterson of the 'strublance of Margaret Smytht & wrangous away taking of hir mantill [cloak or wrap]'.[126] For her offence, the court ordered Paterson to ask Smyth's forgiveness and to pay two pounds of wax to the 'halyblud lycht'. In July 1543 the court convicted James Gelland and the aptly named David Dog for the 'strublens of jonet young & away taking of hir clok'.[127] Three of their neighbours became suretors for their fines as well as for the 'restorans of the said clok'. The Portuis case first mentioned in the introduction to this book provides an explicit example of how theft represented a violent overpowering of the transgressor's victim.[128] The fact that children took away his items while he was helpless reinforced the sense of weakness he may have felt and heightened the humiliation factor. This added element of humiliation, combined with the violence the victim experienced, emphasized his powerlessness against the perpetrators.

It is not clear whether John Fraser and Margaret Paterson had an ongoing dispute, but one night in January 1559 Fraser went to Paterson's house, entered the home and struck Paterson, taking her 'mantyll' before making his quick departure.[129] Not only did Fraser violently attack Paterson and steal her cloak, he did so at night in her own home. As such, Fraser took more than Paterson's cloak, he took away any sense of security she may have felt and thus increased his own sense of power. We may assume Marion Wyntoun felt a similar sense of loss when Alexander Mollison, who had been sufficient enough to act as a cautioner for Andrew Maine and Alex Lasone, attacked her in April 1581. The baillies convicted Mollison for the 'strubling, striking down casting and trapping of marioun wyntounis wares'.[130] Unfortunately, the clerk provided no detail of the motivation behind the attack or whether Wyntoun and Mollison had previously known each other. We do know that Mollison suffered a serious rebuke from another of his neighbours, Jonet Cruikshank, shortly after his attack on Wyntoun.[131]

It is perhaps because of such violations, not only of laws governing the burgh, but also of good neighbourliness and Christian values, that the burgh magistrates tended to dole out more serious punishments on individuals convicted of wrongful away taking.[132] In November 1544, Mage Angous, Mage Cruikshank, Gane Merchand and Margaret Cruikshank went to the home of John Byris and promptly began destroying a dyke built around his yard and removing the stones. For their acts of vandalism and theft, the provost ordered the officers of the town to pass to the homes of the four women and 'baneiss thaim the town for yeir and a day'.[133] One October afternoon in 1551, John Alexander entered a booth belonging to William Ingram and apparently asked to inspect a few swords and scabbards Ingram had in his possession. The court record states that Alexander wrongfully took the weapons from the booth and this resulted in his being convicted for the 'vrangous intromission witht certain swords shone & skaberts owt of wm ingramis cordonaris buytht'.[134] For his actions, the court ordered Alexander to be 'banyst of the town & scurgit naykit threw all the town'. Although the baillies banished Alexander for his wrongdoing the account suggests that there was concern that Alexander would ignore the order to leave the burgh permanently. The public scourging and parading through the town helped to inform the community of Alexander's wrongdoing and was meant to make his punishment part of the public record so that if his neighbours encountered him in the future, they could respond to his presence within the burgh accordingly. The baillies also ordered Alexander to set caution in case 'he beis foundyn in sic faltis againis within the fredome of this bught'. There would be no need to guarantee against Alexander's potential to harm the town again if there was no real concern that he would not abide by the order of banishment. That the burgh authorities instituted a process to regulate his behaviour in the future suggests that they were primarily concerned for his return to proper conduct within the burgh and not necessarily his permanent removal from the town. As this was Alexander's only appearance before the court we may assume that he left town and never returned, or that the court's actions had a lasting impact and he once again resorted to good neighbourliness. The same may be said for Robert Bachelor, who for stealing five fish, was put in the govis and banished from the town.[135]

Such acts committed by members of the community undermined the virtue of neighbourliness and exposed attempts to circumvent both custom and statute through the assertion of individual wants. In this sense, domination and subordination did not have to follow any hierarchical pattern.[136] Rather, the 'settling of a matter' through criminal activities enabled those who lacked access to formal political power to exercise power in an informal manner. Power relations governed behaviour throughout the burgh, and indeed the realm. It is perhaps useful to see the power networks active within the community as overlapping and intersecting at many points. Destruction or removal of property either brought individuals into conflict or elevated already established disputes; in examples of the latter, it is possible to recognize a negotiation between the individuals involved. Through public punishments and restitution, all parties involved, including the community who sustained injury through the breach of proper behaviour, attempted to settle the original disputes that led to such crimes being committed.

Petty Crime and the Negotiation of Social Power

Famine gripped parts of Scotland in each of the last five decades of the sixteenth century, and although local authorities took action to protect the population from rising prices, unscrupulous middlemen and hoarders, it seems clear from the surviving records that most households in Scotland had difficulty achieving minimum subsistence. [137] At the same time, real wages had begun to decline so that between 1540 and 1600 there was an overall drop of 30 per cent in purchasing power.[138] Combined with the rising price of grain, the declining value of real wages contributed to the poverty experienced across the realm. This raised fears of increased vagrancy and crime prompting legislation to curtail the wrongful behaviour that poverty bred.[139] Between 1541 and 1591, Aberdeen confronted the challenges brought on by the Reformation, experienced extensive periods of plague, famine and dearth, witnessed a craft riot that altered the political structure within the burgh and saw the fall of the family that had dominated burgh society for almost the entire sixteenth century. Undoubtedly, these circumstances influenced attitudes towards crime and contributed to the manner in which the burgh magistrates dealt with wrongdoing in the burgh.

The success with which certain penalties were able to deter individuals from committing crimes within the community, the processes of regulating behaviour and determining punishment, as well as the actual acts that contravened custom and statute were equal parts in a negotiation process that sought to establish power within the community. Individuals sought to utilize the power they possessed, whether informal or formal, to expand their control over their own lives and the lives of their neighbours. Through acts of statute breaking and regrating and forestalling, members of the community sought to challenge the authority of the burgh magistrates for personal gain, often at the expense of the entire community. Likewise, property crimes and unruly behaviour served as an extension of interpersonal conflicts often as a 'weapon for settling a dispute'. For the most part all of the petty crimes under consideration in this book continued to be a threat to good neighbourliness throughout this period. However, the overall number of crimes, including assaults, property damage, civil disobedience and theft brought before the burgh court declined over this sixty-year period.

It is unlikely that the sanctions imposed by the burgh's authorities were the reason for this decline. Informal pursuit of retribution, unproven reciprocal violence and wrongdoing (i.e. vigilantism) and a shift in the concerns of the council and kirk likely effected this change. The highest number of cases brought before the court occurred between 1541 and 1551. In the following decades there was a decline of 21 per cent, with the numbers in each decade between 1552 and 1600 remaining almost equal. The fact that hundreds of cases of petty crime continued to be brought before the courts each decade suggests that the authorities had not won the war on crime. After 1551 the incidents of petty crime remained fairly constant, as did the types of crimes prosecuted in the courts, this despite introducing Reformation ideas into the burgh in the 1560s and the adoption of a kirk session to help regulate society. Indeed, what can be taken away from this analysis is that despite occasional changes in the specific concerns the authorities may have had, there was continuity in terms of the manner in which the community perceived and combatted crime.

Table 3.1 found at the end of this chapter reveals that there was an overall increase of approximately 21 per cent in cases of statute breaking, regrating and forestalling between 1542 and 1591. The changes between each decade starting from 1542 reveals a 13.5 per cent increase, followed by a 1 per cent decrease and then a dramatic increase of 63.5 per cent followed by an equally dramatic decrease of 54.8 per cent. When depicted in a line graph, it becomes clear that the overall number of incidents of these crimes brought before the court remained consistent throughout this period.[140] The same cannot be said for vandalic property crimes or 'wrongous away taking'. Between 1542 and 1571 there was virtually no change in the numbers of cases of vandalic property crimes brought before the burgh court; a 20 per cent increase in the first decade after 1551 was followed by a 20 per cent decrease in the proceeding decade. However, between 1572 and 1581 there was a 60 per cent increase from the 1542–51 numbers, and between 1582 and 1591 the numbers dropped by 100 per cent of the figures recorded for 1542–51. The result was an overall 40 per cent decrease in the total number of recorded incidents of this type of crime for the entire period. Over the entire period under consideration, the number of recorded incidents of 'wrongous away taking' or intromission decreased by 50 per cent. A significant drop-off in the number of recorded cases occurred between 1552 and 1561 and again between 1572 and 1581, with decreases of 27.8 per cent and 38.9 per cent respectively. It is interesting to note that the only types of crime other than statute breaking, regrating and forestalling that saw an increase in the number of cases brought before the burgh court, were for disobeying the magistrates and strubling the town. In none of the accounts do we see disobedience or strubling the town manifesting itself in acts of vandalic property crime or theft, nor can the decrease be explained away by a change in record keeping.[141]

That said, given that vandalic property crimes and 'wrongous away taking' were among the lowest total number of petty crimes brought before the burgh court, the overall decrease seems somewhat artificial. It may be tempting to see the imposition of harsh penalties on those individuals convicted of 'wrongous away taking' as being a deterrent. However, the decades that saw the greatest number of banishments prescribed for such behaviour were 1542–51 and 1562–1571. These decades, as one might expect, also had the highest number of recorded incidents. Interestingly enough, in both of these decades 50 per cent of the individuals who were brought before the courts accused of 'wrongous away taking' were banished from the town. This compares with 15 per cent between 1552–61 and 22 per cent between 1572–81 and 1582–91. If indeed such penalties served as a deterrent, they did so in a rather haphazard manner. It would be difficult to argue that the authorities cracked down on this type of crime and that this resulted in the fewer incidents brought before the court. Likewise, it is unlikely that the inhabitants of Aberdeen recognized the detrimental impact such activities had on the common weal and sought to change their ways. It is more likely, when the numbers are taken into consideration, that such activities continued relatively unabated and that the lower number of recorded incidents is indicative of fewer individuals being willing, or able due to court expenses, to prosecute their cases before the courts. As Chapter 5 demonstrates, it is likely that the court, and the magistrates at its helm, were more preoccupied with the activities associated with the 'tumults' surrounding the craftsmen of the burgh's agitation for greater political involvement.

In the next chapter it becomes clear that the number of personal conflicts that erupted into incidents of verbal and physical violence brought before the court also declined over the period under consideration. This supports the idea that individuals may have chosen not to prosecute transgressions committed against them in the court either because they chose to use illegal means to resolve the conflict or because the cost of bringing cases before the court was becoming prohibitive. However, the *total number* of crimes committed within the burgh and brought before the court remained relatively consistent. This suggests that petty crimes continued to challenge the ideal notions of good neighbourliness and, from the perspective of the burgh authorities, threatened the common weal of the burgh. It likewise continued to enable those without any access to formal power to exercise social power in an informal manner. Crime and conflict sought to undermine the control the burgh magistrates had over the social structures within the burgh. Moreover, each of the petty crimes under consideration acted as a form of control and a means of exerting power over other individuals in the community. In large part, the interactions between 'neighbours' helped to outline areas of concern for a magistracy keen to ensure the protection of the common weal and determined that order reigned in the burgh.

Table 3.1: Incidents of petty crimes brought before
the burgh court of Aberdeen, 1542–91

Crime	1542–51	1552–61	1562–71	1572–81	1582–91	Total
Unspecified strublance	94	11	10	5	8	128
Decline each decade vs 1542		-88.3	-1.1	-5.3	3.2	-91.5
Decline from 1542 (cumulative)		-88.3	-89.4	-94.7	-91.5	
Comparison between each decade		-88.3	-9.1	-50.0	60.0	
Physical assault	110	111	91	85	76	473
Decline each decade vs 1542		0.9	-18.2	-5.5	-8.2	**-30.9**
Decline from 1542 (cumulative)		0.9	-17.3	-22.7	-30.9	
Comparison between each decade		0.9	-18.0	-6.6	-10.6	
Verbal assault	109	91	98	47	41	386
Decline each decade vs 1542		-16.5	6.4	-46.8	-5.5	**-62.4**
Decline from 1542 (cumulative)		-16.5	-10.1	-56.9	-62.4	
Comparison between each decade		-16.5	7.7	-52.0	-12.8	
Vandalic property crime	5	6	5	8	3	27
Decline each decade vs 1542		20.0	-20.0	60.0	-100.0	**-40.0**
Decline from 1542 (cumulative)		20.0	0.0	60.0	-40.0	
Comparison between each decade		20.0	-16.7	60.0	-62.5	
Disobedience	9	3	4	21	27	64
Decline each decade vs 1542		-66.7	11.1	188.9	66.7	**200.0**
Decline from 1542 (cumulative)		-66.7	-55.6	133.3	200.0	
Comparison between each decade		-66.7	33.3	425.0	28.6	
Breaking statutes, regrating and forestalling	104	118	117	183	126	648
Decline each decade vs 1542		13.5	-1.0	63.5	-54.8	**21.2**
Decline from 1542 (cumulative)		13.5	12.5	76.0	21.2	
Comparison between each decade		13.5	-0.8	56.4	-31.1	
Wrongous away taking and intromission	18	13	16	9	9	65
Decline each decade vs 1542		-27.8	16.7	-38.9	0.0	**-50.0**
Decline from 1542 (cumulative)		-27.8	-11.1	-50.0	-50.0	
Comparison between each decade		-27.8	23.1	-43.8	0.0	
Strubling the town	7	5	5	17	56	90
Decline each decade vs 1542		-28.6	0.0	171.4	557.1	**700.0**
Decline from 1542 (cumulative)		-28.6	-28.6	142.9	700.0	
Comparison between each decade		-28.6	0.0	240.0	229.4	
Crime totals	456	358	346	375	346	1881
Decline each decade vs 1542		-21.5	-2.6	6.4	-6.4	**-24.1**
Decline from 1542 (cumulative)		-21.5	-24.1	-17.8	-24.1	
Comparison between each decade		-21.5	-3.4	8.4	-7.7	

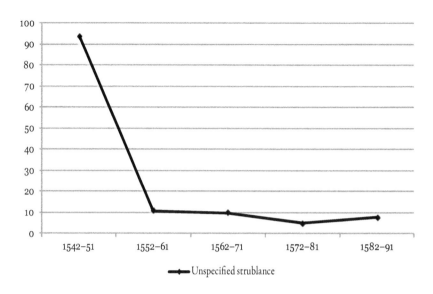

Figure 3.1 Distribution of incidents of unspecified strublance brought before the burgh court of Aberdeen, 1542–91.

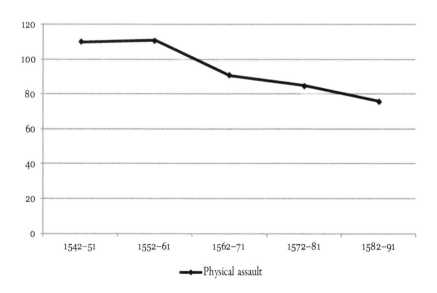

Figure 3.2 Distribution of incidents of physical assault brought before the burgh court of Aberdeen, 1542–91.

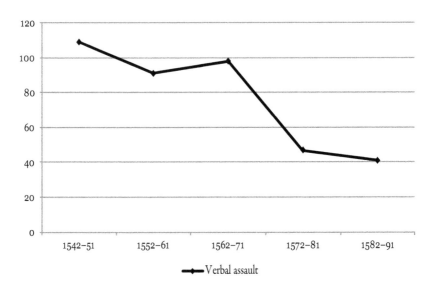

Figure 3.3 Distribution of incidents of verbal assault brought before the burgh court of Aberdeen, 1542–91.

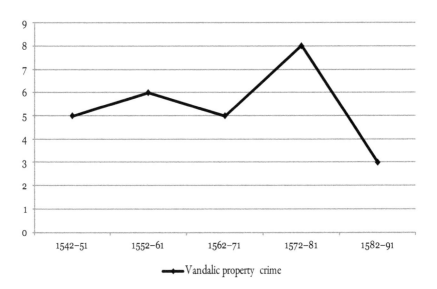

Figure 3.4 Distribution of incidents of vandalic property crime brought before the burgh court of Aberdeen, 1542–91.

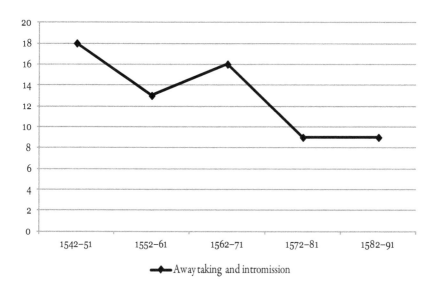

Figure 3.5 Distribution of incidents of away taking and intromission brought before the burgh court of Aberdeen, 1542–91.

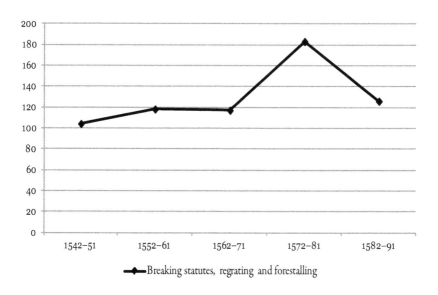

Figure 3.6 Distribution of incidents of breaking statutes, regrating and forestalling brought before the burgh court of Aberdeen, 1542–91.

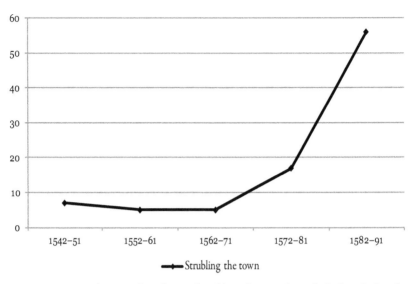

Figure 3.7 Distribution of incidents of strubling the town brought before the burgh court of Aberdeen, 1542–91.

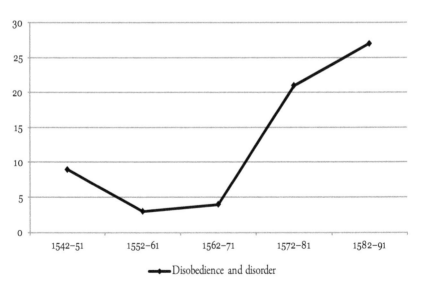

Figure 3.8 Distribution of incidents of disobedience and disorder brought before the burgh court of Aberdeen, 1542–91.

4 VIOLENCE

On 24 July 1562 the town magistrates convicted John Chalmer for the 'iniuring of divers nytbors and inhabitants thereof in deid and sklandering of thaim in word'. The authorities determined that 'for misbehawne of him self in sic sundry wayis' Chalmer was to be declared an unlawful neighbour and banished from the town.[1] Although Chalmer denied the charges levelled at him, a sworn assise found that he 'aucht not to be sufferit to pas at libertie in this town to commit sic misorder and enormities as he daly committis'.[2] While the account does not provide clear details of Chalmers' crimes, the court clerk does suggest that they included a verbal assault as well as some other deed or deeds that threatened the social fabric of the sixteenth-century burgh.[3] This the clerk makes more clear in the later account that Chalmer was responsible for causing disorder within the community on a daily basis. While 'injury' frequently referred to some form of verbal crime, 'injuring in deed' suggests the possibility of physical violence. What is clear is that the town magistrates, acting on behalf of the whole community, determined that Chalmer's behaviour, or rather misbehaviour, required immediate remedy and should result in the loss of his freedom. While we cannot with any certainty know whether the authorities actually banished Chalmer from the town, a lifetime of wrongdoing most likely ended with his removal from the community.[4] Chalmer's case, like so many others, reveals that the leading men of the burgh had a clear idea of what they believed constituted a threat to 'neighbourliness' and that such behaviour had no place in the burgh community.

This chapter examines the incidents of verbal and physical violence tried in the Aberdeen burgh court in the last half of the sixteenth century and the impact such crimes had on the burgh community.[5] As previous chapters have shown, the magistrates were keen to prevent the inhabitants of the burgh from committing any offence that threatened the common weal and to punish those who did. That they punished violent offenders with the same types of punishments, fines, public acts of repentance and, in some cases, banishment from the burgh does not mean that they viewed petty violence as trivial or inconsequential. Rather, it reflects, on the one hand, the extent of the powers the magistrates had to punish crime in the burgh and, on the other hand, the contemporary belief that *all* criminal activities were a threat to the burgh's well-being. Still, when it came to punishing verbal and physical assaults there were some areas of difference. For example, verbal and physical violence frequently generated retaliation from victims, their family and friends or neighbours in the burgh. Court clerks also tended to record accounts of these crimes differently, both in tone and language. Moreover, while both men and women committed a variety of crimes within the burgh, it is quite clear that the frequency in which men and women wronged their neighbours and the broader community differed.

Causing a Disturbance: 'Strublance' as Petty Crime

The language used to describe criminal activities committed in the burgh or to characterize persons involved in such activities helps to inform us of contemporary attitudes, both to the offences committed and to the offenders themselves. However, contemporary language, not unlike its modern counterpart, contained hidden codes that reflect the culture in which it was produced.[6] Perhaps the most obvious example of this is the word 'strublance', with its best understood meaning to be a disturbance through word or by deed.[7] In March 1543, Michael Will strubled Margaret Seton by taking her fish.[8] For his actions he was put in amercement of court. Mr John Fraser and Andrew Crawford came before the baillies in January 1542 and accused each other of strublance and mispersoning. Crawford made a point of stressing to the baillies that Fraser had called him a 'dyor' [a debtor].[9] On the same day, an assise convicted John Rany 'for the strublance of the officiars & mispersoning of thaim & the baizeis'. The assise made note that the officers and baillies 'war maid quytt of all strublans of the said John rany'.[10] In May 1542, James Wat and Ambrose Taylor stood before the baillies and accused each other of strublance and blood drawing. The matter was put to a sworn assise who acquitted Wat of committing these deeds 'bot in his puir defence' and convicted Taylor 'for the masterfull strublans and vnsetting ane the said James'.[11]

In all of these cases, the function that the word 'strublance' performs is not entirely clear. However, examples such as the ones cited are common in both the Council Register and Baillie Court Books. Indeed, strublance, in its different spelling variations, appears in 27 per cent (517 of 1936) of the recorded accounts of petty crime that occurred between October 1541 and August 1596. What is more, the word strublance frequently accompanied descriptions in the accounts of different crimes other than verbal and physical violence. As we saw in the case of Jonet Paterson,[12] the court clerk cited 'strublance' and theft in describing Paterson's transgression against Margaret Smyth. In May 1550, a sworn assise found Riche Ray guilty of the strublance of Besse Collinson and 'als for the vrangous spilling of hir land' [the destruction or spoiling of her land].[13] The records also suggest that clerks used the word strublance to describe disputes in public places.

It is perhaps in these two forms that we might recognize its inherent meaning of 'causing a disturbance'. Between 1541 and 1596 there were 102 incidents where clerks cited the town or the burgh court as victims of various transgressions in the form of 'strublance'. In April 1543 the baillies ordered the officers to warn Gilbert Mar to appear before the council and make his amends 'for the strublance of the court, striking and strublance of Robert Aytkin'.[14] In an account of John Riddell's conviction in March 1586, the clerk makes clear that strublance equated to the causing of a disturbance. The record states that the baillies found Riddell guilty of mispersoning David Fortre, 'calling him coward and knaiff in presens of the balzie in jugement and tharthout convictit als for strubling of the court'.[15] In other words, Riddell's outburst in front of the magistrates placed him in contempt of court.

Frequently, scuffles involving individual townspeople led to convictions in the burgh court for 'strubling the town'.[16] The dispute in April 1583 between Gavin Wishart and David Indeaucht brought the two parties before the burgh court where an assise convicted them both 'for strubling of the town in prs of the ballies'.[17] The actual incident that caught the baillies' attention involved Indeaucht 'geving of ane cuff to the said Gawane' after being provoked by Wishart's slanderous tongue. In February 1584, John Jak stood accused before the provost and baillies 'in the name of the kingis majestie for strubling of this town in hurting & blud drawing of Alex Kyng'.[18] Deemed 'trowbilsom' by the magistrates, Jak received a fine of £10 and the council banished him from the town for a year and a day. The records are unclear as to whether or not Kyng was an officer of the burgh, as suggested by the reference to the king's majesty. While it was not necessary for public acts of violence to involve members of the town's authorities in order to be construed as strubling the town, for the most part, in other instances of 'strubling the town' the court convicted all parties involved in the incident.

Most often, accounts of an attack on authority figures within the burgh directly state the action that took place. Of the seventy-five recorded instances of disobedience in Aberdeen between January 1542 and August 1596, ten accounts refer to 'strubling the court' while none specifically state that the incident involved 'strubling the town'.[19] For this reason Jak's conviction stands out. Similarly, an incident that occurred in the summer of 1587 involving an Aberdeen flesher, one of the town's baillies and one of the town's officers resulted in the flesher facing very serious consequences. Michael Davidson was convicted for disobeying the Baillie 'in execution of his office' and for the 'striking and strubling of Thomas Kyng officer'.[20] For this transgression, Davidson received one of the harshest penalties recorded in the burgh Council Register. The baillies ordered Davidson to be:

put in ward in the kirk there to remane for the space of ten days with breid and water and thereupon to be banyst the burgh ordainis his crag to be put fast in the govis [neck placed in the stocks] instantly there to remane twa houris and the sin be public proclamation in the croce to be banist this burght enduring the counsell's will and gif any person indwellar within this burght resave the said michaell in hous or harborand during the said space to pay the unlaw of ten poundis besyd the punishment befor imponit.[21]

While other incidents of strubling the town involved the disturbance of the community through breach of peace involving verbal or physical violence, the court perceived Jak's attack on an officer of the burgh to constitute an attack on the community.[22]

However, this does not bring us to a completely satisfactory understanding of the word 'strublance' in its historical context. In all of the examples cited, clerks recorded the term alongside a different offence committed by the convicted party. It is somewhat tempting then to read 'strublance' as an adjective modifying the accompanying offence. However, of 1,936 recorded incidents of petty crimes between October 1541 and August 1596, there are 128 incidents where the clerk recorded the convicted party's sole offence as 'strublance'. Besse Myll was convicted and put in amercement of court for the strublance of Maly Gibson in October 1541. The baillies later modified her unlaw, requiring her to publicly seek Gibson's forgiveness on her knees in the parish kirk.[23] In June 1542 John Make was convicted for the strublance of Jerome Blak and ordered to amend as law will. Interestingly enough, in the proceeding entry in the Council Register the council ordered Blak to pay Make 43 shillings 'for his fee within viii days'. This suggests that the original dispute may have arisen from Make's attempts to force Blak to pay for some service he rendered. Unfortunately, the records are silent on Make's occupation.[24] The records only very infrequently offer us the assistance of subsequent entries to decipher the nature of the 'strublance' committed by those convicted of this offence alone. What is more, penalties ascribed for such offences do not offer any deeper insight. The range from amercement to acts of repentance suggests that it was held in comparable light to the other types of petty crime under consideration. Perhaps the only true insight into this word, beyond recognizing that contemporaries perceived it to be a form of disturbance, comes from the decline in usage that occurs over the period.

Table 4.1: Incidents of unspecified strublance, physical and verbal violence before the burgh court, 1542–91

Date Range	Unspecified strublance	Physical assault	Verbal assault
1542–51	94	110	109
1552–61	11	111	91
1562–71	10t	91	98
1572–82	5	85	47
1582–91	8	76	41
Total	**128**	**473**	**386**

As Table 4.1 illustrates, after 1551 there was a considerable decrease in the number of cases recorded solely as 'strublance'. When compared with other forms of crime, the decline is noticeable. For example, while the period 1572–81 marks a significant decline in recorded accounts of verbal crimes within the community, cases of physical violence experienced the smallest decline of all the types of wrongdoing under consideration during the entire period.[25] This decrease corresponds with a subtle change in record keeping during this period. Although it is less easy to quantify, by the 1570s the Council clerk had begun recording incidents of petty crime in brief, omitting details other than the names of the individuals involved and the offence they committed. However, this too is rather inconsistent as fuller entries continue to dot the materials sporadically. As late in our period as 1594 a full entry in the Baillie Court Books states that: 'anabell chalmer [was] convikit for strubling of thomas dwn and his wyf.'[26] This marks the last appearance of 'strublance' on its own in the archival material for this period.

What then, if anything, can we take from cases where the recorded offence is 'strublance' without any other qualifier to help us determine the nature of the wrongful activity? First, it is possible to say, with little qualification, that 'strublance' did, in some form, equate to a disturbance through word or deed. It is also fair to say that its impact was felt by individuals and in some instances the entire community. Second, that contemporaries perceived the act of strubling as detrimental to proper neighbourly behaviour is clear from the accounts left behind. Both the frequency with which clerks employed the term and its association with other harmful behaviour underscores its place in the contemporary lexicon. Third, although it gives the impression of having operated as a catchword[27] for a variety of offences, its frequent appearance alongside more explicitly defined crimes suggests that contemporaries would have understood it to possess a distinct meaning. This is most discernable in cases where the clerk recorded the convicted party's offence as being 'strublance' *and* some other offence. For example, in July 1557 Andrew George and Alex Joffray were convicted for the 'strublens and mispersoning of utheris'.[28] Although there is the possibility here of rhetorical flourish, it seems more likely that the clerk employed the term strublance for a specific purpose that was absent in the numerous cases where mispersoning occurred and that the clerk recorded this offence without reference to any strublance. Ultimately, contemporaries were very aware that to struble was to cause great hurt within the community.

That strublance conveyed a sense of molestation underscores its frequent connection to crimes of verbal and physical violence. Table 4.2 shows that these two types of behaviour account for 46 per cent of the total number of cases of petty crime brought before the burgh court between 1542 and 1591.

Table 4.2: Total cases of petty crime brought before burgh court *c.* 1542–*c.* 1591

Crime	Total
Physical assault	473
Verbal assault	386
Vandalic property crime	25
Breaking statutes	386
Regrating/Forestalling	262
Unspecified strublance	128
Disobedience/Disorder[29]	67
Petty theft	44
Strubling the town	90
Total	**1861**

It also illustrates that with the exception of incidents of regrating and forestalling and incidents where Aberdonians contravened statutes, verbal and physical violence dominate the accounts of petty crimes in the extant source materials.

The accounts of property crimes and strublance have revealed that when individuals committed these crimes they disrupted the proper order within the burgh and threatened the neighbourliness that was to govern a stable and prosperous community. The accounts also suggest that such prescriptive ideas were challenged frequently by the conflicts, tensions and competing interests of the burgh's inhabitants, or what Steve Hindle has called 'the constant jostling and realignments' within the community.[30] Ultimately, the social relationships within the burgh were constantly negotiated and criminal acts, and how they were prosecuted both legally by the burgh court and illegally by offended parties, formed part of that negotiation process.[31] In such manner, accounts of verbal and physical violence provide insight into the burgh community by revealing the dynamics of social relationships between neighbours and between those regulating society. For instance, Heleyne Keyth was found guilty of 'striking and blud drawing of thomas moreis and iniuring heuelye be word off the said Thomas to his greyt sklander and defamation'.[32] Although Moreis himself had been convicted on a few occasions for unlawfully using merchandise, the magistrates recognized the importance of protecting an individual's honour and keenly attempted to curb slanderous attacks. With very few exceptions, those who had been convicted of past offences and who met the required penalty continued to maintain their status within the burgh and participate within the community. This is most recognizable in the form of acting as suretor and cautioner, participating in town elections and as civil magistrates and as sitting on assises.

Casting Aspersions: Verbal Assaults in the Burgh

For those whose status in the burgh prevented them from playing an active role in burgh governance, preserving their good name and their ability to earn a living unscathed was equally important. Craig Muldrew has argued that early modern societies should be seen as markets 'not just where things were bought and sold, but where trust was extended, or not extended, and where the "social" was defined as the need for, and the extent of, such trust'.[33] Reputation, then, was absolutely crucial because individuals (and households) 'sought publicly to define their own reliable and virtuous personalities, and to be reassured about those of others with whom they did business'.[34] But as Muldrew and others have shown, this was not simply the concern of the wealthy elite seeking to protect business interests and to safeguard their social status. In accounts of 'misperson-ing', 'defamining', 'missaying' and 'injuring' where the victim's social status was unclear, the authorities' attitudes towards protecting individuals from verbal assaults did not deviate. In October 1561 the authorities convicted Cristane Annand for the 'missaying, detracting and slandering' of Agnes Leslie 'gretlie reproching hir fame'.[35] The court ordered Annand to appear before the entire congregation the following Sunday to ask Leslie's forgiveness and to revoke the 'said iniurious wordis said be hir als fals and vntrew'. While it is unclear whether or not Agnes belonged to the lairdly family of Leslie who held some influence within the burgh, the baillies determined that her honour had been undermined and required restoration.[36] Another account, made the same day of Annand's conviction, records that 'the wyf of Johne murray was convikit in jugement be the deposition of divers famous witness for the missaying detracting and sclan-dering of jonet galloway the relict of umquhill johne arclay greitlie reproaching hir fame.'[37] The virtually identical phrasing of both accounts suggests that resto-ration of an individual's reputation after it has been damaged by a verbal assault was of fundamental importance to the magistrates regardless of the victim's sta-tus and standing within the burgh community.

In May 1572, Jonet Davidson was found guilty of slandering and defaming Marioun Paterson calling her 'harlot & huir' and for verbally attacking Paterson's mother. The court clerk added that, as well as these very personal attacks, David-son uttered 'other injurious words'.[38] The clerk also named Paterson's husband, George Grigson, in the account, as Davidson had implicitly attacked his good name in the process of maligning her primary target. Although the records do not provide us with any information on Grigson's standing in the community, it is clear that slander and defamation affected more than just the target of abuse; it often affected their entire household.[39] A clear example of this can be found in an account of a verbal attack committed by Andrew Medell on Master George Myddilton, one of the baillies in the town. While verbal attacks on the mag-

istrates are interesting for what they tell us about contemporary challenges to
authority, this particular attack was personal and involved the baillie's wife:

> The said day andrew medell was convikit in jugement ffor the missaying and detract-
> ing of maister george myddilton bailze saying his wyf brewit plak aill and sauld the
> same by the statutis.[40]

Although the account does not indicate how the court punished Medell, based
on similar accounts it is likely to have involved some form of public recantation
of his slanderous words. Regardless, the incident made clear that the reputation
of all members of early modern households had an impact on the rest of the family. Moreover, by implying that Myddilton's wife broke the town's ordinances,
Meddle openly challenged Myddilton's position as an authority figure whose
role in society it was to uphold the very burgh laws Meddle accused Myddilton's wife of breaching.[41] The accusation that Myddilton's wife was defrauding
the community must have struck deeply at someone invested with the right and
authority to protect and defend the town.

Individuals frequently targeted their neighbour's kin and their disparagement
of a victim's family members was equally damaging to social relations. In 1543,
Molly Myll took the good name of Menzies in vain when she attacked the father
of the current provost, a former provost himself, by saying that his now deceased
mother was a common witch.[42] A more telling example can be found in a mispersoning case from October 1557. The baillies convicted John Colle for attacking
Elspet and Marion Wychtane in retaliation for the sisters' attack on Colle's father,
Duncan.[43] While both Myll and John Colle were punished by the court for their
actions, Colle had attempted to take on the role of prosecutor by punishing the
sisters for their attack on his father. A very good example of this sort of personal
justice can be found in the account of Thomas Kyng's conviction for verbally
assaulting the wife of Mr Gilbert Ross. The account states that Kyng was an officer
of the burgh and that because of his attack on Ross's wife, Ross retaliated by drawing his sword. Unfortunately for Ross, Kyng got the better of him and he was
wounded in the scuffle that ensued. The baillies placed both in amercement of
court and ordered the pair to set surety and lawborrow that they would be 'harmless and skaythless of utheris and siclyk the town and inhabitants thereof'.[44]

We have already seen a good example of how verbal attacks could affect the
wider community in Jonet Troup's defamation case from 1581.[45] In October
of that year, Troup stood accused before the Baillie court for the mispersoning
of Elizabeth Irving. While we do not know the exact words used to disparage
Irving, we do know from the account of Troup's conviction that the baillies and
council sought to demonstrate that this was unacceptable behaviour. Upon her
conviction the baillies ordered Troup to 'revoik and agane call the wordis that
she hes spoken vpon elizabeth irving and to ask God and the said forgiveness'.[46]

By forcing Troup to visit two of the most important and populated sites within the burgh, the market cross and the parish kirk, in order to publicly acknowledge her faults, the baillies made the community an integral part of both her penalty and her rehabilitation. What is more, they ensured that Irving's name was restored to its good standing by making certain that the highest number of the town's inhabitants witnessed Troup's punishment and revocation of the false words she had spoken.

Nearly forty years earlier Besse Spring was found guilty of the strublance and mispersoning of Besse Rany 'ryt hauely'. Although the words spoken against Rany did not find their way into the account of Spring's conviction, the nature of the offence stands out in the use of the phrase 'right heavily' and in the baillies' order that Spring be placed in the govis [pillory] for an hour under threat of banishment for committing any future offence.[47] In both of these examples, the public nature of the punishment involved the community in the process of regulating petty crimes. Insuring that the broader community was aware of the crime and of its damaging impact on the victim remained a key part of the restorative nature of this form of punishment. Perhaps more importantly, this was indicative of the deeply interconnected social networks that characterized early modern communities. Despite the fact that in each of the above cases the clerk did not detail the insults used to disparage the victims, we are still able to gain some insight into the nature of the crime and into the manner in which the authorities responded to such acts. Perhaps more telling are the instances where individuals maligned other members of society by referring to them as convicted criminals.[48] Such was the case in January 1582 when Isobel Gibson slandered Katherine Rathe, the spouse of James Menzies, calling her 'baneist theiff and resettar of greyn malt & keil [cabbage]'.[49] In June 1583, Jonet Philip was likewise convicted for the mispersoning of Cristane Cultis, calling her 'comon thieff, wyne staillar and vagabond'.[50] Although neither Rathe's nor Cultis' name appeared in prior accounts, Cultis' husband, Mr James Burnett, had been convicted of breaking statutes in 1558.[51] This may be a case where the husband's misdeeds tarnished the household and contributed to the derision that Cultis experienced. It may also be the case, though unlikely, that Burnett took responsibility for his wife's wrongdoing.

A more extreme example of this type of slanderous behaviour comes from an account found in the Baillie Court Books towards the end of our period. In May 1595 David Low was brought before the baillies and accused of striking Marion Kyntor, the widow of James Ewyn. Ewyn had been convicted in 1575 for disobeying the baillies by removing stakes that were in place to protect a hedge belonging to Andrew Thornton.[52] In addition to his conviction for striking Kyntor 'with his hands & fist' Low was also convicted for the 'sklandering of the said umquhil james saying he wes leid to the gallowis, his hands were bound behind his bak'.[53] For this offence, the provost and baillies ordered Low to appear within the tolbooth and publicly revoke the words spoken against Ewyn as untrue and ask the injured party forgiveness. He was also ordered to pay a fine of £10 to the baillies for his unlawful behaviour. It is clear that the injured party in this case was Ewyn's widow, Marion Kyntor. Kyntor's reputation, after all, was deeply tied to that of her deceased husband's. However, such examples also draw attention to the fact that the community was deeply aware of the crimes committed in the burgh, understood their power and influence and were happy to redirect the power of alleged wrongdoing for alternative purposes. On the one hand it could be used to diminish an individual within the community. On the other hand, it could also be used to highlight the potential dangers of making criminal activities and wrongdoers publicly known.

It is very tempting to conclude – especially given the accusations hurled at individuals – that by publicly acknowledging crimes committed the authorities, and all who participated in public punishments, raised the potential for greater conflict. What should be taken away from these accounts, however, is the fact that the magistrates went to great lengths to make sure the public knew that verbal assaults led to greater disruption of the peace. Regardless of Ewyn's guilt, or whether he had actually been executed for his crimes, the magistrates, and the community at large, believed that it was wrong to verbally assault his wife even if the nature of the insult rang true. However, we must also take into consideration the frequency with which such accusations occurred, or at least led to convictions in the burgh courts. One of the most obvious ways of tracking this type of behaviour is by examining the number of times those accused of petty crimes found themselves the target of verbal assaults in which their previous behaviour figured prominently. Unfortunately, a very small number of accounts exist where the clerk recorded details of the types of insults used to slander, defame and misperson individuals. As such, it is impossible to quantify this type of behaviour. However, the fact that a large number of recidivists lived, relatively unscathed, within Aberdeen society suggests that their actions did not contribute to any ostracism expressed through slanderous attacks.

Over a ten-year span, Molly Abell disturbed her neighbours in word to the point that the baillies convicted her of strublens, mispersoning and defamation on five different occasions. Her first conviction came in May 1543 for the strubling of Margaret Duncan.[54] Eighteen months later Abell was convicted for the mispersoning of Alexander Kay, an officer of the burgh.[55] Having apparently returned to good neighbourliness for nearly five years, or at least having not been convicted of any crime in that period, Abell was again in trouble with the magistrates in March 1549. The baillies convicted her, along with her husband John Myln, for the mispersoning of Canne Balzone and the striking of Balzone's swine.[56] Just one month later, Abell stood before the baillies accused of mispersoning Catte Joffray.[57] The resulting punishments for the strubling of Duncan and the mispersoning of the burgh officer are unknown, but for her next two convictions the baillies ordered Abell to appear in the parish kirk and ask the injured party forgiveness. Despite these four appearances before the burgh magistrates and the community, Abell did not learn to control her slanderous tongue. In October 1553 Abell was yet again convicted for a verbal assault, this time for the defamation and mispersoning of Andrew Gray and his wife Margaret Leyth. The account of her conviction and punishment suggest that the town authorities were becoming increasingly impatient with her unwillingness to change her ways. Once again required by the baillies to perform her act of repentance before the congregation, the provost and baillies also admonished the 'gud men of the town to caus tham forgiv hir'.[58] Perhaps this was the magistrates' method of discouraging members of the community from seeking retribution against Abell.

Despite her repeated offences against both an authority figure and her neighbours, there is no record of any verbal or physical attack on Abell or her family. Abell's husband, John Myln, continued down a similar path and was convicted on numerous occasions for a variety of petty crimes. Perhaps the most grievous offence for which he was convicted came in October 1561 for 'casting of fyir in his awen bed and for ane onlauchtfull nychtbor and ane comond resayttar'.[59] Despite the seriousness of these charges,[60] Myln was put in amercement of court. Like his wife, Myln does not seem to have been subject to any form of verbal or physical abuse despite his wrongful behaviour. Elsewhere I have examined the lives of two Aberdonian women, Besse Barcar and Besse Walcar, who cheated the market, verbally and physically assaulted their neighbours and each other, and threatened the community they lived in for over sixteen years.[61] Yet, despite their numerous convictions, over twenty between the pair, they managed to live within the burgh relatively unscathed. Moreover, despite being very well known to the magistrates for their wrongdoing, the baillies, on at least one occasion, determined that Barcar should live without fear of retaliation in the burgh while Walcar was able to call on the provost's son to act as cautioner following one of her convictions.[62] Just as it was the case that not every regrater and forestaller incurred the wrath of their neighbours, so too was it the case that individuals who acted out violently against members of the community were not driven from the town.

The insults used to disparage victims of verbal assaults often revealed a deeper tension between the parties involved. Impugning one's social status, as well as their honour, was rather standard practice in terms of slanderous or defamatory language. This can be detected in the words Besse Barcar used to disparage Kay Watson the widow of Alexander Kay, the burgh officer who Molly Abell had mispersoned in 1544. Barcar had refered to Kay as a 'theyffis geit beggaris geit [a 'thief's brat' and 'beggar's brat'] commond huir & culzear [dupe] of hir husband witht mony vther wyill wordis'.[63] When Molly Abell had mispersoned Alex Kay she called him a 'skayth karll [mischievous peasant] with uther injurious words'.[64] It is not clear whether Barcar and Abell were close acquaintances, but their independent attack on Kay's household suggests the possibility that the Kays' neighbours took issue with their status or their conduct and it led to the verbal attacks. Regardless, the officer's good reputation was essential for maintaining the authority necessary to effectively fulfill the requirements of his position. As an officer of the burgh he represented the burgh, and how others perceived him and his family reflected on the community. For Barcar's attack the council determined that:

> becaus she hes been divers tymes convikit for siclyk offencis obefor to ask the said kay forgifnes openly at the mercat croce vpon hir kneis & revoke the said ewill sayings as fals & vntrew sayd threw malise in hir first mention of thaim and gif ever the said besse beis convikit for siclyk crymes anes again eftirward to be banist of the town with ane crown of paiper on hir heid as ane bald scald & common flytar.[65]

The fact that Barcar and others could behave in such a manner and still live within the burgh does not negate the fact that contemporaries were deeply concerned about the damage that verbal violence caused in the community. The records make clear that maligning an individual's good name held the potential of very serious consequences.

This can be detected in a defamation case from 1568. In August of that year Robert Paterson was brought before the baillies accused of slandering Mr George Johnstone. The baillies convicted Paterson of 'making ewill report on the said mr george behind his bak allegand that he suld speik ewill of my lord huntly'.[66] It is not clear why Paterson brought such allegations against Johnstone, though it was likely politically motivated. Regardless of the motive behind the attack, in alleging that Johnstone had disparaged the most powerful magnate in the region it is clear that either Paterson was trying to curry favour with Huntly, or realized such an allegation would seriously harm Johnstone's standing in the region. Either way, it suggests that Paterson held considerable animosity towards his victim. By subjecting Johnstone to this type of affront, Paterson put Johnstone at risk for retribution from Huntly or his supporters, or at the very least created the possibility for Paterson to lose standing in the Earl's eyes.[67]

While the overall impact of the verbal assault depended on the type of insult used and the individuals involved, it is fairly clear that most insults and slurs questioned the integrity of the victim. This was certainly the case when James Watson, a burgess of Dundee, found himself in trouble with the Aberdeen authorities for 'missaying and lytleying [belittling] of the guid town'.[68] Watson put himself in the provost and council's will and two burgesses, one from Dundee and another from Aberdeen, became cautioner to Watson that the town, 'inhabiters', ships and gear would be scatheless. A recent study has demonstrated that it was vital for town authorities to ensure that justice was served in order to protect the good standing of both individual and town in such matters.[69] The use of two burgesses, one from Watson's hometown and another from the town he disparaged, illustrates the community involvement as well as the desire to protect against lasting impediments resulting from Watson's actions. The town authorities would have been keen to ensure that Aberdeen's reputation remained unscathed in both Dundee and at home. The town's concern that Watson's misrepresentation of the burgh could have an ill effect on trade may be discerned from the inclusion of 'ships and gear' in the list of items that were to remain 'scatheless'.

A comparable impact was also be felt by individuals who were victims of disparaging remarks. In April 1581 Jonet Cruikshank was ordered by the baillies to present herself at the market cross and revoke the injurious language spoke against Alexander Mollison, the deacon of the baxter craft.[70] A month earlier, witnesses who had heard Cruikshank refer to Mollison as a 'common theif' helped the baillies to convict her for mispersoning. Cruikshank's defamation of Mollison had the same potentially damaging effect as Watson's attack on the town. By bringing into question a leading craftsmen's honesty, a characteristic vital not only for his craft but for his leadership of his craft guild, Cruikshank threatened Mollison's standing in the community as well as his livelihood. Yet, we should recall from an earlier chapter that Alex Mollison had his fair share of trouble with the burgh authorities having been convicted a number of times for breaking statutes and cheating the market.[71] Cruickshank's attack on the deacon illustrates the fact that seemingly minor punishments like public repentance and fines were not always the end of the matter. That the authorities tried to prevent such attacks from occurring underscored the tension between the prescriptive belief that wrongdoers could be reintroduced into society and the reality that the community did not always welcome individuals back with open arms. Mollison's credit, although expected to have been restored after he had paid his fines and performed his acts of repentance, continued to be diminished. That the authorities believed this to be detrimental to the well-being of society, and against the nature of the justice they provided, can be discerned from their keenness to protect Mollison from slander. That members of the community saw things differently is clear from Cruikshank's attack on Mollison's reputation.

Likewise, in January 1591 Margaret Molen became involved in a dispute with Duncan Donaldson over the price of his goods. In anger, Molen lashed out at Donaldson calling him a 'fals commond theif'.[72] Donaldson, concerned over his ability to earn a respectable living, sought action through the court. Like Mollison, Donaldson could express concerns over his own damaged reputation in 1591 despite his own less than upstanding behaviour in the burgh. Ten years earlier he showed no real concern for the community when he slandered and mispersoned the 'Baillies and magestrattis of this burgt'.[73] For his offence, the baillies ordered Donaldson to appear before the congregation the following Sunday and ask God and the injured party for forgiveness. Fourteen years prior to this verbal assault, the baillies and council had found Donaldson guilty of the 'sklandering and defaming of mr thomas fynny calling him mansworn conforme to his lybill and bill of complaint'.[74] Although the details of the situation in which Donaldson accused Fynny of lying under oath are absent from the account of his conviction, the fact that Fynny felt the need to bring a bill of complaint against him underscores his desire to restore his reputation.[75] In a society where credit and reputation were an integral part of interpersonal relationships, mispersoning, defaming, slandering and all such verbal assaults undermined an individual's ability to live free from scorn or ridicule.

It is quite clear that verbal assaults had an impact on nearly all levels of society regardless of gender or social status. Although not all of the records reveal the social standing of either the victim or the perpetrator of the offence, occasionally we do get a glimpse of just who was committing these types of crimes. However, the lack of full detailed descriptions in each of the accounts makes it impossible to provide a statistical analysis based on social status.[76] Bearing this in mind, there are enough details to show that a cross-section of sixteenth-century Aberdeen society participated in such activities. For example, in the relatively small number of incidents where the clerk recorded the social standing of the individuals we see that two authority figures, one Baillie and one officer, were convicted of mispersoning over the entire period. Yet, at least eight baillies, nine officers, one dean of guild, two provosts, an entire assise and two craft deacons were on the receiving end of insults hurled by their neighbours during the same period of time.

In terms of craftsmen and merchants, according to the surviving source materials, far more craftsmen than merchants faced the baillies and council accused of verbally assaulting other members of the community. The same holds true for being on the receiving end of such attacks. Craftsmen figure more prominently than merchants as victims of slander and mispersoning. Indeed, virtually all crafts seem to be represented in the accounts. A cursory glance at the sixty accounts where the details are provided reveals that at least four baxters, two cordiners, two coopers, one flesher, two litsters, one mason, one walker, six websters, two mariners and a white fisherman stood convicted of such crimes.[77] The surviving accounts also indicate that at least five servants were convicted for mispersoning others, while at least three servants suffered this type of abuse. Again, all of this has to be qualified by the fact that the accounts, very infrequently and inconsistently, contain the status or occupation of the individuals involved. We should keep in mind that even when repeat offenders are taken into consideration, it is highly unlikely that the only individuals involved in this type of wrongdoing were unskilled labourers or other members of the lower rungs of society.

Gender is an area where some statistical analysis is possible.[78] Only rarely are the full names of the individuals missing from the accounts and even in these instances there are clues within the text, such as a first name, reference to an occupation or a spouse, or a third person personal pronoun to suggest whether the anonymous individual was male or female. It is possible to break down the frequency of all types of petty crimes according to the sex of the offender(s) and victim(s). For verbal assaults an almost equal number of men and women committed this type of crime. When compared with similar studies, at least in terms of gender, verbal crime committed in Aberdeen was comparable to verbal crime committed elsewhere within the realm.[79] For example, in cases of 'slander/bickering' brought before the St Andrews Kirk Session between 1559 and 1581, seven were committed by men and nine by women.[80] In the Canongate Kirk Session, sixty-five cases of 'slander/bickering' occurred between 1564 and 1567. Of these sixty-five cases, thirty-nine were committed by men and twenty-six by women.[81] Elizabeth Ewan has convincingly argued that men and women 'were equally adept at using their tongues'.[82] In a recent study of defamation and gender, Ewan argued that in pre-Reformation Scotland women were in the 'slight minority among those accused of defamation', but that in the church court of Lothian they 'outnumbered men over the whole period [1518–1551] (82 : 52)'. Perhaps more importantly, Ewan argued that in the burghs men were convicted for a higher number of incidents of 'verbal violence and insult' than were women.[83]

Recent scholarship on crime in England and on the Continent in this period has shown that both men and women were inclined to use their slanderous tongues and that such actions brought them before the courts.[84] Apart from this very important development, one of the most interesting aspects of a recent study on 'scolding' has shown that contemporaries could and did use this term to describe the activities of both men and women.[85] This analysis of the ratio of men to women committing verbal crimes in Aberdeen should go some way to illustrate that in sixteenth-century Scotland, at least, men used their tongues to injure their neighbours as readily as women. That said, the work of Underdown and Ingram for England and Graham for Scotland has shown that by the turn of the seventeenth century women, more than men, increasingly faced charges of committing verbal violence.[86] In Aberdeen, at least, the reason for this may be the shift in responsibility for regulating such behaviour. As Table 4.1 suggests, the number of individuals accused of verbal crimes appearing before the burgh court declined dramatically towards the end of the sixteenth century. With the Kirk Sessions starting to handle the majority of these types of offences towards the end of the period under consideration, it is possible that a shift in emphasis occurred in who was brought before the courts and on what account.

The lack of full church court records for the period 1542–91 makes it impossible to determine if there was a difference in approach before the first decade of the seventeenth century. That said, I would suggest that the large number of individuals brought before the burgh court on account of verbal crimes well into the Reformation period suggests that, as in other types of petty crime, there was little distinction in secular and spiritual social reform. For the period under consideration it is quite clear that gender did not determine who used their tongue to abuse their neighbours and who did not. Likewise, it did not determine the target of such abuse. Table 4.3 illustrates that the ratio of men to women who were victims of verbal crimes roughly parallels the same ratio of men to women who committed them.

Table 4.3: Number of 'cases' of verbal and physical assaults delimited by sex of victim.[87]

Victims	Physical assault	Verbal assault	Unspecified strublance	Total
Male	262	177	60	499
Female	155	153	43	351
Male and female	11	30	10	51
Multiple males	5	8	4	17
Multiple females	5	9	3	17
The 'town'	0	3	0	3
Male/female and town	23	2	3	28
Unknown	16	4	1	21
Total	477	386	124	987

While it is clear that men suffered a higher number of physical assaults than verbal attacks, an almost perfectly even number of men and women were victims of verbal assaults during this period. If we take into account the fact that women could not serve as magistrates, and that in fifteen of the 177 cases where the victim was male the individual was one of these authority figures, the number of individuals who were victims of verbal assault breaks down to an almost equal number of male and female victims.[88] When we consider that a broad cross-section of Aberdeen society participated in such behaviour, either convicted for committing the crimes or dishonoured by an attack committed against them, we may determine that injuring in word was a fairly common occurrence in sixteenth-century Aberdeen. It is important to note that this compares well with other communities during this period.[89]

While the similarities are clear, there certainly were differences in terms of gender and verbal assault. The most obvious difference was the form the insults took. While a man's sexuality was very rarely the subject of the insult used against him, it almost always was the basis for insults used against women. In Aberdeen, as elsewhere, 'whore' and 'harlot' were the most commonly used insults directed towards women. While there is little question that the intention behind such insults was to question the woman's integrity and honesty by attacking the very cornerstone of her reputation, slanderers often used it as a 'catch-all' term that informed the perpetrator's more immediate concern.[90] According to an account in the Council Register, in late August 1589 Agnes Murray confronted Katherine Menzies and verbally assaulted her, calling her common thief, harlot with other injurious words.[91] Two years later, Elspet MacGowrie went to the home of Jonat Forsyt and John Robertson and there slandered Forsyt 'calling hir common huir, common theiff and common reset[tar-damaged] and casting of stanes at the said Jonat's duir'.[92] Forsyt responded to her attacker with both verbal and physical violence. For their actions, both were put in amercement of court and ordered to set caution. Both Katherine Menzies' and Jonet Foryst's honesty were brought into question through attacks on their sexuality. Moreover, both attackers alleged previous wrongdoings on the part of the victim. However, neither Menzies nor Fysset had been convicted by the court for any crime prior to their attacks. It is likely that, in these incidents at least, common whore and common thief were general insults meant to damage the probity of the victim rather than to call into question specific failings on their part.

Of course, such attacks were not unique to women alone. Commonly used insults directed at men also brought their honesty into question but tended to focus more on their financial probity and social standing.[93] We recall that in 1586 John Riddell had been convicted of mispersoning David Fortre in front of the baillies. The Council Register version of this offence notes that Riddell called Fortre a 'coward and knaiff (rogue or scoundrel)'. In the Baillie Court Books, the account indicates that Riddell had called Fortre a 'common theif and knaiff'.[94] While there is no clear explanation for the differing reports, the accounts offer a good example of an attack on a male inhabitant of the burgh where the insults used questioned his social standing, bravery and ability to earn a respectable living. Other insults frequently hurled at men commented on their intelligence and respectability. Thus, in April 1591, David Castell attacked a fellow webster by the name of Henry Dwn calling him a 'common peiff [a clumsy, stupid person, a dolt, clodhopper]'.[95] Likewise, in August 1596 Thomas Johnstone was convicted by the Baillie court for strubling the town by injuring Patrick Best calling him 'fals wod karl [rustic, country-bumpkin]'.[96] On the same day that Johnstone was convicted, Best himself stood accused of cheating the town in using faulty weights in order to increase his profits. Although not specified, it is probable that Johnstone attacked Best in front of the magistrates and on account of Best's alleged dubious activities. While Johnstone's insults did not directly question Best's financial honesty, in calling Best a peasant Johnstone attacked Best's place in society. This was especially damaging given that Best was a member of the Gild Brethren.

Injurious language used to undermine the reputation of individual members of society formed a major component of negotiating social power. By calling into question an individual's good standing in the community or by drawing attention to their failings, members of the community were able to influence how people responded to those individuals. Court records very infrequently offer us a window into the experiences of the parties involved after convictions were made and punishments were executed. Although this limits our ability to see the full impact such crimes had in the community, it does offer us examples of how individuals took it upon themselves to respond to their neighbours. Such insights enable us to see beyond formal regulatory processes and to gain a fuller understanding of community life.

Casting Stones: Physical Assaults in the Burgh

Non-fatal physical violence affords us a similar opportunity to examine social interaction within the burgh community. Such crimes often accompanied verbal assaults. Indeed, the burgh records provide numerous accounts where the town's inhabitants injured in deed as well as in word. Moreover, by physically assaulting members of the community individuals exercised their social power in a truly tangible fashion.[97] Helen Allan, who we met at the start of this book, is first mentioned in the court records in 1553.[98] In late July of that year the court convicted her alongside her sister, Besse, for the strublance and striking of Sande Gray.[99] Helen's sister, Besse, was the same woman that was convicted in 1569 with Thomas Durrant and William Forest for resetting [keeping stolen merchandise], but Helen does not appear in the records again until her perjury conviction in 1581. Helen seemingly stayed out of trouble until May 1587 when the Baillie court convicted her and Anabell Grigson for 'the trubling of Alex Harpar and his spous in their own hous'.[100] Allan and Grigson appeared before the court one week later along with Jonat Thomson, Nannis Thomson and Jonat Galloway and were convicted for the 'strubling of the town as common vagabonds and striking of utheris to forbear in tym cuming and amend as law will'.[101]

Between 1542 and 1591 a total of 1,861 charges of petty crimes were brought before the burgh court.[102] However, the court clerks employed the word 'vagabond' only this once to describe the individuals convicted of a crime committed within the burgh. We should recall that the account of Allan's 1581 conviction for perjury described Allan's continued criminality as 'odious'. The court records very infrequently contain such words describing the crimes brought before the burgh court or Kirk Session. For example, the town magistrates considered Patrick Leslie and George Troup's disturbance in the parish kirk in February 1582 a grave offence because of where it took place; the court clerk described their crime as 'more odious and haynous'.[103] Such description does not appear again in the court records until 1595 when William Gawane, a local tailor, was convicted for the strubling of a town officer within the kirk. The magistrates 'considering the offens was haynous & gryt & odious' ordered that Gawane be put in ward in the kirk for twenty-four hours, to ask the injured party forgiveness and to be banished if he ever did this again.[104] Each of these incidents took place in the kirk suggesting that this was the reason behind the authorities' perception of the crimes as 'odious and heinous'. If that was the case, Helen Allan's activities, although somewhat typical, bore some distinction that caused the authorities to characterize them in terms similar to the crimes committed by Leslie, Troup and Gawane. Although the records do not offer us further insight into Allan's case, further examples of physical violence committed in the burgh illustrate that the community saw such crimes as more than trivial offences.[105]

In July 1591, Agnes Coutts was the victim of a violent attack by Margaret Dempster. Although we do not know the reason Coutts incurred Dempster's wrath, we do know that she suffered both verbal and physical assaults. The Council Register states that Margaret struck and mispersoned Coutts to the 'gryt effusion of hir blud calling hir harlot with uther iniurious wordis'.[106] For her crime, the baillies ordered that Dempster set caution and be placed in the govis. Attacks resulting in the loss of blood are immediately recognizable in the accounts by the language used to describe them. Clerks regularly employed the terms 'blud drawing' and 'bla making' to define physical violence. Terms such as 'striking' 'dinging' 'wounding' and 'besting' also indicate physical violence, while references to drawing weapons or throwing objects underscore an intention to use physical violence even if the individual did not bring themselves to actually assault their victim. In the majority of cases found in the extant sources, 'strublance' appears alongside some form of physical violence. In the same manner that injurious language was used to negotiate social power, inhabitants of the burgh used physical violence to exercise their frustrations and hostility, but in a manner that physically overpowered their victims and exhibited their desire to gain control over situations. Moreover, they used violence to force the resolution of an ongoing conflict.

In May 1561 William Calderheid became involved in a dispute with William Mathewson. Though the details of the events leading up to the clash are patchy, we do know that at some point shortly before 21 May Calderheid and an unnamed servant entered Mathewson's booth and began destroying his wares. Mathewson responded to this attack by hurling stones at the two intruders. The burgh magistrates convicted Calderheid for 'cuming in william mathewsonis bychth and braking of his lynis' and Mathewson 'for casting of stanis and braking of William calderheidis servandis heid'.[107] In a preceding account, a William Mathews had become suretor for Mitchell Buchan who was indebted to Calderheid for £3.8s but refused to pay him any more than 30 shillings. It is possible that Mathews and Mathewson were the same individual or, more likely, that the individual who hurled the stones at Calderheid and his servant was Mathew's son. If that was the case, then the dispute that led to the breaking of 'calderheidis servandis heid' likely resulted from Calderheid seeking full payment for the debt incurred by Buchan. Casting stones and breaking heads do not appear to have been unusual occurrences in Aberdeen. Nor was it unusual for a third party to be on the receiving end of the blows. A dispute similar to the one between Calder-heid and Mathewson occurred in September 1571 between Robert Troup and a local mariner named John Jaseyn. Once again the sources are silent on the details of the initial quarrel; however, we do know that both Troup and Jaseyn were convicted for their violent attacks and that Jaseyn's assault was on Troup's wife.[108]

This case, as well as the Calderhead and Mathewson case, are but two out of numerous cases where individuals used violence to address wrongs committed against them. Such acts demonstrate that physical violence in the burgh was not always random; rather, it tended to serve a purpose regardless of its unlawful and damaging nature. Alexander Fortre apparently had the patience to endure a similar wrong committed against him by William Riddell without resorting to violence. Riddell was convicted by the burgh magistrates for the 'wrongous tirving [tirving: removing roofing material] of alex fortreis hous and takyne away the devettis [divett: thatch] of the same and siclyk for castine stanis and mispersoning of the said Alexander'.[109] Although there are no further details of the conflict that led Riddell to remove the thatch from Fortre's house, or to cast stones and aspersions at Fortre, we get a sense from the account that this was another instance of settling a score. A year prior to Riddell's conviction, the burgh magistrates twice accused and convicted Fortre for acts of property destruction. In early May 1564, Henry Cheyne accused Fortre of cutting down and stealing a tree from his yard.[110] Three weeks later, the master of the Kirk work, Mr Robert Lumisden, accused Fortre of 'brakin of certane growand treis and takin away of stanes of the kirk yard'.[111] Although there does not appear to be any record of a similar transgression committed by Fortre against Riddell, it is likely that Riddell acted 'in kind' in response to Fortre's own wrongdoing. This can be discerned from Riddell's mispersoning of Fortre, likely referring to his previous activities. Riddell was a substantial enough individual that his removing of the thatch from Fortre's house should be seen as willful property destruction rather than theft; here was not a case of want or need but an attempt to resolve an outstanding conflict. Riddell's only previous conviction came in October 1548 for an assault on one of his servants. In this instance Patrick Foulton and Riddell 'his master' were convicted for 'strubling' one another.[112] While it is unclear whether Foulton was Riddell's servant or apprentice, we get a sense from this account that Riddell belonged to the hammersmith guild as he was ordered to pay one pound of wax to St Eloy's light unforgiven.

While the dispute between Fortre and Riddell was over property, the forceful removal of Fortre's roofing materials, the casting of stones and the verbal assault characterize Riddell's response as undeniably violent. If violence begot more vio-lence during this period, then it is no surprise that the attack on William Portuis by the five German sailors should have resulted in the victim's violent response. On 7 October 1549 Cloyes van Holing, Henry Smyt, Cloyes Fultmeir, Benedict

Tymmerman and Clement Tehay were convicted for 'the violent and vrangis taking handling strubling blud drawing and binding of william portuis vnder silence [of the night]'.[113] The five sailors were ordered to set caution for their amends. The account ends by stating that the 'bailzeis continewit the pronunciation of the allegit strublance done be the said Scots men elikvise for thair enteres the said day to sett caution.'[114] The next day the burgh court convicted Portuis along with John Fettes, Riche Gibsoun and David Tailzour for 'the vrangous and violent casting of stanes in cloyes van holing ship vnder silence of nyt within the harbor of aberd[een]'.[115] From these accounts it is not entirely clear which happened first, Portuis and his friends casting stones at the ship belonging to the German sailors or the German sailors' attack on Portuis. In a separate account, the baillies ordered van Holing to return 'or caus deliver again to wm portuis his awn quhingar and his bonat again als guid as thai war quhen thai war takyn fra him be the said skippers childer'.[116] It is hard to tell whether the sailors captured Portuis when he and his friends attacked the ship, or whether Portuis' friends responded to his attack by coming back to the ship and throwing stones. Regardless, the accounts make clear that both parties used violence and it seems likely that at least one of the parties acted out in response to the initial violent act.

Although the involvement of foreigners in an attack on an Aberdonian was a rare occasion, the Burgh Council's response to the attack on Portuis stands out as an example of how the authorities perceived such violent activities. Having found the five sailors guilty of attacking Portuis, the assise declared that:

> tha had offendit thairthrow, fyrst, to the queenis grace of Scotland, in the taking, handling, and binding of the said William at thair avin hand with ony ordour of law or iustice, he beand hir fre liege and subdict; secondly, to the guid town of Abirdene, doand sic offensis at thair awin hand within the fredome and iurisdictioun thairof; thirdly, to the said Wm himself, doand sic strublance and offensis to him in manner forsaid.[117]

From the council's perspective, there were three victims of their crimes: the queen representing the realm, the town and the injured party. The baillies settled the fine to be paid by the convicted sailors at 20 merks for Portuis and 10 pounds for the town, which suggests that the affront to the town was perceived to be greater than the affront to Portuis. This reaction is somewhat reminiscent of the one exhibited by the council when James Watson maligned the town.

In terms of reparations, violent crimes often led to fines or 'bloodwite' to be paid to the town by the convicted party.[118] Victims received monies 'for thair skayth' and/or their attacker's plea for forgiveness. As well, if the victim's wounds required the attention of a barber surgeon, the baillies would add his fees to the fines paid. In June 1563, the court convicted John Forbes 'alias the guidman' for the strublans and blood drawing of an Aberdeen smith by the name of David Cut. For his offence, the baillies ordered Forbes to appear within the parish kirk and ask God, the congregation and Cut forgiveness. As well, Forbes was to pay 'the leiche xx s for curing & heling of the said david and vther xx s to the said david for ane pecuniall payne'.[119] The baillies ordered Walter Duncan to pay the 'barbor lix dd with xl S to the said Andrew and modefeit the townis vnlaw of blud to five pounds to be pait within terme of law' for his violent attack on Andrew Davidson.[120] As stated in the previous chapter, fines were not firmly set and the variation in amounts to be paid often depended on recidivism, the ability of the convicted party to meet the expense, and the status of the victim. A week after Duncan's conviction, the baillies ordered Robert Kay to pay 10 shillings to Andrew Myddilton for striking him and drawing of his blood and ten shillings to the town for the baillies's unlaw.[121] The difference between Duncan's unlaw of 5 pounds and Kay's unlaw of 10 shillings was considerable. Of the individuals mentioned, the only one's status that we can be certain of is Andrew Davidson whom the clerk noted was a tailor.[122]

Occasionally, we gain insight into where the town's authorities redirected monies they collected for violent crimes committed within the burgh. Alexander Lyon incurred a fine of 10 pounds 'to be gevin to the support of the hospitall' for his strubling of the town and 'drawing of ane swerd and strubling' of John Anderson.[123] Alex Robertson had to ask Barbara Davidson for forgiveness for striking her and pay 30 shillings 'to be applyet or gevin to the kirkwark or hospitall'. He was also required to pay 8 shillings to the baillies for their unlaw.[124] For those individuals not required to pay fines as part of their penalty, often the court would warn them that if convicted in the future they would be ordered to pay a fine usually designated to the hospital or the kirk work. When Duncan Colle and Richart Mytt decided to verbally and physically abuse each other in the middle of the town in September 1553, the baillies had little choice but to convict them for strubling the town, striking, blood drawing and mispersoning. For their punishment, the baillies ordered them both to come 'on sunday nixt cumis within the parish kirk of aberdene in tym of highmass and thereto sett down vpoun their kneis and ask utheris forgiveness and gif ony of them beis found in doing siclyk in tym cuming to pay lx s to St. Nicholas wark unforgiven'.[125]

In the case of Colle and Mytt it was clear that because they took their dispute to the streets the authorities saw them as causing a disturbance within the town. Other situations were less clear cut. For example, in April 1590 Lawrens Maser, John Shand and John Bogy stood accused of 'trubling of the town' on account of their 'drawing of wapins swords'.[126] The matter was put to an assise. Unfortunately, the records omit the assise's decision, recording only the order put to the three men to set caution that they 'will not perturb the town'.[127] Another act of violence occurred three weeks later when Thomas Hay went through the town brandishing his weapon. The provost and baillies convicted Hay for 'trubling of this burgt in drawing of ane sword and thairwith striking divers nychtbors of the same'.[128] The clerks' use of the phrase 'diverse neighbours' in this account was not meant to indicate that Hay's victims were random; rather, it should be taken that a number of individuals were attacked and that their relationship to the perpetrator of this crime was not relevant to the magistrates' determination to take this crime seriously. The size of the community and the extensive network connecting individual inhabitants to each other suggests that only infrequently victim and perpetrator had no relationship that contributed to the offence.[129]

The wording of an account that described a dispute between John Duncan and Andrew Jamison that turned violent suggests such a relationship. In May 1590, the Baillie court accused Duncan, a local tailor who had agitated against the town and merchant guild in the 1580s, along with two of his servants, for strubling the town. Likewise, the baillies charged Andrew Jamison with the same offence. Although the Council Register and Baillie Court Books contain numerous accounts of individuals convicted of strubling the town through physical or verbal violence committed in public, this is the only occurrence where the court separated the accused parties in terms of responsibility:

> The said john duncan tailzer thomas gow & rechert blak his servandis on the ane part & andrew jameson mason on the vther part accusit for trubling of the town in blud drawing ilk ane of vtheris & striking of vtheris with swords & vther wapponis.[130]

The only discernible reason for distinguishing the two parties in such a manner is that Jamison confessed to strubling the town whereas Duncan and his servants denied committing this crime. What is more, the clerk further detailed Jamison's offence by stating that he stood accused of 'strubling the said john & blud drawing of *his* servant Thomas gow'. This underscores the relationship between Jamison and Duncan; Jamison offended Duncan through an attack on one of his servants. The separation into two parties in court implies that Duncan pursued retribution for the attack on his household and Jamison was defending his actions.

Strubling the town through acts of physical violence could also have the added dimension of contravening parliamentary statute. Such were the cases where individuals caused disturbances within the burgh by brandishing weapons outlawed by Parliament. In February 1591, Gilbert Fraser strubled the town by 'drawing ane pistol to george laying and thairby manassing and invading him of his lyfe' and for 'haffing & vsing ane pistol within the burgh againis the actis of parliament'.[131] Three years later a local minister, Mr Thomas Bissett, using weapons prohibited by law, attacked Andrew Gray and James Walker on the burgh streets. Despite recognizing that Walker and Gray were simply defending themselves, a sworn assise convicted the three for troubling the town in drawing of swords, quhingars and pistols under silence of the night.[132] Ordinances passed throughout Scotland during this period suggest a continuous concern with 'nytwalkars'.[133] Most accounts suggest that the common perception of such individuals was that of a drunk and idle person, usually masterless or without connection to the burgh, lurking in dark corners, that 'persewit the nychtbouris and inhabitantis of this burgh, bot committit divers robreis and utheris villannyis, unworthy to be hard of in a weele governit citie'.[134] In Edinburgh, for example, the town council ordered that no persons remain on the streets 'after the ringing of the ten-hour bell at night'.[135]

The first example of such behaviour found in the records for our period supports this idea. John Fraser, listed as a 'laborar', was convicted in January 15⁵⁸⁄₉ for striking and strubling Margaret Paterson 'in hir awn hous vnder silence of nyt'.[136] However, there are numerous accounts that suggest that such enormities were being committed within the burghs at night by well-known members of the community. In December 1575, the court convicted a local cordiner, John Myl, for the striking and blood drawing of another Aberdonian craftsmen, Robert Paterson.[137] Paterson was also convicted for striking Myl and his son. The clerk describes both attacks as having occurred 'under silence of the night'.[138] Occasionally the convictions of individuals for committing such acts during the night came after witnesses to the crimes gave testimony indicating their own presence out of doors after hours. Six months prior to Myl and Paterson's conviction, 'divers famous witness' helped to convict Walter Cassy 'for the strubling and striking of Marioune Scherar vnder silence of nycht'.[139] Cassy's first conviction in the burgh occurred twenty years earlier in 1556; in January 1576 Cassy and his wife were on the receiving end of a verbal assault committed by Molly Myll.[140]

The town's concern over such behaviour is clear in an account of the conviction of James Karnoway, a local skipper. Sometime in mid-August 1587, Karnoway set out to the home of Jonet Kelle and her spouse Samson Saffray. Witnesses testified that 'vnder silence of the nycht' Karnoway struck Kelle, drawing her blood.[141] The baillies also convicted Karnoway for strubling another sailor, 'invading of him with ane drawn sword vnder silence of the nycht'.[142] On account of these crimes, Karnoway was ordered to set caution. A testament to Karnoway's familiarity within the burgh, Gilbert Menzies became cautioner for the 'bludwite and that the town salbe skaythless of him'. This was a case where the offender was not charged with 'strubling the town' but where his offences, particularly disconcerting due to when they occurred, were taken to be a threat to the whole community's well-being. Yet, despite the acknowledged threat to both individual and town, Karnoway received a fine and an order to set caution.

One final example of an attack occurring during the night should help to illustrate the type of violent acts committed by Aberdonians. On the night of 26 April 1595, Elspet Lesly and her daughter went to Agnes Cullan's house and there violently attacked Cullan 'vnder silence of the nycht'.[143] With the testimony presented by witnesses to the crime, Lesly and her daughter were convicted for 'putting violent hands on the said agnes rugging hir be the hair and striking her in the face'. For committing this act, both mother and daughter were put in amercement of court. What is most noticeable about the various violent crimes committed at night by the inhabitants of the burgh is that in every account where such an offence was committed the court put the convicted party in amercement of court and ordered them to set caution. This stands in stark contrast to the pre-scribed punishments established by the early statutes regulating such crimes.

In all of the accounts of physical violence found in the records between 1541 and 1595, punishments, when documented, do not provide clear insight into the status of the individuals who committed these crimes, the perceived severity of the violent act or whether recidivists received harsher penalties. Similar to accounts of verbal violence, the opportunity for quantitative analysis of physical violence is limited by the surviving records. That said, the records do provide enough material from which to glean some useful statistics; as in cases of verbal assault, it possible to examine the frequency of physical violence and to delimit the number of incidents of physical violence by the sex of both victim and per-petrator. This should provide some insight into just who was committing violent crimes in Aberdeen during the last three quarters of the sixteenth century.

As Table 4.1 illustrates, over the period 1542–91 recorded incidents of phys-ical violence remained fairly constant with roughly a 31 per cent decline over a fifty-year period.[144] This stands in contrast to the nearly 91 per cent decline in recorded incidents of unspecified strublance and the 62 per cent decline in recorded incidents of verbal crime. As was suggested earlier, the main discernible reasons for the greater decline in recorded incidents of verbal assault and strub-lance are shifts in regulating such crimes (slander and defamation cases possibly being pursued more vigorously in the church courts after 1574) and a shift in record keeping. However, physical violence continued to fall under the jurisdic-tion of the burgh court. As such, the number of incidents remained relatively high. Nonetheless, there is still a noticeable decline in the number of recorded incidents from the decade preceding the Reformation in Scotland and the dec-ade immediately following its establishment. Indeed, that period witnessed a 19 per cent decline compared to the overall 31 per cent decline for the whole period. This would suggest that the Reformed Kirk may have also had some influence on this type of behaviour. By comparison, the main drop-off in recorded incidents of verbal assault corresponds with the visit of the Regent Morton to the burgh and the arrival of John Craig, a more reform-minded minister, to his post at St Nicholas. Yet, given the lack of extant source materials, it is impossible to deter-mine whether or not such a decline in verbal assaults stemmed from a shift in responsibility for regulating such behaviour.

For the entire period, there is only a single 'blasphemy' case that went before the Kirk Session. Interestingly enough, when Andrew Philipson blasphemed the deacons and ministers in 1574, the session ordered the baillies 'to put him fast will' where a 'tryall mycht be had'.[145] Witnesses 'to the said sklandering' came forward five days after the session ordered the baillies to try Philipson in their court and announced that Philipson was 'imparted to drynk'. For the offence of drunkenness, and one suspects for the slander he committed, the session required Philipson to 'present him self in the place of reprentance' the following Sunday and ask god and 'hys kirkmen' forgiveness. The account also specifies that the session 'desyred the magistrates to promis him civilly'. In other words, the burgh court still held responsibility for trying individuals accused of committing verbal assaults. Philipson's case suggests that at least in the 1570s the Kirk Session was still inclined to allow the burgh magistrates to deal with this type of petty crime.[146]

In terms of non-fatal physical violence, there is not a single incident recorded in the St Nicholas Kirk Session records for the period under consideration.[147] As others have shown, the main concern of this session during its infancy was catholic recusancy, rooting out adultery and fornication and enforcing regular marriage practice.[148] As such, the Council Register, Baillie Court Books and to a lesser degree the Guildry Accounts, serve as the most complete source of information on physical violence committed in the burgh. Unlike accounts of verbal assault where details may be lacking, accounts of physical violence present a fairly clear picture of the individuals involved, the type of action committed and the authorities' response to such behaviour. Table 4.4 demonstrates that a significantly higher number of men were accused of committing acts of physical violence than women. It also indicates that in Aberdeen during this period, men were more likely to be charged with committing acts of physical violence than verbal assault whereas women were more prone to be charged with committing a verbal attack than a physical assault.

Table 4.4: Number of 'cases' of petty crime delimited by sex of offender.[149]

Offender by sex	Physical assault	Verbal assault	Unspecified strublance	Total
Male	315	185	75	575
Female	87	176	27	290
Male and female	9	10	3	22
Multiple males	25	1	8	34
Multiple females	3	4	4	11
Total	439	376	117	932

Individuals were also more likely to injure in word or deed on their own than in groups. About 11 per cent of all physical assaults brought before the burgh court were committed by two or more individuals. Groups committed acts of unspecified strublance at a slightly lower 7 per cent. However, roughly 24 per cent of all acts of verbal assault committed in the burgh were committed by two or more persons.

It is equally clear that men more often than women suffered incidents of physical assault. The number of incidents of physical assault where the victim was female matches almost exactly the number of incidents of verbal assault where the victim was female. In contrast, men more frequently fell victim to physical violence than verbal assault, while a third less women were victims of non-specified strublance. As Table 4.3 reveals, in cases of verbal assault there was a higher proportion of multiple targets than in cases of physical violence or non-specified strublance. Although the figures do not speak to this issue, it is clear that in terms of physical assaults, the number of incidents where men attacked women was greater than the number of incidents where women attacked men. Between 1542 and 1591, of the 118 recorded incidents of physical violence committed by women eighteen (or 6.5 per cent) of those incidents indicate that the victim was male. Over the same period of time, of 370 incidents of physical violence where there was only a single victim, eighty (or 22 per cent) of those victims were female.

Despite the numbers, it seems fairly obvious that petty violence was not entirely defined by gender, nor did one's sex influence the decision to commit crimes. Petty violence, both physical and verbal, served as an outlet for 'righting' wrongs within the community and for negotiating social power. Regardless of one's status within the community, through the use of slanderous language or physical violence the inhabitants of the burgh could at times manoeuvre against their neighbours for the purpose of establishing some form of control. In this sense, establishing control usually meant over trade, standing within the community, reputation and day-to-day functions. In this regard, it was a means individuals employed for achieving their goals.[150] Even those individuals without access to formal political arenas found ways to exercise social power. One of the most effective means was through criminal activities, in particular, through acts of verbal and physical violence. Thus, when James Menzies attacked Alex Joffray in May 1595 'injuring him with many diverse injurious words and manessing him on the street with a pistol', Menzies sought to diminish Joffray's power as Baillie.[151] In a similar manner, John Chalmer, who we met at the beginning of this chapter, attempted to increase his own sense of place by acting as his conscience dictated, regardless of the criminal nature of those acts.

Individual concerns as well as individual desires for personal betterment could also take the form of group activism. In the next chapter, I explore how the raising of tumults and explicit disobedience towards authority figures in the community raised the level of petty crimes from transgressions against one's neighbour and the community to an overt attempt at restructuring the political and social spheres within the community. In this way, we may discern the different levels of wrongdoing within the community. What is more, through explicit attacks on authority we may better understand how the wider community perceived social power and social space within the burgh. Such examples also enable us to examine smaller groups interacting with other groups within the community and the impact such interactions had on the entire burgh.

5 DISOBEDIENCE AND EXCLUSION

An entry in the Council Register for 20 November 1588 states that:

> the power, place, dignitie, and authoritie of the counsall of this burgh (as of all uther burrowis of this realme) is and cheiflie dois consist past memorie of man unto this day, in treating, aduysing, and consulting upoun all materis concerning the commoun weill of this burght, making and setting down of lawis, statutis, and ordinances, be the quhilkis the same is estableschit and governit.[1]

The Council's chief motive for (re)asserting their 'power, place, dignitie [sic], and authoritie' on this particular day was to put an end to the practice among the burgh inhabitants to 'gather and convene' to vote on 'any mater of weycht and importance' without the Council's express permission. Although a seemingly banal administrative memorandum, the last portion of the entry hints at an underlying current of political unrest within the burgh's magistracy. The entry states that 'it sall na vayis be lesum [legally permissible] to the prouest, bailleis, deanis of gild, nor yit cousalour, to gif command to warne and convocat the town to the tolbuith or any uther publict place....without ane ordinance of the counsall.'[2] This entry reveals the continuing power struggle among senior officers of the burgh, namely the provost, baillies and deans of guild and the larger, elected council. This episode needs to be considered within the larger context of the tensions between the craftsmen, merchants and magistracy in the burgh in the 1580s. In that context, it is clear that the disobedience and disruptive behaviour within the burgh, and among every level of burgh society, constituted a genuine threat to the burgh's 'common weal' and the authority of the local magistrates.

This chapter explores the interplay between petty crimes and community membership in Aberdeen in the last half of the sixteenth century. In particular, it explores a variety of ways individuals sought to circumvent burgh statute and custom in order to increase their social standing, earning potential and political voice within the burgh. Such activities cast a light on the anxiety the magistracy felt over perceived threats to their authority and the maintenance of the burgh's social order while contributing to the political changes that were unfolding within the burgh in the 1580s and 1590s.[3] In particular, this chapter focuses on the conflict between Aberdonian craftsmen and merchants in the 1580s, a conflict generated by the increased frequency of craftsmen participating in illegal trade, usurping rights and privileges guaranteed to the prestigious merchant guild, contravening burgh statutes and ordinances and circumventing the customs of the burgh. Seen by those who committed such acts as an effective way for individuals to redefine their place within the town's social order, they were perceived by the burgh magistracy as a threat to the 'common weal of the burgh' and a reason behind the merchant guildry's increased impoverishment.

Historians interested in questions of poverty have demonstrated that this term possessed a variety of meanings in the late middle ages and early modern period. In particular, they have shown that it could equally refer to a lack of power, political involvement, citizenship, military capability or economic wherewithal.[4] This stands out in Aberdeen where for the most part indwellers, unfree and free craftsmen, and minor merchants as well as their more established neighbours negotiated their social power in an attempt to redress the very poverty they experienced whether political, social or economic. It is telling that tumults often associated with the economically poorer sorts in other parts of the British Isles and the Continent were instigated in Aberdeen by members of Aberdonian society who had achieved some social standing within the burgh and sought to continue improving upon their condition.[5] The burgh statutes barring the poorer sorts from the kirk, like those passed in the late 1570s and 1580s barring the craftsmen from the merchant guild and burgh council, stand out as attempts to keep the 'impoverished' from interfering with those more fortunate. Such concerns are on display in a number of the cases of civil disobedience and attacks on officers of the burgh that occurred throughout this period.

Craftsmen and Merchants and the Governance of the Burgh

Although contemporary records refer to the 'gryt part of the communite' or the 'hail community of the burgh' they are not always explicit about who exactly constituted the 'community'.[6] Clearly, there were multiple smaller communities within the burghs to which individual inhabitants claimed membership and to which they owed loyalty. As Elizabeth Ewan has shown, 'people could belong to overlapping communities, just as they do today, without their participation in any community being diminished for it.'[7] And while such communities were part of the fabric of urban social life in early modern Scotland, membership in these smaller groups was not always clear and the relationship between the component parts of the 'gryt part of the communite' was frequently uneasy. There has been a tendency among Scottish urban historians to focus on the tumultuous relationship between craftsmen and merchants who vied for positions of status and power within the burghs. In Aberdeen, where the merchants outnumbered craftsmen by a ratio of three to one, their influence on local government and trade was significant. [8] This was not unique to Aberdeen; throughout most of the sixteenth century merchants controlled burgh politics and barred craftsmen from holding office throughout Scotland. The only exception came in 1534 and 1538 when Perth and Edinburgh respectively elected two craftsmen to sit on their burgh councils.[9] In large part, the relationship between the merchant guildry and the burgh councils emphasized the contemporary notion that burghs were organized for the purpose of trade.[10] But within the Aberdeen merchant community a hierarchy based on access to foreign trade and wealth meant that minor merchants also found themselves on the margins of belonging. This relegation prompted them to play a significant role in agitating for greater access and political rights in the burgh in the 1570s and 1580s.[11]

The Aberdeen Council Register and Guildry Accounts reveal that, regardless of the social and economic interactions between craftsmen and merchants, the privileges each group enjoyed often proved enticing to anyone excluded from these groups. To make matters worse, from about the middle of the sixteenth century, the burgh council began to interfere with the admissions process into these communities. Seeing it as a way of increasing burgh revenue, the council increased the charges for admission to the Guild and began to admit anyone who could pay the fees regardless of their status. Inevitably, tensions began to emerge over rights of access and the roles played by each group in determining the other's involvement (and arguably place) in burgh government as well as within the smaller exclusive communities themselves.[12] In the surviving accounts recording the entrance into the free crafts, merchant guild and burgessship in Aberdeen between 1582 and 1603, there is a dramatic increase in the monies paid by new members as part of their initiation into these communities. For example, in 1582 those seeking entry into the guildry paid on average £6.5.[13] By 1585 the deposition had risen to £10, and by the 1590s some individuals were paying £20 to £24.[14] The records show that the burgh's total intake for creating freemen in 1584 was less than half the £58.13*s*.4*d*. brought in the following year. This suggests that increased revenue for the burgh became a motivating factor in determining entrance to the guildry. Even more revealing, the total amount recorded in the accounts for 1593/94 was £246.4*s*.4*d*.[15]

So when the guildry complained of its 'poverty' in the 1590s, it was not solely their finances they were concerned about; rather, it was the diminished character and make-up of its membership due to the increased admittance of so many minor merchants and craftsmen to the guild. The increased inclusion of such individuals exacerbated the rising tensions between the various smaller communities within the burgh and drew attention to the resentment these groups had felt towards the Menzies' control and management of burgh government. Just prior to the downfall of the Menzies in 1590, such tensions and the concern over the potential impoverishment of the guildry had led to a rise in civil disobedience. Extensive burgh court records reveal a connection between the civil disobedience that disrupted the burgh in the 1560s, 1570s and 1580s, and the restructuring of burgh politics in the late 1580s and early 1590s. The records also reveal that while other petty crimes were in decline in this period, the number of individuals charged with statute breaking and civil disobedience rose. By examining this form of wrongdoing, concepts of belonging, areas of conflict and control, as well as social differentiation within the smaller communities, become clearer.[16]

Those who were not fortunate enough to gain entrance into the guildry or incorporated crafts through the proper channels often attempted to enjoy the privileges associated with these communities. In January 1542 the baillies and deacon of the barber craft brought Robert Barber 'alias Coull' before the court for 'the wrang done be him throw the intromitting [dealing with] & leiching of ane hurt man'.[17] Barber's conviction arose from practising his profession despite the fact that he was 'unfre of his craft'. In February 1559, John Cruickshank, a local flesher, stood before the baillies and confessed to practising his craft despite the fact that he had not gained the freedom to do so. For his wrongdoing, the baillies put him in amercement of court.[18]

As the many examples provided in Chapter 3 illustrate, individuals attempted to enjoy both the privileges of a guild merchant and those of a free craftsman. That the motive behind such attempts was more than a desire for greater political access and the potential to climb the social order can be discerned from the fact that members of the more prestigious, and arguably more powerful, merchant guild attempted to enjoy the fruits of labouring as a free craftsmen. In July 1571 the baillies placed William Robertson, a free burgess of guild, in amercement of court for working as a flesher in the burgh. The court ordered him to make amends according to the laws and statutes of the burgh.[19] Wilson Burley, likewise a local merchant and member of the guild, came before the burgh court accused of working as a tailor. For his wrongdoing the court ordered him to pay a fine of 40 shillings.[20] In August 1583, the Dean of Guild brought Alexander Litster before the burgh court and accused him of labouring as a litster despite 'beand a free burgess of guild'. The records indicate that Litster had been warned before by the Dean of Guild and the burgh council to either quit working at the craft or revoke his oath of 'guilderie & burgesship'.[21] Litster confessed to having ignored the inhibition and was convicted for disregarding the council's orders and placed in amercement of court. Some merchants were willing to risk the privileges associated with being a part of the merchant guild by seeking out the benefits of labouring as craftsmen.[22] The potential risk factor suggests the depth of personal interest in expanding one's social power, income and access to exclusive communities.

We should recall that five months after Litster appeared before the court, three other Aberdonian burgesses of guild, Andrew Kelly, Thomas Moreis and James Robertson, were convicted for labouring as craftsmen. Robertson confessed before the court to working as a goldsmith in his father's booth and placed himself in the 'provost bailleis and consale will to be corectit be thame'.[23] Moreis and Kelly, however, denied working as free craftsmen and their matter was put before a sworn assise made up of both craftsmen and guild brethren. Ultimately, the court convicted the pair for 'working at the walker craft thay beand fre burgess of guild *joining* the said craft with the office of the guild brethren'.[24] Although there was concern over the possibility of individuals having increased economic opportunities, the case of John Walker suggests that the real issue was the merchant guild's desire to prevent the impoverishment of this exclusive group. Walker, a guild member, was convicted two weeks after Moreis and Kelly for 'using of the walker craft againis the *ordour* and *honor* of ane frie burges of gild and the statutis of yis burt'.[25] These cases reveal that these activities were not solely about masters and men, or rulers and ruled, but also about individuals looking to expand their social, economic and political network by availing themselves of opportunities the burgh's laws and customs had put out of their reach.

The actions of an Aberdonian cordwainer named John Deuchar illustrate further how individuals attempted to redefine community membership through wrongful behaviour.[26] Between 1565 and 1582 Deuchar appeared before the baillies at least thirteen times to answer for a number of charges that included physical assault, slander, statute breaking, forestalling and practising his craft despite having lost the privilege to do so freely. Although Deuchar could be dismissed as a malcontent eager to wrong his neighbours, the records suggest that he was motivated by the belief that the magistrates were arbitrary in their attempts to limit his earning capacity and restrict his social mobility. His challenge to local authority stands out in a number of the transgressions he committed. A dossier prepared by Aberdeen's burgh council and presented to the King's Privy Council in the early 1580s linked Deuchar's wrongdoing with the organized efforts of a group of craftsmen in the 1580s to remove the Menzies from power, to change the guidelines for electing burgh officials and to gain entry into the exclusive merchant guildry.[27] What linked Deuchar's wrongdoing in the 1560s and 1570s to the craft riot in 1581–2 was the method, notably illegal activities, by which both parties sought to expand their social power in the burgh.[28]

Deuchar first appears in the court records in December 1565 where he is mentioned as having been ordered to remain in ward while he 'satisfeit an act obtenit aganis him be Duncan Blak'.[29] Deuchar, however, defied the order and threatened one of the burgh officers, Hildebrand Menzies. For this act of disobedience, Deuchar was 'decernit to have tynt [lost] his fredom and prevelege of this burgh'.[30] Despite the court's readiness to deprive Deuchar of the economic

and social benefits of belonging to one of the incorporated crafts there is no indication that the penalty was enforced. Moreover, a further six convictions over
the next decade for regrating and forestalling alone did not result in Deuchar
suffering any real restriction on his way of life; Deuchar continued to pay his
fines and to live within the community relatively unscathed. We recall that John
Mannis had been convicted for physically and verbally assaulting Deuchar. [31]
Although the records do not include the insults Mannis used to attack Deuchar,
it is likely that Mannis called into question Deuchar's honesty by referring to his
past indiscretions. [32] Despite Deuchar's flouting of burgh laws and the authority
of the baillies to enforce them, the court believed that he still possessed the right
to be protected from attacks from other members of the community.

During the 1570s the burgh court convicted Deuchar on several occasions
for contravening town ordinances. In particular, Deuchar frequently attempted
to sell goods at prices that were higher than that decreed by acts of the town
council. The frequency at which Deuchar broke these statutes suggests a pattern
of open defiance of the local authorities and the powers they had at their disposal.
In November 1571, Deuchar was convicted of 'his awn confessionne' for buying
hides in Old Aberdeen 'contrair the libertie of his craft'.[33] Despite having lost his
freedom in 1565 to practise his craft freely, this account states that Deuchar's
fault was primarily for buying merchandise contrary to the rights granted to free
craftsmen.[34] Clearly, Deuchar's status as a craftsman was not altered by the fact
that he was no longer able to practise his profession legally within the burgh;
nor were the exclusionary limits associated with his place among the burgh's
craft community diminished by his conviction. Regardless of whether Deuchar
believed he was still entitled to practise his craft freely, he knew from the oath
that he took when he had become a free craftsman that 'using' merchandise was
prohibited. Therefore, any attempt to do so would have been interpreted by the
members of the merchant guild and the burgh magistrates as a contravention
of his oath, an overstepping of the boundaries of the exclusive community and
a defiance of the authorities. That Deuchar was little inconvenienced by such
concerns stands out in his conviction in 1574 for:

> braking of the command and ordinance giffin to him be the Baillies and consalle pre-
> sent for the tyme makand inhibitionne to him to use & occupy ane bark pott recentlie
> biggit be him vpoune the myll brone quhair neuer na bark pott was obefoir.[35]

While Deuchar's was one of 179 separate convictions for breaking statutes, disobedience or regrating and forestalling committed by members of the community
between 1571 and 1585,[36] the growing concern over his behaviour was obvious
in the language used by the clerk who recorded his conviction. The clerk noted
that 'in disobeying of the said ordinance be his *manifest* contempt' Deuchar 'was

in *manifest* amercement off court'.[37] After ten years of wrongdoing in the community, the baillies were starting to lose their patience with John Deuchar.

Deuchar continued to push the boundaries of acceptable behaviour throughout the rest of the 1570s and well into the 1580s. In July 1578 the baillies charged
him with flagrantly disobeying the magistrates for operating an open booth and
working freely at his craft having been 'dischargit of his fredome of the burgh'.[38]
The court reminded Deuchar that his loss of freedom had resulted from the
many previous transgressions he had committed within the burgh. The account
also states that Deuchar had promised to abstain from practising his craft within
the burgh under threat of incurring a fine of £20. This is a notable sum given that
in the account of his previous convictions the largest fine he had incurred had
been 40 shillings.[39] As I argued in Chapters 3 and 4, fines for committing petty
crimes in the burgh ranged from a few shillings to quite a few pounds. There is
no indication in the records, however, that fines were based on the severity of
the crime, the status of the individual convicted, or the ability of the convicted
party to pay. Most accounts do suggest that repeat offenders were expected to
pay higher fines if convicted again. Thus, when the baillies modified Deuchar's
unlaw for working openly within the burgh, they surely used his past offences to
help set the fine at £20. They also ordered the officers of the burgh to 'pass and
poynd his redress guids and geir wherever thai may be apprehendit'.[40]

In November of that year, Deuchar was convicted again for buying hides and
holding an open booth 'not beand free of his craft'. For this offence the court
ordered him to pay a fine of £20.[41] In this instance, the court also ordered that
Gilbert Collison, who was one of the burgh's baillies in the mid-1570s, be 'poyn-
dit' as Deuchar's cautioner. In spite of his previous convictions and regardless
of his social status, Deuchar had been able to secure one of the town's upstanding citizens as his cautioner; this says a fair bit about the impact his crimes had
on his credit and standing in the community. More importantly, his continued
efforts to force the issue of both practising a craft and using merchandise within
the burgh involved Deuchar in a negotiation with the authorities over rights
and privileges. That he was able to remain within the town, continue to earn a
living and practise his craft, despite attempts by the authorities to curtail these
activities, is telling. Deuchar raised the level of the negotiations in 1581 when he
brought a complaint against the burgh before the Privy Council.

Despite his past convictions, Deuchar believed that the restrictions imposed
on him by the provost, baillies and council were an encroachment on his earned
rights and freedoms. This is clear in the complaint Deuchar brought before the
King's Privy Council in 1581 against the provost and baillies of Aberdeen for
having wrongfully 'discharged him from the using of his vocatioun'.[42] Before the
burgh magistracy had the opportunity to appear before the Privy Council, the
King ordered them to restore Deuchar to his previous freedoms. Despite the

King's order, the provost, baillies and council refused to do so even under the
threat of being put to the horn [declared outlaws]. When Deuchar and Alexander Cullan, who represented the provost and baillies, finally appeared before the
Privy Council, Cullen stated the burgh's case by arguing that:

> the said Johnne, for his continewing in the filthye vice of adulterie, without amend-
> ment or repentance, he being divers tymes admoneist thairto be the assemblie and
> counsale of the kirk of Abirdene wes, in the moneth of Maii the yeir of God jmvclxviii
> yeris, denuncit, excommunicat, and cutt of fra the societie of the faithfull thairefter ...
> the said Johnn, for missaying, detracting, and sclandering of the Baillies of Abirdene
> for the tyme in the sessioun of the same, wes, be a decrete gevin be the provost and
> Baillies thairof in the moneth of Februar the yeir of God j^{m}v^{c}lxxvii yeris, dischargeit
> of his fredome and privilege of the said burgh in all tymes thairefter.[43]

The list of Deuchar's criminal offences was damning indeed, even if it was
incomplete. While singling out his disobedience to the secular authorities and
his disregard for the spiritual leaders within the burgh, not to mention his grievous sins, Cullan left out that Deuchar had been convicted in June 1575 for
'causing' his son, Alexander, to strike a local woman by the name of Cristane
Many. This particular conviction is interesting in that it is the only instance, in
nearly 2,000 cases, where the court charged an individual not directly involved
in the act for inducing another to commit the crime.[44] For his involvement in the
assault on Many, the baillies ordered Deuchar to pay 10 shillings to the barber
for tending to the victim's wounds and 5 pounds for the baillies' unlaw. Other
than the notice in the Privy Council records, there is no record of Deuchar having been brought before the Kirk Session for committing adultery or any record
of his excommunication. Nonetheless, the language used in Cullan's testimony
– 'denuncit, excommunicat, and cutt of fra the societie of the faithfull' – highlights the magistrates' belief that criminal activities put the individual outside
the boundaries of the community, cut off from the benefits of belonging.

There is no clear indication of how the Lords ruled in the complaint Deuchar
brought before them. Deuchar appears for the last time in the extant records
in December 1582 when he was convicted for labouring at the cordiner's craft
despite being unfree, buying and barking hides, and selling to unfreemen.[45] The
fact that the court continued to not recognize Deuchar's freedom to practise his
craft suggests that the King and his Privy Council had either decided in favour
of the burgh, or that the burgh magistrates chose to ignore the Council's decision, as they had done in 1581. Although Deuchar chose to exercise his legal right
by bringing a complaint against the magistrates and the burgh before the Privy
Council, his frequent disregard for burgh statutes reveals his greater inclination
to use illegal and extra-legal activities to negotiate his power and space within the
community. Through his numerous transgressions Deuchar delimited the parameters of the negotiation between himself, the guildry and the burgh council. More

importantly, he raised the stakes by bringing the King and his Privy Council into the negotiations.[46] In the 1580s, a concerted effort by craftsmen and minor merchants to effect change in their position within the burgh built on Deuchar's precedent by drawing the King and his Privy Council into greater involvement in regulating the burgh. The response by the provost and council reveals their sensitivity to what they considered was external interference, and their keen desire to maintain order and reassert their authority. The so-called 'craft riots' between 1580 and 1582 not only mirrored previous transgressions committed by other inhabitants of the burgh, such as John Deuchar, they significantly magnified such behaviour. From the perspective of the burgh magistrates such flagrant disregard for their authority and contempt for what was deemed proper behaviour by 'honest nychtbors' was construed as entirely harmful to the 'common weil'.

There was perhaps no more pronounced exploitation of the sensitivity of the local magistrates to outside interference in the regulating of the burgh than in the expanded involvement of the King and his Privy Council in the growing conflict between the merchant guild and the craftsmen in the 1570s and 1580s.[47] The illegal activities undertaken by the craftsmen in this period, and in particular the exploits of John Duncan, John Bannerman, John Rory and Patrick Leith, were akin to those of John Deuchar whose own petty crimes challenged the established boundaries of proper behaviour. Collectively they can be taken as an explicit example of the way in which members of the community sought to challenge authority as part of a process to redefine their place in urban society. From the perspective of the burgh magistrates, such flagrant disregard for the established authority within the burgh and contempt for what was deemed acceptable behaviour by 'honest nychtbors' could only be construed as inviting God's wrath upon the town and entirely harmful to the 'common weil'. Their actions, however, do not reflect a dichotomous model wherein the rulers and the ruled jostled for power and the results of their conflicts established the social order. Throughout this period nearly every level of society participated on different sides of this negotiating table. In a number of cases, town officials, wealthy merchants and prosperous craftsmen found themselves before the courts on account of disobedience, contravention of acts of the burgh, kirk and Parliament, and almost every other form of petty crime, as readily as those whose social status and economic well-being were much further down the scale. The experience of the four men mentioned supports the idea that nearly every level of Aberdonian society could, and did on occasion, exercise some measure of social power and attempt to elevate their position within the community. Their activities between 1578 and 1582 are demonstrative of some of the attempts made by members of the burgh community to redefine the social boundaries of late sixteenth-century Aberdeen.

In December 1580, the Dean of Guild convicted John Duncan, along with two other tailors, for passing to the market and 'bying of clayth in gryt selling & topping of the same thereby usurping the privilege of a free burgess of guild'.[48] There was nothing extraordinary in the accusation; many Aberdonians had faced similar charges in the past. Indeed, regrating and forestalling accounted for nearly 25 per cent of the cases brought before the burgh court between 1571 and 1580. Even the more serious charge of usurping the privileges of the merchant guildry was fairly common during this period. Two months earlier the baillies convicted an armourer by the name of Patrick Leith with regrating and forestalling 'in bying of raw clayth in gryt' and ordered him to abstain under the threat of a fine of 40 pounds.[49] On the same day that the baillies modified John Duncan's unlaw to 8 merks, they also modified the unlaw of another Aberdeen tailor, John Rory. Rory had been convicted on a number of occasions between 1563 and 1582 for forestalling, using merchandise and breaking statutes.[50] Like Duncan, Leith and Rory, John Bannerman, the deacon of the baxter craft, participated in this familiar process of challenging the ordinances set by the burgh magistrates. Bannerman was keenly aware of the profit margin in his craft and sought to increase his potential earnings at every possible opportunity, even if this meant contravening the statutes that governed both the price and quality of bread in the town.[51] Only within the context of the events of the next two years do these seemingly common activities stand out as part of a much larger process of redefining the established boundaries within the community.

Throughout the sixteenth century the craftsmen and merchants in Aberdeen, as in other parts of Scotland and Europe, struggled to establish a privileged position within the larger urban community. While some historians may be keen to downplay the growing tension between the two groups, others have shown that the nature of such conflicts, and the degree to which it escalated, depended largely on the urban centre.[52] Thus, the shape, the ferocity and the motivations behind merchant/craftsmen conflict differed in Perth, as it did in Elgin, Edinburgh, Dundee, Dunfermline and of course Aberdeen. The work of Alan White and Michael Lynch have shown that the needs of the Aberdeen burgh council to raise funds to cover the cost of taxation offered increased opportunity to those who normally would not have met the established requirements outlined by statute and custom for entrance into the prestigious merchant guildry.[53] Indeed, as we saw earlier, it was often possible for those individuals convicted of usurping the privileges and liberties of a free burgess of guild to immediately purchase entrance into the merchant guildry as a means of preventing them from future transgressions.[54] However, this was not an assured possibility nor did the local authorities perceive this to be a procedure implemented outside the discretion of the council.

Thus, when in August 1581 a group of craftsmen purchased the liberties and rights associated with the merchant guild from the King and his 'secreit consale', this was taken to be an affront to the authority of the burgh, the burgh magistrates and the liberties of the guildry. The council convened a meeting of the 'haill craftismen free and unfree' to address their involvement in purchasing these liberties. Once assembled in the townhouse, the magistrates informed the craftsmen that they perceived their actions 'to raise and engender seditioun schisme and tumult betwixt the saidis free burgessis of gild and the saidis craftismen of this burt'.[55] The magistrates demanded that each of the craftsmen answer whether or not they would abstain from pursuing the liberties they purchased from the king and return to their 'awin craft & vocatioun'. Of the sixty names mentioned in the account, none 'wald avow afferme nor adhere' to the rights purchased by the craftsmen from the King.[56] Bannerman appeared in this list as a denier of the purchase and agreed not to pursue the associated rights and liberties. This list of names did not include Duncan, Rory and Leith, but in a subsequent list found in the Baillie Court Books they appear as adherers to the purchased liberties.[57] The next day, both Leith and Rory, along with twenty-three other craftsmen, appeared before the provost and baillies where they confessed that 'thai had rashly and unadvysably approvit in jugement the purchasing new pretendit privilege'.[58]

What is interesting about this account is the explicit response given by the magistrates to these adherents. The court record states that such men 'vnderstand now [that their actions] tendis to engender uproar schisme tumult and seditioun betwixt thame and thair superiors & magistrates the provost balleis consall and free burgessis of gild of this burt'.[59] Moreover, they were ordered to 'newer to do the lyk in tym cuming bot to be subvertit to all obedience of the said provost balleis & consall'. Although Leith acknowledged that he had 'rashly' supported the cause, a subsequent account makes it clear that he was unwilling to give up the fight as readily as the magistrates may have hoped. Leith promptly showed his disdain for their authority by attacking William Gray, the brother of one of the baillies, in what appears to be a scuffle within the courtroom. The provost, baillies and council determined that this was not a separate incident but that it was 'done in more contempt tending so far as lay in the said Patrick to caus tumult & sedition betwixt the free burges of gild of this burt and the craftismen thereof'.[60] For his violent actions, the court discharged Leith of his freedom and banished him from the burgh 'for all tyme cuming'. Clearly, the magistrates viewed the current actions undertaken by the craftsmen as a serious attack on their authority. The fact that these individuals involved an outside party to mediate the conflict could only be taken by the provost and town council as a hostile action.

From the different accounts in the Baillie Court Book and the Council Register the magistrates had demanded John Duncan to appear in court a number of times in the month of August 1581 to answer to charges of instigating the craft riot.[61] On 28 August 1581 Duncan was called again to answer for 'certane crymes and enormities committit and done be him and specialie for the resing of schisme and seditioun in this burt betwixt the bredder of gild and craftis-men'.[62] The provost and baillies were particularly put out by what they referred to as Duncan 'obstinatlie' refusing to appear. Duncan, for his own part, allegedly argued that 'he had utheris quhome he wald prefer to the saidis provest and bal-leis'.[63] Such disregard for the 'power, place, dignitie [sic], and authoritie' of the magistrates could not be tolerated. When Duncan failed to appear in court, the provost and baillies determined that he was the 'principall inventar beginner and author of the said tumult schisme and dissentioun resit' between the craftsmen and burgess of guild. For his crimes, the court deprived Duncan of the freedom to use his craft within the burgh noting his 'wilfull and obstinate inobediens'.[64]

What stands out in this account is the penalty imposed on Duncan for rais-ing a tumult within the burgh and for flagrant disobedience. The leniency is striking when compared with other such examples of disobedience. For exam-ple, on 1 May 1562 John Kello and Alex Burnett had passed through the streets of Aberdeen with a handbell and called on the community to march with them to the woods to welcome in the new summer. The provost and baillies deter-mined that such a breach of the Queen's grace and ordinance from the Lords of Council was meant 'eppeirandlie to rais tumult and ingender discord betwixt the craftismen and the fre burgesses of gild'.[65] More perniciously, the magistrates believed this action would induce the 'saidis craftismen to disobey and attempt aganis the superioris of the town gif it stuid in thair power'.[66] Kello and Burnett admitted to the charge denying that they were of 'ewill mynd' claiming only to be following the 'auld use'. In other words, the craftsmen claimed to be maintain-ing traditions associated with their crafts in celebrating the change of season.[67] Perhaps more crucial to their defence, they claimed to have been acting under the command of John Grant who was a 'fre burgess and brothir of gild'.

The matter was put before a sworn assise who determined that Grant, Kello and Burnett had acted out of 'ignorance' and ordered them to appear the follow-ing Sunday before the magistrates and congregation in the parish kirk and ask God and the congregation forgiveness. The council included in their sentence a stern warning that should they ever commit such crimes in the future they would lose their freedom of the burgh 'and to be separate and expulat fra the societie thereof'. This is the same language that was used to describe the council's belief that John Deuchar's actions had put himself outside acceptable society. When Grant failed to perform his penance before the congregation he immediately forfeited his freedom and was ordered banished from the burgh. The pronounce-ment of his offence and penalty was to be proclaimed at the market cross.[68]

Grant's treatment before the court, his subsequent refusal to perform his repentance and the eventual proclamation announcing his banishment from the town informs us of contemporary attitudes towards authority, hierarchy and dis-cipline prevalent within Aberdonian society. First, it is clear that Grant's status as a free burgess and guild brother did not prevent the council from finding him guilty of his crime or from imposing the same sentence that they also bestowed upon individuals deemed his inferior. Second, it is equally clear that his own perception of his place in Aberdonian society prevented him from demeaning himself in public through an admittance of guilt and a lowering of himself to the level of Kello and Burnett or being brought low by his equals. Third, despite their involvement in raising a tumult and allegedly sowing discord between the craftsmen and free burgesses of guild, Kello and Burnett did not suffer the ultimate penalty of banishment that the council imposed on Grant. Undoubtedly, rehabilitation through public penance was part of the process of (re)including the convicted party in the community after they had excluded themselves through their crimes. Grant's unwillingness to participate in this process ensured that he remain outside the community.

Likewise, in May 1565 the court convicted James Maser, Lawrens Masar, Mathew Guild, Thomas Huntar and Andrew Wysman for 'cuming throw the town vpoun Sunday last was efter nowne with an wistell playand be for thame throw the gallowgait in contemption of the town's actis and parliamentis and contravening of same'.[69] For causing this disturbance, they were put in amercement of court and ordered to remain in the tolbooth until they had found surety to satisfy and fulfill the amends. Three days later, the baillies modified their unlaws. The court determined that they should each be discharged of their freedom and 'fra all execution of thair craftis conform to an act of parliament'.[70] Again, by public proclamation the community was to know that these particular craftsmen had lost their right to use their craft within the burgh. The convicted craftsmen were not the only individuals affected by their activities; an open proclamation at the market cross made known that no craftsmen would be made free of their craft for seven years with the exception of the sons of free craftsmen. This was a concerted effort to stem the apparent abuses of the craftsmen and to demonstrate the full authority of the council. It is interesting to note that in 1581 Mathew Guild and Lawrens Maser's names appear in the list of the craftsmen who adhered to the purchase of rights and liberties from the King.[71] While John Grant suffered banishment for his disobedience and Maser and his colleagues lost their freedom and instigated a reform in the number of craftsmen who were to be made free, their experience was not dissimilar from John Duncan's experience with the burgh magistrates.

Although Duncan lost his freedom for being the instigator and author of the tumult and schism in the summer of 1581, he continued to agitate for change and repeatedly found himself called before the court. In late September 1581, the council warned Duncan, along with John Bannerman, John Rory and Patrick Leith to answer to the charges of raising tumult and sedition within the burgh.[72] In an alternative account, the council order named only Bannerman and Rory to compear before the court. This makes sense if we consider that Duncan had already lost his freedom and Leith had been banished for his attack on William Gray.[73] The language used in this account stresses the discord sowed by the actions of the craftsmen and emphasizes the threat posed by challenging the authority of the council and the established social order. Accordingly, the provost, baillies and council ordered Bannerman and Rory to appear before them to answer for:

> certane crymes demerits and enormities committit & done be thame and in speciall
> for resing of schesme and sedition within the bowalls of this common welth betwixt
> brethren of gild and the craftismen of the same attempting to seik new liberties and
> vocations quhilk thay had newer befor.[74]

Bannerman and Rory firmly denied the charges and the matter was put before a sworn assise where the charges were 'verifeit tryit and prowen'. The court clerk recorded that the two men were also accused of convincing John Duncan to purchase new 'liberties & innovations which the craftismen newer had before'.[75] Regardless, in determining Bannerman and Rory's fate, the council took into consideration the two men's record of behaviour. Recounting that both men had been convicted numerous times in the past for a variety of offences and been made to promise to never offend again, the council ordered that both were to lose the freedom and privileges associated with their craft.

According to the earlier charge brought against the craftsmen in August of 1581, the so-called 'new liberties and vocations quhilk thay had newer befor' sought by Duncan, Bannerman, Rory and their followers were designed to 'vsurp thair [the free burgesses of guild] libertie and commodite in bying and selling of merchandice'.[76] The incendiary aspect of their action was not the trespass of the liberties of the burgesses of guild, but rather the attempt to circumvent the authority of the provost, baillies and council by attempting to purchase these liberties from the King and his Privy Council. The involvement of outside parties shone a light too brightly on a house not in order. Such actions threatened to destabilize the burgh magistracy by undermining their authority within the burgh, not to mention causing the provost, baillies and council a serious embarrassment. This is not to diminish the affront felt by the guild brethren who were keenly aware of the need to protect their place within burgh society. Given that there had been a steady increase in the number of craftsmen and lesser merchants welcomed into the merchant guild over the course of the sixteenth century, these events cannot be viewed solely as a craftsmen/merchant conflict.[77] It was as much about jostling for power as it was about order, authority and discretion.

The fact that the authorities in Aberdeen chose to put their own complaint before the Privy Council in September 1581 does not undermine the argument that they had felt their authority challenged by the craftsmen and their rights

and liberties interfered with by the King and his council. By sending commissioners to Edinburgh, the provost, baillies and council not only sought to level
their complaint against the craftsmen but also to indicate their displeasure with
having the rights of the burgh transgressed by the powers in Edinburgh.[78] It is
not entirely clear how the King or Privy Council responded to this complaint. In
December 1581, the provost, baillies and council passed an ordinance stating that
'na craftismen of this burgh salbe admittit free burgesses of gild of this burgh in
na tym cuming to quhene any license or previlege salbe grantit for any tym.'[79] Not
wanting to entirely cut off a valuable source of income, the council determined
that craftsmen desiring to become burgesses of guild would have to 'leif the craft'
in order to 'use the office of an free burges of gild'. This was not innovative, nor
was it meant to be. By reinforcing the statutes already in place governing entrance
to the merchant guild the council ignored the rights purchased by the craftsmen
earlier that year and upheld the rights granted to the burgh by the King's predecessors in its foundation charter. The conflict rose to a greater level in February
the following year when Bannerman, Duncan, Leith and Rory purchased letters
of lawborrow from the King seeking to have their freedom restored.[80]

The accounts in the Council Register and Register of the Privy Council for
this period reveal just how deep the conflict between the craftsmen, merchants
and burgh magistrates had become. The magistrates not only saw the injustice
in the craftsmen seeking to enjoy the liberties and rights of the merchant guild
which they believed were illegally attained, but saw these individuals as eschew-
ing order. By bringing letters of lawborrow against the provost, baillies, council
and the 'gryt part of the communite', the baillies claimed that Duncan, Bannerman, Leith and Rory intended 'thairby to leive within this burght without ony
correctioun or ordor by an act or the accustome & lawis and lautfull constitu-
tions of this burt'.[81] The council's sole purpose for convening the 'hail brethren
and burges of gild' in February 1582 was to prepare the case to be brought before
the Privy Council that would best demonstrate the transgressions committed
against them by the craftsmen.[82] Moreover, the council took the opportunity
to pronounce further judgment on Bannerman, Duncan and Rory. The baillies
determined that by 'causing vproar schisme and division within the burght and
bowalls thairof' and 'refusing all dewtifull obediens to thair superiors and magistrate vnder the kings maiestie to the ewill example of the rest of the nichtbors
and trubling of the quietnes of the guid town' these men were to be shunned.

By open proclamation all guild brothers were prohibited from offering these
men any employment and from keeping company with them. According to the
complaint Bannerman, Duncan and Rory put before the Privy Council on 11
April 1582, the ban on keeping company with the accused had been extended to
the entire community of craftsmen within the burgh:

The said provost and Baillies not only refuse to obey by opening the booth doors of
the complainers, bot banesis tham the toun for seeking of the samin, and hes, be thair
act of court, concludit that na burges of Abirdene sall at ony tyme efter the dait of the
said act quhilk wes maid at Abirdene the xvii day of Februar last bypast beir company,
eat or drink, gif ony kind of work or sett houssis to duell or work in, to ony craftismen
of Abirdene at ony tyme heirefeter; the lyke of quhilk pernitious and ungodly act
wes nevir hard nor sene amangis ony Christian people, subject to the discipline of a
Christian prince, as the said complainers ar.[83]

The complaint continues by emphasizing that the action taken by the burgh
council was 'slanderous' to God and the true religion and in 'contempt of the
kingis majestie'.[84] It also bears witness to contemporary perspectives on the role
of humiliation in penalties doled out by the provost and baillies. Not only had
craftsmen been banished, shunned and refused opportunities to earn a living,
but the actions of the council had made 'the saidis compliners mair odious to
the warld'. The baillies achieved this by having 'affixt the catholog of thair names
upoun the maist patent tolbuith dur and on all thair awin durris intitulit The
Names of the Perjurit Craftismen'.[85]

The craftsmen followed up their intial complaint of 11 April 1582 with
another dated at Stirling 16 April 1582 and on behalf of 'the hail craftismen
of the burgh of Abirdene'.[86] Much of the second complaint follows the original
in terms of structure and content. However, a number of important elements
emerge in the second complaint that indicates a change in tactics by the craftsmen.[87] First, in the opening section of the complaint the complainants cite the
many abuses perpetrated by the Menzies family in circumventing the proper
election of the provost, baillies, officers and dean of guild. Each of these offices
had been occupied by individuals connected by blood or marriage or through
an unwavering support of the Menzies over the course of the sixteenth century.
The craftsmen also called into question the entire electoral process stating that
the 'provost, Baillies, elderman and counsale of the said burgh' were not 'electit
thairto be commoun consent and voit of the haill inhabitantis as use is'.[88] Second,
in a number of clauses the complainants made certain to stress the serious plight
they have found themselves in since losing the ability to earn a living. In one section, they argue that on account of the Menzies family and the present council
'not onlie the saidis compliners, bot the haill communitie of the said burgh, is
brocht to extreme indigence and povertie'.[89] This simply reiterated a clause in the
first complaint of 11 April 1582 which argued that the King had prompted the
provost, baillies and council to remedy the situation 'desiring thame to lett the
saidis compliners use thair honest occupations within the said burgh, to the help
and confort of thair pure wyffis and fameleis'. Third, the complainants employed
the language used by the council in the open proclamation against the craftsmen
on February 1582 against the council. For example, they referred to the 'sedi-
tious devices' and 'evill example' of the magistrates who oppress their neighbours

within the burgh. Interestingly enough, the craftsmen's complaint referred to those individuals who denied endorsing the purchase of the liberties from the King back in the summer of 1581 as 'perjurit craftismen', arguing that the council had coerced these men 'partlie throw menassing and boisting' and 'partlie be brybis'.[90] Finally, the craftsmen laid before the Council the full extent of their concern over the policy adopted by the burgh magistrates:

> Thay have in contempt thairof not only baneist the toun a part of the saidis compliners, bot als lokkit in the rest of thair buith durris, making tham thairthrow unable to wyn thair leving, sindre of tham remaning heir banesit fra thair native toun and cuntre, quhair thay dar not repair for feir of thair lyffes, speciallie Johnne Duncan, John Rowry, tailyeouris, John Duequhair, cordiner, and James Banerman, Baxter, - the rest being in na bettir cais.[91]

It is interesting to note that while the clerk omitted Patrick Leith from the specified names, he included John Deuchar's name, attaching his previous conflict with the magistrates to the current cause before the Council. Again the matter was put before the Lords of Council and Session. The Privy Council determined that while the judges deliberated, both parties were to 'behave thameselffis within the said burgh as thay did befoir the purchessing of the said confirmatioun'.[92] It is clear that the matter dragged on for some time. At the Head Court on 1 October 1582 the craftsmen refused to vote a new town council 'quhill thai be restorit to thair libertie and admittit to the societie of utheris freemen of burght'.[93] In reaction, one of the baillies, Robert Menzies, protested that they should lose their right to vote in the future. In fact, the matter did not resolve itself until the 'Common Indenture' of 1587 established guidelines for elections, the mode and composition for making craftsmen free, and defined the trading privileges of both merchants and craftsmen; even then the resolution was quite limited. Overall, historians have viewed the 'Common Indenture' as having not served the craftsmen nor quieted the town.[94] Rather, it consolidated the council's control over the crafts by restricting the voice they had in determining their own course. This was largely achieved by restricting admittance to the craft to only candidates approved by the council, barring craftsmen from representation on the council and determining the two candidates out of a leet of six from the craftsmen that would audit the burgh compts.[95]

The individuals involved in putting the Indenture in place included the old adversaries John Duncan for the craftsmen and Alexander Cullan for the guild brethren. By the 1590s the Indenture's failings had become obvious as craft deacons continued to admit craftsmen without the consent of the council and craftsmen continued to 'usurp the privileges and liberties of a free burgess of gild'. Perhaps more indicative of the impact the preceding ten years had on the social order in the burgh was a complaint brought before the Privy Council in 1590 by the 'hail communitie, burgessis and craftismen of the burgh of Abirdene'.[96] The complaint outlined the 'grit hurte and detriment of the commounwele of the said burgh proceding upoun the misreule and misgovernament' of the Menzies family. Moreover, echoing the complaint issued by Bannerman, Duncan and Rory in April 1582, the 'hail communitie' charged the 'race of Menzies' with perverting the electoral process.[97] The community sent Mr John Cheyne and Andrew Kyng to prosecute their case. These 'commissioners' called for 'sum gude reformatioun in matteris concerning the common weill' and in particular the election of a council representing both craftsmen and burgesses of guild. More critically, they demanded that the Common Good [the funds allocated for the town's upkeep] be put towards the improvement of the town so that 'sindrie utheris abuses and enormities within the said burgh micht be repairit and reformeit'.[98] While the Indenture may not have completely altered the political and social landscape within Aberdeen, it certainly augured the changing perspectives of the day. In this sense, it is clear that the organized conflict under the leadership of Duncan, Bannerman, Rory and Leythe was part of a much larger process. Equally, smaller scale individual attacks on authority, such as those committed by Kello, Grant, Moris and Deuchar, played a part in the same process.

Attacks on Authority Figures in the Burgh

Collective agitation was not the only form of civil disobedience within the burgh in the sixteenth century, nor was it the only matter that occupied the minds of those 'honest men' whose duty it was to maintain the common weal. Individuals challenged the courts, slandered or threatened town officials and behaved in a manner that caused upset amongst the good neighbours of the burgh. In August 1587 a flesher by the name of Michael Davidson openly disobeyed Alexander Cullan 'in execution of his office' and struck Thomas King, one of the burgh officers.[99] While verbal and physical attacks on authority figures accounted for approximately 3 per cent of all cases of verbal and physical assaults recorded in Aberdeen between 1542 and 1591, no other conviction for a similar offence carried the punishment Davidson received for his transgression. The baillies determined that for his disobedience and his attack on one of the officers, Davidson should be put in ward within the kirk for ten days with only bread and water. Before his incarceration commenced, the baillies ordered that:

> his crag to be put fast in the govis instantly there to remane twa houris and the sin be public proclamation at the croce to be banist this burght enduring the counsells will and gif any person indwellar within this burght resave the said michaell in hous or harborand during the said space to pay the unlaw of ten poundis besyd the punishment befor imponit.[100]

The severity of Davidson's punishment cannot be ascribed to recidivism; his only other recorded transgression occurred in September 1584 when he was convicted alongside David Roals, another flesher, for striking John Adamson and his spouse.[101]

Only twice before had the baillies imposed sentences of comparable severity for attacks on authority figures. In February 1565 the court convicted Henry Pantome for mispersoning the provost and the baillies. For his offence he was ordered to put in the govis and banished from the town.[102] Unlike Davidson, he did not spend any time incarcerated within the kirk. Likewise, William Leith found himself in the govis for his own verbal attack on the baillies in November 1567.[103] What links both of these cases is the fact that their abuse of the authorities appears to have originated with the displeasure they felt over an earlier conviction. Pantome had been convicted of breaking the common ordinance of the town in baking 'quhyt breid being forbiddyne be the Baillies befoir'.[104] As a result of this transgression, the baillies discharged Pantome of 'his fremanship and inhibit him to baik ony forther in tym cuming'. This apparently induced Pantome to call the provost and baillies 'common oppresors and dyors [debtor] & bystors [bastards]'[105] and resulted in his being placed in the govis and banished from the town. Leith's original order to appear before the baillies was for a physical and verbal attack he committed with his wife on Alexander Reidfurd and his wife. While the records do not present a full narration of the events, Leith at some point in the proceedings began to abuse the baillies. It was for this offence that he found himself placed in the govis.[106]

When we take into consideration other cases where individuals maligned the officers, baillies, provost and other town officials it is clear that Davidson's conviction stands out for the harsh sentence he received. For example, in sixteen other recorded cases where the convicted party explicitly defamed, mispersoned or slandered town officials, four were required to perform public acts of repentance in the parish kirk revoking the words they had spoken while the rest were put in amercement of court and ordered to amend as law will.[107] Alexander Snalby called a sworn assise 'common learis [liars] and mensworne persons [perjured persons]' after they convicted his colleagues in the webster craft for regrating and forestalling.[108] For this outburst, the court ordered Snalby to revoke the words as untrue and having been spoken rashly. None of these punishments, however, equal that which was doled out to Michael Davidson for his disobedience.

Unless we take into consideration the more earnest attempts made by the magistrates to maintain order within the burgh in the 1580s and 1590s, it is not clear why the baillies passed such a severe sentence on Davidson. Other cases of physical assaults on authority figures did not end with the convicted party placed in the govis, incarcerated in the kirk and then publicly banished from the burgh. For example, on 11 February 1585 the baillies convicted Margaret Anderson of strubling Thomas King and ordered her to pay a fine of 8 shillings for her offence.[109] Including Anderson's attack on King, there are only seven other recorded incidents where individuals physically attacked town officials between

1543 and 1593.[110] Again the penalty prescribed for such activities was either public repentance or a fine with most individuals being amerced. The only other stipulation often attached to such convictions was for the convicted party to set caution or lawborrow guaranteeing the safety and well-being of the injured party. None, however, received any form of corporal punishment, none of the convicted individuals were put in the govis and none were banished for their actions. We cannot, however, assume that Davidson was a one-off occurrence. More likely, his actions were perceived in the same way as Patrick Leith's attack on the brother of Alexander Gray, the Baillie, at the meeting of craftsmen in August 1581. Moreover, it is clear that during the 1580s and into the 1590s, the court treated such attacks as threats not only to the authority of the individual attacked but to the authority of the entire burgh magistracy and the welfare of the community.

In the previous chapter I suggested that Alexander Mollison's neighbours had failed to restore to him his credit and reputation following his payment of fines and acts of repentance contrary to the prescriptive nature of the form of justice magistrates employed in Aberdeen. Yet, despite the court's attempts to punish individuals who slandered Mollison's name, Mollison did not feel any obligation to be neighbourly towards the magistrates or his fellow Aberdonians. Mollison's activities within the burgh in the 1580s stand out as illustrative of this type of affront to the authority of the magistracy as well as indicative of the clampdown imposed on such behaviour. Mollison first appears in the records in September 1574 when the court ordered him to 'mak his public repentans for his douball relaps in fornication twa Sundays'.[111] Despite his own sinful behaviour, the Kirk Session did not deem him unworthy to act as a cautioner for Christian Sinclair in 1575 when she was called before the Kirk Session to answer to the charge of fornication with Duncan Philip.[112] In December 1576 Mollison was ordered to make his repentance and to pay 20 shillings to the council magistrate for relapse fornication.[113] Roughly around the same time that Mollison acted as a cautioner for Sinclair he also acted as lawborrow, cautioner and surety for a wright by the name of George Leslie who was convicted of 'molesting, trubling and striking of Marion Wychton'.[114] While Leslie was put in amercement of court for this act, Mollison, only five years later, needed to find his own cautioner and lawborrow after a sworn assise convicted him for strubling and striking of Wychton and down casting and trapping of her wares.[115] While these incidents reflect more on individual wrongdoing within the burgh, they also shed some insight into Mollison's character. In September 1581 Mollison's less than neighbourly conduct extended beyond personal attacks when he was convicted along with John Rolland and Alex Collison 'for the strubling of the burgh court in plane visage thereof'.[116] All three were ordered to set caution; however, Mollison took an act of court that he did not 'struble' the provost and baillies. Mollison lost his case, and found himself on his knees within the tolbooth seeking forgiveness from the magistrates and ordered to pay a fine of £10 under threat of the greater fine of £100 if he committed such acts in the future.

What stands out here is that Mollison was required to seek forgiveness from the font of authority within the burgh, the King's majestie, as well as the provost and baillies. Interestingly enough Mollison received the harshest penalty of the three. Collison's unlaw was 'devisit in lyk manner exceptit his penalty is midigat to 10 merks because he was provokit'. John Rolland, on the other hand, the court ordered:

> to mak the lyk amends & dischargit with his penalty because his falt is considerate to be the lithest and provit upon sic motion as was to mentione the honor & validuty of the juge to the reproach of their disobediens[117]

Rolland's recanting of his attack on the authority of the court helped him to escape the full penalty Mollison received. Nonetheless, the original questioning of the 'honor and vailduty of the juge' had struck a nerve.

If we consider that Mollison's affront to the court, the baillies and provost occurred within days of the trial of John Duncan and Patrick Leith, as well as the uproar caused by the craftsmen in July and August of that year, it is likely that by provoking the authorities through taking an act of court Mollison incurred the more severe penalty. His apparent indifference towards the court and the burgh authorities can be detected from the fact that three days later Mollison and another deacon of the baxter craft, John Bannerman, appeared before the baillies accused of breaking the common ordinances of the town that regulated the quality of bread.[118] Although the records are silent on Mollison's activities over the next few years he reappears again in August 1587 when the baillies convicted him for the 'strubling of the court and contempting of the provost and Baillies in administration of thair office in judgment'.[119] The baillies modified his unlaw on 26 August 1587 ordering him:

> to comper within the tollbuyth where the falt was committit & thair in the presens of the hail counsall that beis present for the tym sit down his kneis and grantit his offens & ask the king's grace & the provost, Baillies forgifness & gif he beis convikit for sic offens in tym cuming to pay the sowme of ane hundrethh poundis & penaltie to pay to the dein of gild ten pounds and the forsaid sowme to be payt be George straquhin sourte for the said Alex & he to relief the said George thereof.

Despite his obvious lack of respect for the burgh authorities there is no indication in the records that Mollison lost his freedom to use his craft nor is there any suggestion of possible banishment for his affront. Instead, the provost and baillies employed the threat of a hefty fine and the imposition of public repentance as a means of curbing his disobedience.

Although Mollison was the recipient of a more severe penalty than his partners in crime, Alexander Collison and John Rolland, none of their punishments matched that of Michael Davidson. Despite challenging the authorities during the 'tumults' caused by the leading craftsmen within the burgh, Mollison never faced a loss of his freedom or the threat of banishment. Davidson's conviction and subsequent punishment in August 1587 can only be taken as an indication that the local authorities had reached the end of their tether and were keen on rooting out such threats to their authority. That his conviction occurred shortly after the passing of the Common Indenture suggests that the severity of his punishment stemmed from a post-tumult mentality and a reassertion of local authority that had witnessed serious challenges from within and outwith the burgh. The growing concern over threats posed to the common weal dominates the regulations passed by the council in the late 1580s and 1590s underscoring the need to reaffirm the local magistrates' prominent place within the social order as well as outlining acceptable behaviour within the burgh.

CONCLUSION: (RE)DEFINING THE COMMUNITY OF THE BURGH

The various accounts left behind in the records for the burgh of Aberdeen consistently acknowledge a very pronounced concern both the magistracy and the burgh community had regarding the clear danger criminal activities posed to the burgh's well-being. This underlying concern, rooted in the desire to maintain stability and 'neighbourliness' within the community, demonstrates that contemporaries recognized the inherent power of petty crimes, particularly as a means of achieving goals, settling disputes or challenging established dynamics. In this regard, petty crimes were a means of continuing the negotiation of social relations and power dynamics within the burgh. In their keenness to maintain already established social structures, magistrates used their role in punishing wrongdoers to restore those convicted of crimes 'to the ordor of discipline'[1] thus diminishing the impact their wrongful actions had on the community. But in doing so the burgh magistrates implicitly acknowledged that petty crimes could reshape the boundaries of belonging by challenging accepted norms, customs and statutes that were in place to help maintain an orderly society. This is most obvious in the fact that the magistrates expected the wider community to play a role in regulating crime, thus enabling a much greater number of the burgh's inhabitants to participate in defining and redefining the social boundaries of the burgh.

By using burgh court records and through an examination of the various crimes committed in Aberdeen, this book has explored the methods used to regulate social relations and political dynamics, power structures and social obligations that defined burgh life in the last half of the sixteenth century. As the previous chapters have shown, the study of criminality offers the historian a way of exploring the social dynamics present in burgh communities as well as the processes at work that defined membership in the various communities that made up the burgh. The book focused on three largely connected, yet distinct, areas of inquiry: that of the early modern community of the burgh, of social power and its negotiation, and of the processes that regulate inclusion in, and exclusion from, collectivities. The thread that bound these areas of inquiry together was the idea that in committing petty crimes individuals exercised power over their victims as a means of achieving their goals. Ultimately, this study has shown that in their attempts to protect what contemporaries called the 'common weal of the burgh', local magistrates strove to curb such activities by reinforcing established mechanisms in place to maintain order and to construct the boundaries, statutes and customs that reinforced a sense of place in the minds of the burgh's inhabitants.[2] It was here that the ideals and actualities of sixteenth-century burgh life frequently intersected.

The many examples used throughout this book to demonstrate how petty crimes were part of the ongoing negotiation of social power and space support this conclusion. For example, Margaret Molen's dispute with Duncan Donaldson over the price of his goods led Molen to call Donaldson a 'fals commond theif', thus undermining his standing in the burgh, diminishing his credit and threatening his livelihood.[3] When the magistrates convicted Molen for her crime they sought to mitigate the damage done and restore Donaldson's reputation.[4] Similarly, when James Wilson attempted to cheat the market by 'cutting and diminissing ane firlot' he challenged the regulations that governed the sale of goods within the burgh and sought to increase his potential for greater gain.[5] This was an attempt to increase his own power and control over certain aspects of life within the burgh, in this case, his economic well-being at the expense of his neighbours and the town.

While the chapters in this book have sought to draw out some of the more nuanced aspects of life in the burgh community, one of the most obvious characteristics of sixteenth-century Aberdonian society was the interconnected role of the spiritual and secular authorities in regulating the burgh community. Despite the intrusion of Reformation ideas and a new kirk administrative apparatus after 1560, the conviction accounts suggest little change occurred in terms of attitudes towards wrongdoing, punishments doled out and actions taken to ensure proper behaviour. The continued presence of the Menzies family and their network of supporters in both the civil and spiritual spheres of influence meant a continuity in how local government operated. Underpinning this outlook was a very genuine fear of God's wrath being unleashed in the community on account of wrongful behaviour; a fear that can be detected in accounts found in both secular and ecclesiastical records. Indeed, at least until the start of the seventeenth century it would be unproductive to try and separate secular and spiritual concerns in terms of behaviour within the community. The simple fact that both the burgh courts and the Kirk Session prosecuted the same offences and often included the other in the processes of regulating behaviour, either by invoking their authority or inviting them to apply sanctions, suggests a coordinated effort to govern behaviour within the community.

Even the most cursory examination of the court records reveals a community concerned by the threat crime posed to the common weal. That the community perceived such threats in both spiritual and secular terms, though they most likely would not have made the distinction, should not come as a surprise. What does stand out in the case of Aberdeen during the Reformation period is that there was not the type of religious zeal guiding social reform as seen elsewhere in the British Isles.[6] That is not to say that social reform and social welfare was strictly a secular project. Rather, concern over evoking God's displeasure through continuous wrongdoing remained relatively constant throughout this period. The shape and form such concern took slowly began to change keeping in line with some of the tenets of the new Kirk, but the essence of Godly discipline did not change dramatically until the seventeenth century.[7]

Thus, when the burgh magistrates raised the spectre of God's wrath visiting the town on account of crimes committed or challenges to the social order in 1592 it was not a sign of a significant shift in social discipline.[8] The immediate cause for alarm in 1592 stemmed from an apparent rise in blaspheming, although the activities of the past decade helped to shape such fears. In response, the magistrates demanded that the community police itself, ordering individual homes to be fitted with a 'swear jar' with the contents to be given to the poor for their relief. A year earlier, Patrick Prat was accused by the provost, baillies and council of incest:

> ane sin sa odious that it procuris the wraith and displeasour of God, to be pured on that citie and congregatioun quhair the same is committit, except consign punischement to be imouit to the committeris, and that heirtofoir to be ressone the said cryme of incest hes bene rair within this burght and freedome thairof comittit.[9]

While blasphemy and incest may seem far removed from riotous acts and causing sedition within the burgh, the authorities perceived such acts to be equally ruinous for the community. What stands out in the account of Prat's conviction is the expressed idea that through execution of the penalties prescribed by the burgh magistrates not only had this specific crime 'bene rair within this burght', but the local authorities had made certain that God's wrath had not visited the community.

A good indication of the continuity in how the community perceived the relation between proper behaviour and God's impact on the welfare of that community is in the retention of penitential acts, acts of repentance in the Reformation and post-Reformation era, requiring the convicted party to ask God for forgiveness. Despite the majority of the attacks on authority during this period being directed towards secular magistrates, it was paramount for the provost and baillies that the convicted party ask God, the magistrates and the injured party for forgiveness. That said, a slight change in the practices of the burgh magistrates followed hard on the heels of the disruption caused by the tumults of the 1580s and the pressure placed on the burgh to remove the conservative and Catholic influence of the Menzies family. Indicative of this shift is the implementation in Aberdeen of national legislation coming out of Edinburgh. For example, the concern over blasphemy and the imposition of the swear box or swear jar in 1592 mirrored an act passed by Parliament in 1581.[10] Likewise, promulgation of Acts in Edinburgh between 1587 and 1592 for punishing adulterers and fornicators, preventing the holding of markets on the Sabbath and curtailing disturbances within the kirk had counterparts in Aberdeen willing to implement the original acts. For example, at the Head Court in October 1593 the council passed ordinances for the keeping of sermons given the 'willful remaining from the paroche kirk' for the purpose of 'gaming and playing and passing to tavernis'.[11] Imbedded in this ordinance was the impact such behaviour had on the community: 'procuring nytbors the wrath and displeasor of god'.[12] Again, the magistrates believed there was a need to pass the ordinance for the remedy of such behaviour. Likewise, the provost, baillies and council passed ordinances preventing the holding of fish and flesh markets on the Sabbath seen to be causing 'gryt dishonor to god'.[13]

The council also passed statutes regulating the housing of strangers within the community, managing the burgh accounts, riding the boundaries of the burgh and the price and quality of food commodities.[14] Taken together they represent the primary concerns of the burgh magistrates. They also reflect a sensitivity towards disorder with the burgh and the need to more firmly establish order and discipline. Interestingly enough most of these attempts to regulate the community have earlier precedents. One of the most interesting was the 1551 Act concerning oaths sworn by members of both great and lesser estates.[15] The Act against Blasphemy of 1587 maintains the penalties prescribed in the earlier Act but omits the concern over God's wrath visiting the community. Likewise, an act of 1551 concerning disturbances within the kirk indicates that those convicted of committing this act who will not stop 'for na spirituall monitioun that the kirkmen may vse' would be brought before the secular authorities.[16] A similar Act passed during the reign of James VI in 1587 indicates that the convicted parties would escheat their goods to the king. Any additional activities that disturbed the kirk were to incur the 'appropriate punishment' including excommunication. What is important to take from such Acts is the interconnected role of civil and spiritual authorities in regulating behaviour both before and after the Reformation.

Indications of similarly interconnected roles in Aberdeen can be discerned from the penalties incurred by individuals convicted of disturbing the kirk. Patrick Leslie and George Troupe's conviction in February 1584 for causing a disturbance in the kirk stand out.[17] The Council Register states that such behaviour within the kirk was entirely unacceptable 'being the house and place dedicat to God making the cryme more odious and haynous'. In January 1553 the baillies convicted Alexander Ferguson for disturbing the kirk. For his actions he was:

> to appear at the time of high mass with two pounds of wax in his hands and ask God and the town forgiveness of his offence, offer the said candil on his knees to the provost And gif he does siklik in tym to cum to be banist of the town.[18]

On the day the baillies modified Ferguson's unlaw they likewise convicted John Dwne and Alexander Incheson of strubling the town in their strublens of Alexander Ferguson. While the details are not available, it is tempting to see a connection between Ferguson's disturbance of the community and kirk and the subsequent abuse he endured from his neighbours. Nonetheless, these examples present a picture of a wider community keen on maintaining the spiritual and social welfare of all its members. That the secular magistrates saw it as one of their responsibilities should not come as a surprise. It was their duty, as they would have seen it, to play an integral role in the processes that maintained the common weal of the burgh and ensured that the community did not incur God's wrath.

Still, due to the incomplete nature of the burgh records it is difficult to determine whether the powers the magistrates held were sufficient for rooting out unwanted elements in the burgh. The fact that in 1593 the council was concerned about 'sindrie vtheris gryt disorder laitlie creppin in within the burght' suggests that despite the tandem of kirk and council, crime continued to pose a major threat to the common weal of the burgh.[19] While certain crimes appeared to be on the decline over the period under consideration, such as unspecified strublance, verbal and physical assault and 'wrongous away taking', as well as an overall decline of 24 per cent in prosecuted crimes, it is unlikely that the sanctions imposed by the burgh's authorities were the only reason for this decline. More likely, rising court costs, informal pursuit of retribution, unproven reciprocal misbehaviour (i.e. vigilantism) and a shift in the concerns of the council effected this change. This last point is perhaps the easiest to support. As the discussion on unspecified strublance in Chapter 4 revealed, a change in how court clerks documented convictions in the burgh corresponded with a decline in the number of accounts where the charges against individual wrongdoers were recorded as 'strublance'. As well, the rising number of cases of statute breaking and disobedience during the 1570s and 1580s reveal the council's concern with protecting the established social hierarchy. That we also witness a rise in incidents of 'strubling the town' brought before the court during this same period underscores this concern.

Table 6.1: Number of 'cases' of petty crimes brought before the burgh court, 1562–91

Crime	1562–71	1572–81	1582–91	Total
Physical assault	91	85	76	252
Verbal assault	98	47	41	186
Vandalic property crime	5	8	3	16
Breaking statutes, regrating and forestalling	117	183	126	426
Unspecified strublance	10	5	8	23
Disobedience and disorder	4	21	27	52
'Wrongous away taking' (petty theft)	16	9	9	34
'Strubling the town'	5	17	56	78
Total	346	375	346	1067

Although there were only 29 more cases brought before the court between 1572 and 1581 than there were for the period 1562 to 1571, there was a 56 per cent increase in the number of cases of statute breaking before the court, a 425 per cent increase in incidents of disobedience and a 240 per cent increase in incidents of 'strubling the town'. In contrast, there was a decline or plateau in the number of incidents of physical violence, verbal violence, property crime and 'wrongous away taking' brought before the court during this same period. From what we know of the threats posed to the merchant guildry and the political establishment in Aberdeen in the 1570s and 1580s, it seems entirely consistent that the authorities would focus on the crimes that posed an immediate threat to those areas of burgh society. What is telling about the figures found in Table 3.1 (p. 94) is that the most significant decline in the number of petty crime cases brought before the court occurred in the decade immediately preceding the Reformation Parliament of 1560 and the establishment of the Kirk Session in Aberdeen in 1562. A decrease in numbers by 21 per cent from the 1542–51 numbers is followed by a further decline of 2.6 per cent, an increase of 6.4 per cent and another decline of 6.4 per cent in subsequent decades. Despite introducing Reformation ideas into the burgh and adopting another body to regulate society, there does not seem to be a significant decrease in the overall number of tried criminal cases committed in the community. Indeed, what can be taken away from this analysis is that despite occasional changes in the specific concerns the authorities may have had, there was greater continuity in terms of the manner in which the community combated wrongdoing and in the general belief that any and all criminal acts challenged the boundaries of good neighbourliness, altered the burgh's social structures and affected the power dynamics within the burgh.

This book has made no attempt to examine all aspects of community life in Aberdeen; it does, however, provide a basis for further studies of the community of the burgh. In particular, by offering numerous insights on power structures within an early modern town it contributes to our understanding of early modern peoples and the societies they construct. Indeed, through an analysis of petty crimes captured in existing court records, guildry accounts, town council statutes and Kirk Session records, this book examined how sixteenth-century Aberdonians interacted within the burgh community. Moreover, it highlighted areas where personal necessity and personal desire conflicted with the concerns/wishes/needs of the wider community and, in particular, with those elites or 'guid men' of the burgh who considered themselves to represent *the community*.[20] More importantly, it shed light on one area where elite and non-elite both actively participated in the restructuring of social space and exercise of social power. Often this exercise of power resulted in very tangible results such as affecting change in the prices of goods, gaining access to the exclusive communities within the burgh and altering the political landscape. While most individual crimes were in response to immediate individual concerns or disputes or to achieve some goal that impacted on social relations that were already established, collectively all petty crimes committed in the burgh represented a force that defined and (re)defined the community of the burgh.

From the examples given, it should be clear that the concern in 1593 over the 'gryt disorder laitlie creppin in within the burght' needs to be considered in the context of the tensions within Aberdonian society that pervaded burgh life during the latter half of the sixteenth century. Although these activities dominate the extant records for this period, there were a number of other elements, such as famine and dearth and the problems such things produced, that threatened the social order and prompted the magistrates to attempt to reaffirm their control. Together they helped to usher in the more thorough reform discipline that defined Aberdonian society well into the seventeenth century.[21] That their experiences reflect a greater course of agitation amongst the non-enfranchised groups in Aberdeen can be discerned in the statutes passed by the burgh council attempting to restrict the activities of the craftsmen, the actions taken by a number of craftsmen to pursue their goals through outside channels, and the increased focus on statute-breaking by free and unfree craftsmen as the provost, baillies, merchant guildry and council put the activities of all the inhabitants of Aberdeen under the metaphorical microscope for, at the very least, the remainder of the last decade of the sixteenth century.[22] As Robert Shoemaker demonstrated in his study of London, the types of crimes this book examined had an impact in every corner, and on every level, of burgh society.[23] As such, the history of petty crimes committed in the last half of the sixteenth century in Aberdeen offers, as I hope this book has shown, insights into the social relations, power dynamics and boundaries of belonging that shaped this early modern burgh community.

NOTES

Introduction

1. Aberdeen City Archives, Council Register (hereafter ACA, CR), xx, 301–2 (7 October 1549).
2. *Extracts from the Council Register of the Burgh of Aberdeen,* ed. J. Stuart, 4 vols (Aberdeen: Spalding Club & SBRS, 1844–72) (Hereafter *Abdn. Counc.*), vol. 1, pp. 271–2.
3. ACA, CR, xxvi, 147 (13 May 1566)
4. ACA MSS Baillie Court Book 1 (15 December 1581).
5. Ibid.
6. K. Wrightson, 'Mutualities and Obligations: Changing Social Relationships in Early Modern England' (The Raleigh Lecture, 2005), pp. 1–37, on p. 3; S. Hindle, *The State and Social Change in Early Modern England, 1550–1640* (Basingstoke: Palgrave, 2000), p. 59.
7. On this voluminous subject see for example A. Fletcher and J. Stevenson (eds), *Order and Disorder in Early Modern England* (Cambridge: Cambridge University Press, 1985); R. Po-chia Hsia, *Social Discipline in the Reformation: Central Europe 1550–1750,* (London: Routledge, 1989); R. Jutte, *Poverty and Deviance in Early Modern Europe* (Cambridge: Cambridge University Press, 1994); S. Hindle, 'The Shaming of Margaret Knowsley: Gossip, Gender and the Experience of Authority in Early Modern England', *Continuity and Change,* 9:3 (1994), pp. 391–419; K. Wrightson and D. Levine, *Poverty and Piety in an English Village, 1525–1700,* 2nd edn (Oxford: Oxford University Press, 1995); P. Slack, *From Reformation to Improvement: Public Welfare in Early Modern England* (Oxford: Clarendon Press, 1999).
8. M. Lynch, *Edinburgh and the Reformation* (Edinburgh: John Donald Publishers, 1981); E. P. Dennison, D. Ditchburn and M. Lynch (eds) *Aberdeen Before 1800: A New History* (East Linton: Tuckwell Press, 2002); E. Ewan, *Townlife in Fourteenth-Century Scotland* (Edinburgh: Edinburgh University Press, 1990); M. H. B. Sanderson, *Ayrshire and the Reformation: People and Change, 1490 – 1600* (East Linton: Tuckwell Press, 1997); E. P. D. Torrie, *Medieval Dundee: A Town and its People* (Dundee: Abertay Historical Society, 1990); M. Graham, *The Uses of Reform: Godly Discipline and Popular Behaviour in Scotland and Beyond, 1560–1610* (Leiden: E. J. Brill, 1996).
9. The relatively limited number of studies examining misbehaviour and power structures and authority in Scotland during the middle ages and early modern period underscores the real need to begin exploring such topics. See for example Y. G. Brown and R. Ferguson, *Twisted Sisters: Women, Crime and Deviance in Scotland since 1400* (East Linton: Tuckwell Press, 2002); E. Ewan, '"Many Injurious Words": Defamation and Gender in Late Medieval Scotland' in R. A. McDonald (ed.), *History, Literature, and Music in Scot-*

land, 700–1560 (Toronto: University of Toronto Press, 2002), pp. 163–86; M. Todd, 'Profane Pastimes and the Reformed Community: The Persistence of Popular Festivities in Early Modern Scotland', *Journal of British Studies*, 39:2 (2000), pp. 123–56; M. Todd, *Culture of Protestantism in Early Modern Scotland* (New Haven, CT: Yale University Press, 2002). In terms of full-length studies, Brown, *Bloodfeud in Scotland, 1573–1625* (Edinburgh: John Donald, 1986), Todd, *Culture of Protestantism* and Graham, *Uses of Reform* stand out as possible exceptions.

10. J. Goodare, *State and Society in Early Modern Scotland* (Oxford: Oxford University Press, 1999), p. 178.

11. J. A. Sharpe, '"Such Disagreement betwyx Neighbours': Litigation and Human Relations in Early Modern England', in J. Bossy (ed.), *Disputes and Settlements: Law and Human Relations in the West* (Cambridge: Cambridge University Press, 1983), pp.167–87; K. Wrightson, 'The Politics of the Parish in Early Modern England', in P. Griffiths, A. Fox and S. Hindle (eds), *The Experience of Authority in Early Modern England* (Basingstoke: Macmillan Press, 1996), pp. 10–46; P. Griffiths, 'Meanings of Nightwalking in Early Modern England', *Seventeenth Century*, 13:2 (Autumn 1998), pp. 212–38; J. Walter, *Understanding Popular Violence in the English Revolution: The Colchester Plunderers* (Cambridge: Cambridge University Press, 1999); D. Rollison, 'Discourse and Class Struggle: The Politics of Industry in Early Modern England', *Social History*, 26:2 (May 2001), pp. 166–89; A. Wood, '"Poor Men Woll Speke One Day": Plebeian Languages of Deference and Defiance in England, *c.* 1520–1640', in T. Harris (ed.), *The Politics of the Excluded, 1500–1850* (Basingstoke: Macmillan Press, 2001), pp. 67–98; S. Hindle, 'The Keeping of the Public Peace', in P. Griffiths, A. Fox and S. Hindle (eds), *The Experience of Authority*, pp. 213–48.

12. See for example E. P. Thompson, *The Making of the English Working Class* (London, 1963); A. Wood, *Riot, Rebellion and Popular Politics in Early Modern England* (London and New York: Palgrave), p. 200.

13. On these subjects see for example K. Wrightson, 'Alehouses, Order and Reformation in Rural England, 1590–1660', in E. and S. Yeo (eds), *Popular Culture and Class Conflict, 1590–1914: Explorations in the History of Labour and Leisure* (Sussex: Harvester Press, 1981), pp. 1–27; M. Ingram, 'Religion, Communities and Moral Discipline in Late Sixteenth- and Early-Seventeenth-Century England: Case Studies', in K. von Greyerz (ed.), *Religion and Society in Early Modern Europe* (Boston: Allen & Unwin, 1984); M. Spufford, 'Puritanism and Social Control?', in Fletcher and Stevenson (eds), *Order and Disorder in Early Modern England* (Cambridge: Cambridge University Press, 1985), pp. 41–57; S. Amussen, *An Ordered Society: Gender and Class in Early Modern England* (Oxford: Oxford University Press, 1988); S. Hindle, 'The Shaming of Margaret Knowsley', pp. 391–419; P. Griffiths, *Youth and Authority: Formative Experiences in England, 1560–1640* (Oxford: Oxford University Press, 1996); P. Slack, *From Reformation to Improvement*; A. Shepard and P. Withington (eds), *Communities in Early Modern England* (Manchester: Manchester University Press, 2000); G. Walker, *Crime, Gender and Social Order in Early Modern England* (Cambridge: Cambridge University Press, 2003).

14. S. Hindle, 'Power, Poor Relief, and Social Relations in Holland Fen, *c.* 1600–1800', *Historical Journal*, 41:1 (1998), pp. 67–96, on p. 67.

15. Ibid., p. 68. See also M. Braddick and J. Walter (eds), *Negotiating Power in Early Modern Society: Order, Hierarchy and Subordination in Britain and Ireland* (Cambridge: Cambridge University Press, 2001), p. 4; Mann, *The Sources of Social Power: vol. 1, A History of Power from the Beginning to AD 1760* (Cambridge: Cambridge University

Press, 1986); M. Foucault, *Discipline and Punish: The Birth of the Prison* (New York: Random House, 1978).

16. Braddick and Walter (eds), *Negotiating Power in Early Modern Society*, p. 2.

17. 'Social power', according to Michael Mann, 'restricts its meaning to mastery exercised over other people' and 'whereby persons in cooperation can enhance their joint power over third parties or over nature.' M. Mann, *Sources of Social Power*, pp. 6–7.

18. C. Tilly, *Coercion, Capital, and European States, AD 990–1992* (Cambridge, M.A.: Blackwell Publishing, 1992); J. Goodare, *State and Society in Early Modern Scotland*.

19. A. Gramsci, *Selections From the Prison Notebooks*, ed. Q. Hoare and G. N. Smith. (New York: International Publishers, 1971); S. Gunn, 'From Hegemony to Governmentality: Changing Conceptions of Power in Social History', *Journal of Social History*, 39:3 (2006), pp. 705–20.

20. M. Foucault, 'The Subject and the Power', *Critical Inquiry*, 8:4 (1982), pp. 777–95, esp. pp. 778–81.

21. M. Mann, *Sources of Social Power*, p. 6; T. Parsons, 'The Distribution of Power in American Society', in *Structure and Process in Modern Societies*, (New York: Free Press, 1960), pp. 199–225.

22. S. Gunn, 'From Hegemony to Governmentality', p. 705.

23. J. A. Sharpe, 'The History of Crime in Late Medieval and Early Modern England: A Review of the Field' *Social History*, 7:2 (1981), pp. 187–203.

24. Ibid., p. 187, fn. 2.

25. See for example V. A. C. Gatrell, B. Lenman and G. Parker (eds), *Crime and the Law: The Social History of Crime in Western Europe since 1500* (London: Europa, 1980); B. Lenman and G. Parker, 'Crime and Control in Scotland, 1500–1800', *History Today*, (January 1980), pp. 13–17; C. B. Herrup, 'The Law and Morality in Seventeenth-Century England', *Past and Present*, vol. 106 (1985), pp. 102–23; M. Ingram, *Church Courts, Sex and Marriage, 1560–1640* (Cambridge: Cambridge University Press, 1987); H. Schilling, '"History of Crime" or "History of Sin"? Some Reflections on the Social History of Early Modern Church Discipline', in E Kouri and T. Scott (eds), *Politics and Society in Reformation Europe.* (New York: St. Martin's Press, 1987), pp. 289–310; S. Amussen, 'Punishment, Discipline and Power: The Social Meanings of Violence in Early Modern England', *Journal of British Studies,* 34 (January 1995), pp. 1–34; M. Gaskill, *Crime and Mentalities in Early Modern England* (Cambridge: Cambridge University Press, 2000); T. Harris, (ed.), *The Politics of the Excluded, c. 1500–1850*; G. Walker, *Crime, Gender and Social Order in Early Modern England*; B. Capp, *When Gossips Meet: Women, Family and Neighbourhood in Early Modern* England (Oxford: Oxford University Press, 2003).

26. B. Hanawalt and D. Wallace (eds), *Medieval Crime and Social Control* (Minneapolis, MN: University of Minnesota Press, 1999), pp. ix–x; J. P. Pickett (ed.), *The American Heritage Dictionary of the English Language*, 4th edn (Boston, MA: Houghton Mifflin, 2000), Appendix 1.

27. See F. de Saussure, *Course in General Linguistics*, ed. C. Bally and A. Sechehaye (Toronto, ON: McGraw-Hill, 1966); P. Burke, *The Historical Anthropology of Early Modern Italy* (Cambridge: Cambridge University Press, 1987), pp. 3–7.

28. G. R. Elton, 'Introduction: Crime and the Historian', in J. S. Cockburn (ed.), *Crime in England 1550–1800* (Princeton, NJ: Princeton University Press, 1977), pp. 2–6; Sharpe, *Crime in Early Modern England, 1550–1750*, 2nd edn (London: Longman, 1999), pp. 6–7. Sharpe points out that contemporary writers could indeed put adultery and theft

on an equal plane and counters Elton's claim that contemporary attitudes towards theft and treason were similar.

29. For a discussion of this see P. Burke, *Historical Anthropology of Early Modern Italy*, pp. 3–7; see E. Durkheim's 'Introduction' in *The Elementary Forms of the Religious Life* translated by J. W. Swain (London: George Allen & Unwin Ltd., 1976), pp. 1–20.

30. Elton, 'Introduction: Crime and the Historian', pp. 2–6; see the editors' 'Introduction' in Gattrell, Lenman and Parker (eds), *The Social History of Crime*; M. R. Boes, 'Public Appearance and Criminal Judicial Practices in Early Modern Germany', *Social Science History*, 20:2 (1996), pp. 259–279; R. Shoemaker, *Prosecution and Punishment: Petty Crime and the Law in London and Rural Middlesex, c. 1660–1725* (Cambridge: Cambridge University Press, 1991); K. Jones, *Gender and Petty Crime in Late Medieval England: The Local Courts in Kent, 1460–1560* (Woodbridge: Boydell, 2006); P. Griffiths, 'Bodies and Souls in Norwich: Punishing Petty Crime, 1540–1700,' in S. Devereaux and P. Griffiths (eds), *Penal Practice and Culture, 1500–1900* (New York: Palgrave, 2004), pp. 85–120.

31. C. Herrup, 'Law and Morality in Seventeenth-Century England', pp. 106–11. Trevor Dean argues that this was the case in medieval England wherein jurors who believed the accused did not deserve to die for the crime would often acquit or re-grade the crime from a felonious action. See T. Dean, *Crime in Medieval Europe, 1200–1550* (New York: Longman, 2001), p. 12. Peter King has shown this also to be the case for the eighteenth century. See P. King, *Crime, Justice and Discretion in England, 1740–1820.* (Oxford: Oxford University Press, 2000).

32. B. Lenman and G. Parker, 'Crime and Control in Scotland, 1500–1800', p. 15.

33. According to Lenman and Parker, in the localities the authorities exercised their power more rigidly to root out disreputable characters. This was certainly the case when an individual accused of theft was sentenced to be scourged and banished. Lenman and Parker, 'Crime and Control in Scotland, 1500–1800', p. 15.

34. National Archives Scotland (hereafter NAS) CH2/448/1, 36 (4 May 1574).

35. A. J. Finch, 'The Nature of Violence in the Middle Ages: An Alternative Perspective', *Historical Research*, 70 (1997), pp. 249–68, argues that local courts in England dealt with the 'banal and mundane' as opposed to the more serious offences tried in the higher courts of the realm.

36. B. Lenman and G. Parker, 'Crime and Control in Scotland, 1500–1800', p. 15.

37. S. Amussen, 'Punishment, Discipline and Power', pp. 2, 32. While acknowledging that the common perception during this period was that the 'use' and 'extent' of violence was limited, Amussen contrasted the key difference amongst those who used violence: In spite of the structural similarities between the use of violence by an officer of the state and by a witch, we must remember the difference in context: for the one, it was a demonstration of power; for the other, it served as a claim to power generally denied her.

38. Ibid., p. 32.

39. B. Capp, 'Arson, Threats of Arson and Incivility in Early Modern England', in P. Burke, B. Harrison and P. Slack (eds), *Civil Histories: Essays in Honour of Sir Keith Thomas* (Oxford, 2000), pp.197–213, pp. 197–8.

40. Ibid., p. 202.

41. Ibid., pp. 212–13. Capp addresses this issue in the concluding paragraphs of his essay. In particular he acknowledges the changes in legislation concerning arson that arose in the seventeenth century as a result of previous wrongdoing. He also highlighted a shift in contemporary attitudes towards arson as the landed classes and middling sorts moved

away from using it to settle their disputes. 'Arson had become, for the most part, a crime of the uncivil poor, in quarrels among themselves or as a weapon against their superiors.'

42. S. Amussen, 'Punishment, Discipline and Power', p. 3; B. Capp, 'Arson, Threats of Arson and Incivility in Early Modern England', pp. 197–8.

43. On this subject see A. Gibson and T. C. Smout, *Prices, Food and Wages in Scotland 1550–1780* (Cambridge: Cambridge University Press, 1995); E. Gemmill and N. Mayhew, *Changing Values in Medieval Scotland: A Study of Prices, Money, and Weights and Measures* (Cambridge: Cambridge University Press, 1995). See ch.3 p. 77.

44. S. Hindle, 'The Keeping of the Public Peace', in P. Griffiths, A. Fox and S. Hindle (eds), *The Experience of Authority*, p. 217.

45. P. King, *Crime, Justice and Discretion in England*, p. 361.

46. Christopher Marsh has recently drawn attention to some of the limitations of this 'interpretative model that appears to be gathering quite a head of steam among historians of early modern social relations'. Marsh's interest lies in assessing 'order' in early modern societies as witnessed from the pew; he does not actually comment on crime. He does, however, take issue with using James Scott's 'public transcript' and Keith Wrightson's analysis of the 'hidden transcript' to assess social interactions in the early modern period. C. Marsh, 'Order and Place in England, 1580–1640: The View from the Pew', *Journal of British Studies*, 44:1 (January, 2005), pp. 3–26.

47. S. Amussen, 'Punishment, Discipline and Power', p. 27. Amussen argues that 'violence was used to assert one's place and to try and make the world conform to an ideal'.

48. See above p. 160, n. 31.

49. See ch. 1, pp. 34–5.

50. These individuals figure prominently throughout the book.

51. ACA, CR, xix, 351 (30 April 1547)

52. The other possibility is that this was an instance of vagrancy. If that was the case then the magistrates employed the same type of punishment used for removing other unwanted elements from the burgh in order to protect its 'common weil'.

53. NAS CH2/448/1, 36 (4 May 1574).

54. ACA, CR, xvii, 55 (13 December 1541).

55. ACA, CR, xvii, 51 (9 December 1541).

56. The 'riotous' behaviour of the craftsmen within the burgh who agitated for greater enfranchisement and sought to redefine the boundaries between merchants and themselves, is explored in ch. 5, pp. 127–44.

57. This phrase was used to describe criminal activities that occurred in secrecy or which disturbed the quiet of the night.

58. ACA, CR, xxiii, 92 (26 January 1558/9).

59. The records show that an Andrew Forbes and his brother John were convicted of property destruction in May 1575, ACA Baillie Court Books 1–1 (Pen May 1575). It is unclear if this Andrew Forbes and the Andrew Forbes convicted in 1595 were the same person.

60. ACA MSS Baillie Court Book 1 (12 July 1595).

61. Peter King has argued that crime functioned as a form of negotiation in the seventeenth and eighteenth centuries. See in particular, P. King, *Crime, Justice and Discretion in England*, pp. 17–46, 253–373; P. King, 'Punishing Assault: The Transformation of Attitudes in the English Courts' in *Journal of Interdisciplinary History*, 27:1 (1996), pp. 43–74; P. King, 'Legal Change, Customary Right, and Social Conflict in Late Eighteenth-Century England: The Origins of the Great Gleaning Case of 1788' in *Law and History Review*, 10:1 (1992), pp. 1–31.

62. W. C. Dickenson has argued that in Aberdeen the burgh council was responsible for framing statutes. See his introduction to *Early Records of the Burgh of Aberdeen, 1317, 1398–1407* (Edinburgh: T. and A. Constable for the Scottish History Society, 1957), pp. lxxxii–iii.

63. *Ancient Laws and Customs of the Burghs of Scotland, 1124–1424 and 1424–1707*, ed. C. Innes, 2 vols (Edinburgh: SBRS, 1868–1910), *Statuta Gilde*, c. 37.

64. The following discussion is based largely on the work of Ewan, *Townlife in Fourteenth-Century Scotland*, pp. 54–8; J. Finlay, *Men of Law in Pre-Reformation Scotland* (East Linton: Tuckwell Press, 2000), pp. 90–6; D. M. Walker, *Legal History of Scotland vol. 3, The Sixteenth Century* (Edinburgh: T & T Clarke Ltd., 1995), pp. 335–41.

65. Ewan, *Townlife in Fourteenth-Century Scotland*, p. 55; Walker, *Legal History of Scotland*, p. 335.

66. Walker, *Legal History of Scotland*, p. 335. However, numerous accounts found in the Council Register and Baillie Court Books invoke the authority of the 'provosts, Baillies and council'.

67. J. Balfour, *The Practicks of Sir James Balfour of Pittendreich*, ed. P. G. B. McNeill, 2 vols (Edinburgh: Stair Society, 1962), c. 69–72.

68. Walker, *Legal History of Scotland*, p. 337.

69. An account of Alex Forbes, Dean of Guild Alex Forbes from 'michelmas 1582–michelmas 1583' indicates that on 13 December 1582 the town spent 19*d*. 'for bedding the floor of the tolbooth and taking measure of the orlage.' On 10 January 1582/3 they spent £4 'for ane duir to the battolinter of the tolbooth to lock in the stand.' As well, on 14 August 1583 the council paid an unspecified amount 'for making of ane knok and mending of the lok on the counselhouse', ACA MSS Guildry Accounts (unnumbered). Finlay and Walker both note the lack of information on the chamber housing the court, though it is apparent from references made in conviction accounts of a bar in the court where persons stood to address the magistrates. Finlay, *Men of Law*, p. 92; Walker, *Legal History of Scotland*, p. 337.

70. ACA Baillie Court Books 1 (1 May 1581). Blak was convicted of breaking statutes governing the production and sale of beer in the burgh; for her wrongdoing the court ordered her to pay 6 merks before she departed the tolbooth and to abstain from brewing for a year.

71. For example, the court clerk noted for Helen Allan, whose numerous convictions will be examined in later chapters, that she had been 'accusit of divers tymes upon sic crymes and of many tym dyvers odious crymes committit be hir obefore' ACA MSS Baillie Court Book 1 (15 December 1581).

72. E. P. Dennison, 'Power to the People? The Myth of the Medieval Burgh Community' in S. Foster, A. Macinnes and R. Macinnes (eds), *Scottish Power Centres: from the Early Middle Ages to the Twentieth Century* (Glasgow: Cruithne Press, 1998), pp. 100–31, pp. 112–13.

73. M. Lynch, G. DesBrisay and M. Pittock, 'The Faith of the People', in Dennison, Ditchburn and Lynch (eds), *Aberdeen before 1800*, p. 293.

74. On the impact of the Reformation in Aberdeen see for example B. McLennan, 'The Reformation in the Burgh of Aberdeen', *Northern Scotland*, 2:2 (1976–7), pp. 119–44; A. White, 'The Impact of the Reformation on a Burgh Community: The Case of Aberdeen', in M. Lynch (ed.), *The Early Modern Town in Scotland* (London: Croom Helm, 1987), pp. 81–101; M. Graham, *Uses of Reform*, esp. pp. 49–64, 114–25.

75. For a discussion of the kirk session's attitude towards such practices see M. Graham, *Uses of Reform*, pp. 118–19.

76. Ibid., p. 114. The Cullens, Forbes, Grays, Knowles, Chalmers, Rutherfords and Middletons all found spots on the session.
77. B. McLennan, 'The Reformation in the Burgh of Aberdeen,' p. 138.
78. A. White, 'The Menzies Era: Sixteenth-Century Politics', in Dennison, Ditchburn and Lynch (eds), *Aberdeen Before 1800*, p. 233.
79. ACA, CR, xxi, 539 (27 October 1553).
80. See M. Graham, *Uses of Reform*; M. H. B. Sanderson, *Ayrshire and the Reformation*.
81. I. Flett and J. Cripps, 'Documentary Sources', in M. Lynch, M. Spearman and G. Stell (eds), *The Scottish Medieval Town* (Edinburgh: John Donald Publishers Ltd., 1988), p. 25.
82. Community issues such as the 'remedy of lawborrows' and setting caution and surety, in other words vouching for your neighbour's return to good behaviour, also shine through in the accounts found in the Council Register.
83. This statistic is based on the forty-eight incidents where town officials were the specific target of physical or verbal violence out of a total of 1,234 cases of misconduct found in the Council Register and Baillie Court Books between 1541 and 1592. In terms of status, kin relationship is included in this category where the individual's socio-economic background is missing, but where the records specifically mention their connection to another individual within the burgh based on marriage and consanguinity. There are also a number of recorded violent and non-violent acts perpetrated against officers or the town (including the magistrate) during each decade under consideration. As such, it needs to be determined to what extent, if any, this represented a concerted response to authority and shifts in attitude toward social regulation. For example, in April of 1598 a certain Baxter was convicted of 'usurping the office of the magistrates of this burgh', and his unlaw (penalty) modified to £3.6s.8d., ACA *Guildry Accounts*, 26 April 1598; likewise, James Martyn was convicted for 'mispersoning' of one of the officers of the town 'with a quhingar', and his unlaw also modified to £3.6s.8d., ACA *Guildry Accounts*, 19 May 1599.
84. ACA, Baillie Court Books, 1 1572–6; 1 7 April 1581–28 September 1582; 1 10 February 1585–2 September 1587; 1 18 November 1594–23 September 1595; 1 21 June 1596–September 1597.
85. ACA, Guildry Accounts, 1581–4, 1587, 1594–1603.
86. NAS CH2/448/1. 1562, 1568, 1573–77.
87. See Braddick and Walter (eds), *Negotiating Power in Early Modern Society*, p. 6; J. Scott, *The Moral Economy of the Peasant: Rebellion and Subsistence in Southeast Asia* (New Haven, CT: Yale University Press, 1976).
88. Any quantitative analysis of crime and punishment during this period requires strong statistical evidence including definitive population accounts. While hearth taxes provide a decent overview, the problems with using such evidence for this type of research are numerous. As such, numerical references are used sparingly and only when a conclusive assessment can be provided.
89. The most conclusive analysis to come from using this program is that for the most part Aberdeen clerks very infrequently recorded the status or occupation of those individuals convicted of wronging their neighbour.
90. For a fuller discussion of how the incidents of recorded crimes were quantified see ch. 3 and 4.
91. These ideas are considered in the collection edited by M. Braddick and J. Walter, *Negotiating Power in Early Modern Society*. In particular, see S. Hindle's 'Exhortation and Entitlement: Negotiating Social Inequality in English Rural Communities, 1550–1650', pp. 102–22; R. Gillespie, 'Negotiating Order in Early Seventeenth-Century Ireland', pp. 188–205.

92. In 1546 the baillies ordered Thom Moidart to pay the Dean of Guild 20*s* for inviting a potential threat into the community by 'housing strangearis', ACA, CR vol. xix, 212 (13 September 1546). A similar concern over misbehaviour bringing 'the Ire and wraith of God vpone the pepill heirfoir' can be found in an Act of Parliament of 1551 concerning blasphemy. Interestingly enough, 'oaths sworn' against other individuals fell under both civil and spiritual jurisdiction. *APS*, 2, p. 485.

93. On similar processes see the essays in A. Shepard and P. Withington (eds), *Communities in Early Modern England*; S. Amussen, *An Ordered Society*; P. Griffiths, *Youth and Authority*; S. Hindle, 'Custom, Festival and Protest in Early Modern England: The Little Budworth Wakes, St Peter's Day, 1596', *Rural History*, 6:2 (1995), pp. 155–78; C. Muldrew, 'The Culture of Reconciliation: Community and the Settlement of Economic Disputes in Early Modern England', *Historical Journal*, 39:4 (1996), pp. 915–42; G. Walker, 'Women, Theft and the World of Stolen Goods', in J. Kermode and G. Walker (eds), *Women, Crime and the Courts in Early Modern England* (London: University College London, 1994), pp. 81–105.

94. M. Meyerson, D. Thiery and O. Falk. (eds), *'A Great Effusion of Blood'? Interpreting Medieval Violence* (Toronto: University of Toronto Press, 2004), p. 6.

95. Amussen argued that 'violence was understood as part of a strategy to impose one's beliefs or perceptions on another, to claim authority, power, or rights that would not otherwise be accorded one.' S. Amussen, 'Punishment, Discipline and Power', p. 31.

96. For example, in April of 1598 a certain Baxter was convicted of 'usurping the office of the magistrates of this burgh', his unlaw modified to £3.6*s*.8*d*. ACA Guildry Accounts, 26 April 1598; Likewise, James Martyn was convicted for 'mispersoning' of one of the officers of the town 'with a quhingar' his unlaw also modified to £3.6*s*.8*d*. ACA Guildry Accounts, (19 May 1599).

1 Crime, Community and Belonging

1. P. Slack, *From Reformation to Improvement,* p. 6

2. R. A. Mason, *Kingship and the Commonweal: Political Thought in Renaissance and Reformation Scotland* (East Linton: Tuckwell Press, 1998). Mason argues that 'sixteenth-century Scots tended to use *commonweal* and *commonwealth* interchangeably: both could mean either the common good or with increasing frequency as the century wore on, the community whose welfare was at issue', p. 1. See also R. Mason, 'Covenant and Commonweal: The Language of Politics in Reformation Scotland,' in N. MacDougall (ed.) *Church, Politics and Society: Scotland 1408–1929* (Edinburgh: John Donald Publishers, 1983), pp. 97–126.

3. ACA, MSS Baillie Court Records, 1 (25 July 1575)

4. Marjorie McIntosh has argued that in England 'private suits, regardless of the venue in which they were heard, were primarily a reflection of the individual concerns of the parties, [and] not necessarily focussed upon the well-being of the community as a whole'. See M. McIntosh, *Controlling Misbehaviour in England, 1370–1600* (Cambridge: Cambridge University Press, 1998), p. 27.

5. For example, Lynch, *Edinburgh and the Reformation*; Lynch, 'Urbanisation and Urban Networks in Seventeenth Century Scotland'; E. P. D. Torrie, *Medieval Dundee*; E. P. Dennison, 'Power to the People?'; M. Verschuur, 'Merchants and Craftsmen in Sixteenth-Century Perth' in M. Lynch (ed.) *The Early Modern Town in Scotland*, pp. 36–54.

6. See Introduction on pp. 8–9; also I. Whyte, *Scotland before the Industrial Revolution: An Economic and Social History, c. 1050–c.1750* (Harlow, Essex: Longman, 1995), p. 193.
7. Elizabeth Ewan demonstrates this effectively for Scotland in her study of townlife in the fourteenth century. See especially her chapter on 'the community' in *Townlife in Fourteenth-Century Scotland*, pp. 136–60; see also M. Lynch, *Edinburgh in the Reformation*, esp. chap. 3 'The Burgh Church', pp. 26–48.
8. R. Shoemaker, *Prosecution and Punishment*; K. Jones, *Gender and Petty Crime*; J. Hurl-Eamon, *Gender and Petty Violence in London, 1680–1720* (Ohio: Ohio State University Press, 2005).
9. See above, p. 157, n. 7.
10. A few select studies of French and English urban centres include D. Parker, *La Rochelle and the French Monarch: Conflict and Order in 17th Century France* (London: Royal Historical Society, 1980); K. Robbins, *City on the Ocean Sea: La Rochelle, 1530–1650: Urban Society, Religion, and Politics on the French Atlantic Frontier* ((New York: E. J. Brill, 1997); P. Roberts, *City in Conflict: Troyes during the French Wars of Religion* (Manchester: Manchester University Press, 1996); Wrightson and Levine, *Poverty and Piety in an English Village*; P. J. Corfield 'East Anglia', in P. Clark (ed.), *The Cambridge Urban History of Britain* (Cambridge: Cambridge University Press, 2000), pp. 31–48. For Scotland see Lynch, *Edinburgh and the Reformation*; Dennison, Ditchburn and Lynch (eds), *Aberdeen Before 1800*; Torrie, *Medieval Dundee*; Sanderson, *Ayrshire and the Reformation*.
11. See for example Brown, *Bloodfeud in Scotland*; Brown and Ferguson, *Twisted Sisters*; E. Ewan, 'Many Injurious Words'; E. Ewan, 'There was nae Justice to be got in this Tolbooth': Insults against Officials in Sixteenth-Century Scottish Towns' (paper presented at the Sixteenth-Century Studies Conference, Toronto, Ontario, 29–31 October 2004); M. Graham, *Uses of Reform*; M. Graham, 'The Civil Sword and the Scottish Kirk in the Late Sixteenth Century', in W. Fred Graham (ed.) *Later Calvinism: International Perspectives* (Kirksville: Sixteenth Century Publishers, 1994), pp. 237–48; M. Todd, *Culture of Protestantism*.
12. For an overview of pre-modern Scottish burghs see Falconer, 'Surveying Scotland's Urban Past: The Pre-Modern Burgh,' *History Compass*, 9:1 (2011), pp. 34–44.
13. M. Lynch, 'What Ever Happened to the Medieval Burgh? Some Guidelines for Sixteenth and Seventeenth Century Historians', *Scottish Economic and Social History*, 4 (1984), pp. 5–20; E. Ewan, 'The Community of the Burgh in the Fourteenth Century', in M. Lynch, M. Spearman and G. Stell (eds), *The Scottish Medieval Town* (Edinburgh: John Donald, 1988), pp. 32–45; E. Ewan, *Townlife in Fourteenth-Century Scotland*; M. Lynch, (ed.), *The Early Modern Town in Scotland*; I. D. Whyte, 'Urbanisation in Early-Modern Scotland: A Preliminary Analysis', in *Scottish Economic and Social History*, 9 (1989), pp. 21–37; I. D. Whyte, *Scotland Before the Industrial Revolution: An Economic and Social History, c. 1050–c. 1750* (Harlow, Essex, 1995); Sanderson, *Ayrshire and the Reformation*; E. P. Dennison, 'Recreating the Urban Past', in T. Brotherstone and D. Ditchburn, (eds), *Freedom and Authority, Scotland c. 1050–c. 1650: Historical and Historiographical Essays presented to Grant G. Simpson.* (East Linton: Tuckwell Press, 2000), pp. 275–84.
14. M. Lynch, 'What Ever Happened to the Medieval Burgh?', p. 14.
15. Torrie, *Medieval Dundee*, pp. 34–5.
16. J. Thomas, 'The Craftsmen of Elgin, 1540–1660' in Brotherstone and Ditchburn, (eds), *Freedom and Authority, Scotland c. 1050– c. 1650*, pp. 143–54.
17. Ewan, *Townlife in Fourteenth-Century Scotland*, pp. 136–60.

18. Ewan, *Townlife in Fourteenth-Century Scotland* , pp. 1–4; Gibson and Smout, *Prices, Food and Wages in Scotland*, p. 23; Falconer, 'Surveying Scotland's Urban Past', p. 34–44.
19. Hereafter 'Aberdeen' refers to the royal burgh of Aberdeen or New Aberdeen. Any examples taken from Old Aberdeen will make explicit mention of that town.
20. *Abredoniae vtrivsque descriptio: A description of both touns of Aberdeen*, eds. C. Innes and J. Gordon (Edinburgh: Spalding Club, 1842), p. 3.
21. Ibid.
22. David Walker has demonstrated that 'burgesses were entitled not to be brought before a court of the king, lord or regality, baron or even another burgh, and if indicted, attached and presented in court were entitled to plead the freedom of their burgh and be granted it.' Walker, *A Legal History of Scotland, vol. 3*, p. 335.
23. E. P. Dennison, A. Simpson and G. Simpson, 'The Growth of Two Towns', in Dennison, Ditchburn and Lynch (eds), *Aberdeen Before 1800*, pp. 13–43, on p. 18.
24. James V had provided the burgh with a license to erect 'fortalices, ditches and munitions' for the protection of the town and its inhabitants. Ibid., p. 21; *Abdn. Coun.*, vol. 1 (20 July 1529), p. 123.
25. Gibson and Smout argued, 'the burgh was a restricted trading community founded upon a monopolistic control of trade, but its privileges were to be enjoyed in common by all who had a right to them.' Gibson and Smout, *Prices, Food and Wages in Scotland*, p. 23; E. P. D. Torrie also singled out 'the market as the hub of the burgh; the location of the tron, the tolbooth, the mercat cross as the secular focal points of burghal life'. Torrie, *Medieval Dundee*, pp. 34–6.
26. Aberdeen's tolbooth was first erected in the early fifteenth century, 'when each man was required to give a day's labour or pay 4*d* towards its construction'. It was here that those seeking to access the market paid their dues, where town officials stored the town weights. E. P. Dennison, A. Simpson and G. Simpson, 'The Growth of Two Towns', p. 19.
27. Gordon, *Abredoniae vtrivsque descriptio*, p. 4.
28. W. Kennedy, *Annals of Aberdeen From the Reign of King William the Lion to the End of the Year 1818; With an Account of the City, Cathedral, and University of Old Aberdeen* (London: A. Brown & Co., 1818) (hereafter *Annals*), p. 112.
29. A. Keith, *A Thousand Years of Aberdeen* (Aberdeen: Aberdeen University Press, 1972), p. 148.
30. Perhaps indicative of the 'conservative approach to religion', it took fourteen years from the establishment of the Reformed kirk in Aberdeen for the removal of the stained glass and organ from the parish kirk of St Nicholas and the destruction of the choir stalls. It is likely that this came about only after the very Protestant-minded Regent, the Earl Morton, paid the town a visit in 1574. On this subject see A. White, 'The Menzies Era', p. 233.
31. A. M. Munro, *Memorials of the Aldermen, Provosts, and Lord Provosts of Aberdeen, 1272–1895* (Aberdeen: Spalding Club, 1897), p. 96.
32. Ibid.
33. This became rather acute when, in the middle of the sixteenth century, the fourth Earl of Huntly became provost of the burgh (1545–46).
34. The Gordon Earls of Huntly have not yet been the subject of any full-length study. However, Alan White's doctoral thesis considers this family in some detail. See A. White, 'Religion, Politics and Society in Aberdeen, 1543–1593' (University of Edinburgh, unpublished PhD thesis, 1985).
35. On this subject see A. White, 'Queen Mary's Northern Province' in M. Lynch (ed.), *Mary Stewart Queen in Three Kingdoms* (Oxford: B. Blackwell, 1988), pp. 53–70; J.

Wormald, *Mary Queen of Scots: Politics, Passion and a Kingdom Lost* (London: Tauris, 2001), pp. 124–48.

36. ACA, CR, xxviii, 22 (2 September 1574); *Abdn. Counc.*, vol. 2, pp. 11–19, on p. 19.

37. *Abdn. Counc.,* vol. 2 (2 September 1574), p. 17.

38. On the role of the Gordon Earls of Huntly in the civil unrest within the kingdom during this period see *Annals,* pp. 116–20; J. Wormald, *Mary Queen of Scots,* pp. 124–25; A. White, 'Queen Mary's Northern Province', pp. 53–70.

39. *Abdn. Counc.,* vol. 2, p. 17.

40. See M. Lynch and H. Dingwall, 'Elite Society in Town and Country' in Dennison, Ditchburn and Lynch (eds), *Aberdeen Before 1800,* pp. 181–200, on p. 189.

41. *Abdn. Counc.,* vol. 1 (15 August 1543), p. 190.

42. *Abdn. Counc.,* vol. 1 (29 March 1545), p. 217.

43. Other landed families, such as the Forbes, Leslies and Keith Earls Marischal, involved themselves in the town's business and affected the political and social landscape at varying times throughout the sixteenth and seventeenth centuries. See Kennedy, *Annals,* pp. 79–109; Keith, *A Thousand Years of Aberdeen,* pp. 55–78. An Act of Parliament in 1535 statuted that landed men – earls, lords, barons – were not to 'molest' burgh magistrates in the execution of their offices, *APS,* 2, p. 349, c. 36.

44. ACA MSS Guildry Accounts (no numbers) (9 May 1582). This most likely reflected the town's need to increase revenue in the 1570s and 1580s.

45. *Abdn. Counc.,* vol. 2 (4 October 1572), p. 7.

46. On this subject see Munro, *Memorials.* Here is a list of Menzies provosts in the sixteenth century: Alexander Menzies (1501–3), Gilbert Menzies of Findon (1505, 1507–13, 1516–20, 1522–4), Thomas Menzies of Pitfoddels (1525), Gilbert Menzies of Findon (1526–32), Thomas Menzies of Pitfoddels (1533–4), Gilbert Menzies of Findon (1536), Thomas Menzies of Pitfoddels (1537–44, 1547–75), Gilbert Menzies of Cowlie and Pitfoddels (1576–87), Thomas Menzies of Kirkhill and Durn (1588–9), Thomas Menzies of Durn and Cults (1592), Sir Thomas Menzies of Cults (1595).

47. R. Tyson, 'People in the Two Towns', in Dennison, Ditchburn and Lynch (eds), *Aberdeen Before 1800,* pp. 111–28, on p. 111. Michael Lynch has estimated that the population in Aberdeen in 1639 could have been as high as 10,000 people. See. M. Lynch, 'Urbanisation and Urban Networks in Seventeenth Century Scotland', pp. 25–6.

48. Tyson, 'People in the Two Towns', p. 112.

49. See G. Stell, 'Housing in the Two Towns', in Dennison, Ditchburn and Lynch (eds) *Aberdeen Before 1800,* pp. 97–108, esp. p. 108.

50. *Abdn. Counc.,* vol. 1, p. 315.

51. *Abdn. Counc.,* vol. 2, p. 49; See also Ewan, *Townlife,* p. 142, where she argues that the guild was a 'community within a community'.

52. *Abdn. Counc.,* vol. 2, p. 66. It is possible that the account could be read as a burgess who is also an indweller. This raises the important element of residency as a requirement of burgess-ship. Such requirements also speak to the mechanisms at work for inclusion in the community.

53. Ian Whyte offers the most concise description of this in his *Scotland Before the Industrial Revolution,* p. 202. In Aberdeen, the criteria for non-native born inhabitants were that they had lived there for at least seven years, or had at least one parent who had been born in the town.

54. *APS,* 3, (1567), p. 38; *APS,* 3, (1574), p. 86; *Abdn. Counc.,* vol. 1, (17 October 1549, 23 January 1565) pp. 273, 358; *Abdn. Counc.,* vol. 2, (15 November 1574) pp. 20–1.

55. Lynch and Dingwall, 'Elite Society in Town and Country', p. 185.
56. A. White, 'Religion, Politics and Society in Aberdeen', pp. 327–29.
57. The Hammermen craft included cutlers, saddlers, goldsmiths, blacksmiths, tinsmiths and watchmakers. See Tyson, 'People in the Two Towns', pp. 121–22.
58. R. Tyson, 'People in the Two Towns', p. 122; I. Whyte, *Scotland Before the Industrial Revolution*, p. 201. Whyte argues that two-thirds of the population were unfree; this designation included both the labouring poor and some professional men who had not formed associations with the guildry. See also D. M. Walker, *Legal History of Scotland*, p, 329.
59. I. Whyte, *Scotland Before the Industrial Revolution*, p. 202.
60. Ibid. Torrie argued against the characterizations that urban historians make about medieval burghs as solely 'self-regulating municipal units, an entrepot and market, or a growing townscape', see *Medieval Dundee*, pp. 34–6.
61. Ibid.
62. On this subject see M. Lynch, 'What Ever Happened to the Medieval Burgh?', pp. 5–20; M. Lynch, *Edinburgh and the Reformation*, esp. pp. 2–66; M. Lynch, 'The Crown and the Burghs 1500–1625', in Lynch (ed.), *The Early Modern Town in Scotland*, pp. 55–80; M. Verschuur, 'Merchants and Craftsmen in Sixteenth-Century Perth', in Lynch (ed.), *The Early Modern Town in Scotland*, pp. 36–54; A. White, 'The Impact of the Reformation on a Burgh Community'.
63. Barbara Diefendorf makes an excellent case for the existence of multiple corporate identities in sixteenth-century Paris. B. Diefendorf, *Beneath the Cross: Catholics and Huguenots in Sixteenth-century Paris* (Oxford: Oxford University Press, 1991).
64. *Leges Burgorum*, c. 70.
65. Balfour, *Practicks*, p. 42. Balfour cites the *Leges Burgorum*, c. 74 and *Statuta Gilde*, c. 54 as his sources.
66. *The Acts of the Parliaments of Scotland*, T. Thomson and C. Innes (eds), 12 vols (Edinburgh, 1814–75) (Hereafter *APS*), vol. 3, Acta, 21.
67. Ibid.
68. *Leges Burgorum*, c. 40; *Statuta Gilde*, c. 17. Burgesses agreed to attend each court in the oath sworn on the day they gained their freedom.
69. *APS*, 2, p. 244.
70. On the role of the burgh provost see Ewan, *Townlife in Fourteenth-Century Scotland*, pp. 42–3; Dennison, 'Power to the People?', pp. 102–3; Whyte, *Scotland before the Industrial Revolution*, p. 67–9.
71. On the subject of Pope Gelasius I's two sword or 'dualist' theory which argued that the two governments of *sacerdotium* and *regnum*, each with distinct and separate powers, were the spiritual and the temporal arms of a single Christian commonwealth, see A. Black, *Political Thought in Europe 1250–1450* (Cambridge: Cambridge University Press, 1993), pp. 44–5. A much older, but still useful guide to this subject is R. W. Carlyle and A. J. Carlyle, *A History of Mediaeval Political Theory in the West* (Edinburgh: William Blackwood & Sons, Ltd., 1922) vol. 4, pp. 384–95.
72. White, 'Religion, Politics and Society in Aberdeen, 1543–1593'; White, 'The Menzies Era'.
73. White, 'The Menzies Era', pp. 229–30.
74. A. White, 'The Impact of the Reformation on a Burgh Community', p. 82. Steve Hindle has made a similar claim for early modern English locales. Hindle argued that by the early modern period even though the 'meaning of community narrowed ... The recasting of the community, then, implied that traditional values of solidarity and reciprocity

remained, and perhaps even thrived, but in more socially restricted ways.' S. Hindle, 'A Sense of Place? Becoming and Belonging in the Rural Parish, 1550–1650', in Shepard and Withington (eds), *Communities in Early Modern England*, p. 98.

75. See E. Ewan, 'The Community of the Burgh in the Fourteenth Century', in Lynch (ed.), *The Scottish Medieval Town*; Ewan, *Townlife*; Dennison, 'Power to the People?'; Walker, *A Legal History of Scotland*, vol. 3, pp. 324–41.

76. *APS*, 2, p. 349. This Act also lays out the justification for enabling only substantial merchants who made residence within the burgh to hold office: 'Item because all our souerane lordis burrowis are putt to pouertie waistit and distroyit in their gudis and policy and almaist Ruynous throw falt of vsing of merchandice And that throw being of outland men provest ballies and aldermen within burt for thare awine particular wele In consuming of the comoun gudis of burrowis gratit to thame be our souerane lord and his predecessouris kingis of Scotland for the vphald of honeste and policy within burcht.'

77. For a good evaluation of the push for greater enfranchisement by craftsmen in a Scottish burgh see M. Verschuur, 'Merchants and Craftsmen in Sixteenth-century Perth'.

78. This is the subject of ch. 5, pp. 127–48.

79. See Walker, *A Legal History of Scotland*, p. 331 for discussion of this Act of Parliament; see also the discussion of the history behind interference within the burgh by 'outmen' in Munro, *Memorials of the Aldermen, Provosts and Lord Provosts of Aberdeen*, pp. 95–8.

80. Hindle suggests that 'since an infinite community is by definition a contradiction in terms, community necessarily implies exclusion'. Hindle, 'A Sense of Place?', p. 97; Hindle, *On the Parish? The Micro-Politics of Poor Relief in Rural England, c. 1550–1750* (Oxford: Oxford University Press, 2004), esp. ch, 5, 'Exclusion'.

81. On the subject of the multifarious nature of early modern identities see R. Connors and J. R. D. Falconer, 'Cornering the Cheshire Cat: Reflections on the "New British History" and Studies in Early Modern British Identities', *Canadian Journal of History*, 36 (April 2001), pp. 85–108.

82. On this see E. P. Dennison, 'Power to the People?', p. 102.

83. This compared to three individuals banished for acts of physical violence out of 355 cases and three individuals banished for acts of verbal crime out of 339 cases. Another individual was banished for disobeying the magistrate, another for being an unlawful neighbour, and a group of four individuals for regrating and forestalling.

84. ACA, CR, xxviii, 46 (26 June 1573).

85. M. Todd, *Culture of Protestantism*, pp. 133–34; E. Ewan, '"Tongue You Lied"', pp. 115–36.

86. ACA, CR, xxvii, 174 (24 October 1569).

87. APS, 3, 461, c. 59. See also Walker, *A Legal History*, p. 489. There is no indication why Durrant escaped the govis, the scourging and the banishment. A much later statute, perhaps legislating what was already custom in most parts of Scotland, states that resetters were to be tried only after the 'principal theif' had been convicted. It is possible that the authorities considered Forest the principal thief and therefore Durrant escaped with only a fine.

88. Graham, *Uses of Reform*, p. 43.

89. Foucault, *Discipline and Punish*, p. 48.

90. ACA Baillie Court Book, 1 (21 May 1581). The account continues by stating that the punishment conformed: 'to the act and ordinans made thereupon the quhilk ordains the said Jonet to obey and fulfil the hours here forsaid in presens of Robert Menzies and Gilbert Gray twa of the Baillies of the said burght being personally p[rese]nt at the mercat croce for the tym and the said Alex personally p[rese]nt and requyrit to accept the said amends.'

91. In a slightly different context Barbara Myeroff demonstrates the importance of separation and reintegration in ritual performance. See B. Myeroff, 'Rites of Passage: Process and Paradox', pp. 109–35; M. Todd, *Culture of Protestantism*, p. 130.
92. ACA, CR, xxvi, 91 (11 February 1565/6).
93. ACA, CR, xxvii, 22 (Ultimo March 1569).
94. It may be that the clerks kept a separate register for theft convictions that is no longer extant. There are, however, no references or indication that this was the case. A cursory examination of the Sheriff Court records does not yield any reference to the Stewarts.
95. See the legislation against petty thefts in APS, 3, 461.
96. For instance, ACA, CR, xix, 314 (28 March 1547), ACA, CR, xxvi, 208 (30 August 1566), ACA, CR, xxix, 32 (9 November 1576), ACA Baillie Court Books 1–2 (15 December 1581).
97. C. Herrup, 'The Law and Morality in Seventeenth-Century England', pp. 106–11.
98. ACA, CR, xxviii, 404 (25 February 1574/5).
99. ACA, CR, xviii, 226 (Pen July 1544); ACA, CR, xix, 395 (28 September 1547); ACA, CR, 192–3 (25 February 1548/9).
100. ACA, CR, xix, 395 (28 September 1547).
101. ACA, CR, xxiv, 520 (22 September 1562).
102. ACA, CR, xxvii, 328 (5 June 1570). It is uncertain whether this is the same Alex Burnett or possibly a son. In all appearances of Alex Burnett in the Register his occupation as a potter appears beside his name.
103. This of course may be a problem of extent sources or contemporary record keeping. See ch. 4, p. 103.
104. ACA, CR, xix, 314 (28 March 1547).
105. ACA, xxxi, 560 (5 February 1584/5).
106. ACA, CR, xxiv, 479 (24 July 1562).
107. Ibid.
108. ACA, CR, xvii, 586 (17 September 1543).
109. ACA, CR, xxi, 562 (11 December 1553).
110. In 1546 and 1552 the burgh court convicted the 'wife of John Chalmer' of regrating and breaking town statutes respectively. Her name is not given. Instead, she appears as the 'wife of John Chalmer'. ACA, CR, xix, 252 (22 November 1546); ACA, CR, xxi, 259 (8 November 1552).
111. ACA, CR, xxii, 190 (6 November 1555).
112. The members of the assise convened to determine whether John Chalmer was guilty of mispersoning David Mar included Henry Forbes, John Dwne, James Litster, James Blak, Jerome Blak, James Leslie, Thomas Branche, Andrew Lawson, Alex Collison, master Patrick Rayford, Gilbert Brabnar, John Lawson, Alexander Howeson, John Cheyne, John Bruce, Alexander Scot and Robert Knollis. Forbes, Dwne, Litster, Jerome and James Blak, Branche and Scot had previous convictions. Forbes had been convicted of strublens in January 1543/4 and June 1555, ACA, CR, xxi, 590 (21 January 1553/4); ACA, CR, xxii, 71 (10 June 1555). John Dwne was convicted of strubling the town in 1553, ACA, CR, xxi, 302 (16 January 1552/3). James Litster found himself before the burgh court in 1542 for the strublens of Thomas Philipson, ACA, CR, xvii, 176 (8 May 1542). James Blak was convicted of strubling Marjorie Gray in August 1544, ACA, CR, xviii, 239–40 (24 August 1544). Thomas Branche broke town statutes by buying goods in great quantity and selling them at higher than statuted prices in 1552, ACA, CR, xxi,

228 (6 October 1552). Alexander Scot was convicted of strublens in 1544, ACA, CR, xviii, 252 (14 September 1544).

113. ACA, CR, xxix, 122 (23 February 1576/7); ACA, CR, xxxi, 104 (15 March 1582). Elspett Chalmer also appears in the Council Register as the victim of Agnes Chalmer's mispersoning and injuring, ACA, CR, xxix, 123 (23 February 1576/7). As tempting as it may be to see a connection between John Chalmer and the Elseptt Chalmer married to Howeson, there is no evidence to support such a connection.

114. See M. Todd, *Culture of Protestantism*, pp. 129–30.

115. ACA, CR, xvii, 16 (24 October 1541).

116. ACA, CR, xviii, 17 (12 November 1543).

117. It is possible that the court had convicted them for some fault prior to 1541 when this study begins.

118. ACA, CR, xviii, 128 (22 March 1543/4); ACA, CR, xix, 474 (12 February 1547/8).

119. ACA, CR, xxi, 73 (2 November 1551).

120. ACA, CR, xxii, 120 (9 August 1555).

121. ACA, CR, xxii, 571 (28 June 1557).

122. ACA, CR, xxii, 120 (9 August 1555) (my emphasis).

123. A tailor named Ambrose Littlejohn found himself before the baillies in March and May of 1552 for strublens and 'blud drawing' of James Wat and James Nicholson respectively. In both cases he was put in amercement of court and there is no indication that the baillies modified his unlaw. Littlejohn appears again in the Council Register in 1551 after breaking the 'glass' windows of James Walker. The baillies ordered Littlejohn to mend the windows 'and mak them as good as thai war within xlviii houris' and to pay 8*s* for the baillies' unlaw and to 'abstane fra siclyk' under the threat of 40*s*. See ACR vol. 17, 141 (27 March 1542), ACR vol. 17, 187 (24 May 1542) for Littlejohn's convictions for strublens and blud drawing; ACA, CR, xx, 570 (29 May 1551) for his conviction for breaking Walker's window.

124. While a number of modifications appear in the Council Register, more frequently these were recorded by the dean of guild in the guildry accounts. Unfortunately, these records are incomplete with only fragmentary evidence surviving for the period under consideration. These records, ACA MSS Guildry Accounts, are extant for the period 1581–4, 1587 and 1594–1603. They do exist in fragmentary form for the earlier period.

2 Godly Discipline

1. See p. 157, n. 7.

2. P. Collinson, *From Iconoclasm to Iconophobia: The Cultural Impact of the Second English Reformation*, p. 6; see also Collinson, *The Birthpangs of Protestant England: Religious and Cultural Change in the Sixteenth and Seventeenth Centuries*; Collinson, *Godly People: Essays on English Protestantism and Puritanism*.

3. K. Wrightson and D. Levine, *Poverty and Piety in an English Village*, p. 197–211.

4. M. Spufford, 'Puritanism and Social Control?', p. 43, 57; see also M. McIntosh, *Autonomy and Community: The Royal Manor of Havering, 1200–1500* (Cambridge: Cambridge University Press, 1986); McIntosh, *Controlling Misbehaviour in England*.

5. M. Graham, *Uses of Reform*, p. 1.

6. K. Wrightson, 'Postscript: Terling Revisited', in Wrightson and Levine, *Poverty and Piety in an English Village*, p. 203; See also M. Graham, *Uses of Reform; M. Todd, A Culture of Protestantism*; M. Todd, 'Profane Pastimes and the Reformed Community'.

7. This is the thrust of Spufford's argument. Wrightson, conversely, suggests that Spufford entirely missed the point. See K. Wrightson, 'Postscript', in Wrightson and Levine, *Poverty and Piety in an English Village*, pp. 198–201.
8. NAS CH2/448/1, 5, 8.
9. S. Hindle, 'A Sense of Place?', pp. 96–114.
10. Balfour in particular focused more on criminal procedure, offering very little insight into the types and variations of criminal activities and even less on societal concerns over the impact such behaviour had on the community. See Walker, *The Scottish Jurists* (Edinburgh: W. Green, 1985), pp. 33–80; McNeill (ed.), *The Practicks of Sir James Balfour of Pittendreich*, pp. xlii, xlviii.
11. Walker, *The Scottish Jurists*, pp. 21–2, 41. All three suffered considerable criticism by contemporaries and modern commentators alike. For example, John Knox referred to Balfour as a 'blasphemer' while Balfour's adeptness at switching sides in the fierce political battles that embroiled the realm in the middle of the sixteenth century earned him the enmity of Mary, Queen of Scots and those closest to her.
12. *APS*, 3, pp. 3, c. 46. See also McNeill (ed.), *The Practicks of Sir James Balfour of Pittendreich*, pp. xlii–xliii.
13. Quoted in Walker, *The Scottish Jurists*, p. 60.
14. Skene's categories included capital crimes, corporal crimes and pecunial crimes. For discussion of this treatise see Walker, *The Scottish Jurists*, p. 73.
15. In the sixteenth century the Aberdonian lawyer and 'minor jurist' William Hay argued that adultery, perceived as sinful wrongdoing, should be punished according to statute. See J. C. Barry (ed.), *William Hay's Lectures on Marriage* (Edinburgh: Stair Society, 1967), pp. 57–61.
16. S. Hindle, *The State and Social Change*, pp. 139–40.
17. Quoted in Ibid., p. 139.
18. Ibid., p. 140. Whitelock posited three types of criminal activity: '*onus sacramenti, onus civilus officii*, and *onus providential*'.
19. M. Graham, *Uses of Reform*, pp. 45–6.
20. Sharpe, 'The History of Crime', pp. 188, 201. See also C. Herrup, 'Crime, Law and Society: A Review Article', *Society for Comparative Study of Society and History*, 27:1 (January 1985), pp. 159–70, on pp. 162–163; J. Brundage 'Sin, Crime and the Pleasures of the Flesh: The Medieval Church Judges Sexual Offences', in P. Linehan and J. L. Nelson (eds), *The Medieval World* (London and New York: Routledge, 2001), pp. 294–307, esp. pp. 294–98; H. Schilling, '"History of Crime" or "History of Sin"?', pp. 289–310.
21. Quoted in Graham, *Uses of Reform*, p. 41.
22. See also M. Todd, *Culture of Protestantism*; M. H. B Sanderson, *Ayrshire and the Reformation*.
23. NAS CH2/448/1, 1 (my emphasis).
24. NAS CH2/448/1, 4.
25. Apart from similarity in language, what is perhaps most interesting is the overlap in terms of the statutes emanating from the kirk session and those promulgated by secular authorities. For instance, the St Nicholas Kirk Session outlined penalties for those convicted of blaspheming, nightwalking, vagrancy, petty theft, slaughter, blood drawing, slander and 'iniurious and evill speche' as well as those offences more frequently associated with the Church, adultery, fornication, irregular marriage, breach of the Sabbath, drunkenness, gaming, and Papistry. NAS CH2/448/1, 1–13.
26. *APS*, 2, p. 485.

27. M. Graham, *Uses of Reform.*
28. NAS CH2/448/1, 3.
29. *APS,* 2, p. 486.
30. *APS,* 2, p. 486. On this subject see J. Goodare, *State and Society in Early Modern Scotland,* pp. 172–88.
31. NAS CH2/448/1, 14.
32. Ibid.
33. For the statute against adultery promulgated by the St Nicholas Kirk Session, see NAS CH2/448/1, pp. 5–6. This statute prescribed death for those convicted of this crime, though it acknowledged that 'because the assemblie and magistrat of this town had na power to punish the samyn be dethe for the provost hes not resavit God's law' that the punishment would be commuted to forgiveness for the first offence, carting and dunking for the second and banishment for the third.
34. See the many examples offered in ch. 3, 4 and 5, pp. 67–148.
35. NAS CH2/448/1, 79 (10 November 1575).
36. NAS CH2/448/1, 92 (24 May 1576).
37. For fornication with a member of the Menzies family, Arthur Chalmer was ordered to pay a fine of 53*s*.4*d*. 'befor he resave ony benefit of the kirk.' NAS CH2/448/1, 81 (24 November 1575).
38. In November 1575, the Kirk Session records note that 'Robert [Sederis] cowper & Margaret Lamb to pay 20s to the magistrate for the crym of fornication committed be hir who he is professit to marie' NAS CH2/448/1, 81 (24 Nov Sept 1575). Likewise, the session ordered Ado Young to pay 6*s*.4*d*. 'to the magistrat' for his fornication with Marion Clerk and to perform his 'repentans befor the banns of matrimony completit.' NAS CH2/448/1, 88 (23 February 1575/6).
39. See M. Graham, *Uses of Reform,* pp. 42–3; M. Todd, *Culture of Protestantism,* pp. 132–34.
40. NAS CH2/448/1, 6.
41. NAS CH2/448/1, 110 (7 March 1576/7).
42. Ibid.
43. For a discussion of the Menzies family, pre-eminent in terms of their secure hold on positions of power in Aberdeen throughout this period, see A. White, 'The Menzies Era', pp. 224–37; A. White, 'The Reformation in Aberdeen', in J. Smith (ed.), *New Light on Medieval Aberdeen* (Aberdeen: Aberdeen University Press, 1985), pp. 58–66; White, 'The Impact of the Reformation on a Burgh Community', pp. 81–101; White, 'Religion, Politics and Society in Aberdeen, 1543–1593'; Munro, *Memorialls of the Aldermen, Provosts and Lord Provosts of Aberdeen, 1357–1895*; H. Booton, 'Burgesses and Landed Men in North-East Scotland in the Later Middle Ages: A Study in Social Interaction' (PhD dissertation, University of Aberdeen, 1987); H. Booton, 'Economic and Social Change in Later Medieval Aberdeen', in Smith (ed.), *New Light on Medieval Aberdeen,* pp. 46–55.
44. This included the town provost Thomas Menzies. See NAS CH2/448/1, 34 (20 April 1574); NAS CH2/448/1, 46 (17 August 1574).
45. Michael Graham in his *Uses of Reform* has argued that Scotland during the Reformation period experienced 'social engineering on a societal scale', p. 2. This chapter seeks to redefine Graham's argument and the idea that the Kirk was in the main part responsible for such modification of behaviour.
46. ACA, CR, xxii, 275 (9 March 1555/6).
47. Ibid. The account notes that Forbes also agreed to 'oblyst him[self] to stand abyd & fulfill at his will & ordinance for the said offence'.

48. NAS CH2/448/1, 36 (4 May 1574).
49. NAS CH2/448/1, 73 (14 September 1575).
50. NAS CH2/448/1, 73 (15 September 1575).
51. ACA, CR, xxvii, 516 (Ultimo April 1571).
52. The magistrates often put individuals convicted of various crimes in amercement of court with the acknowledgement that they would at some specified time determine and decree, or in contemporary parlance 'modify', the nature and extent of the penalties to be imposed.
53. ACA, CR, xxvii, 527 (18 May 1571).
54. ACA, CR, xxvii, 701 (23 May 1572).
55. Both Michael Graham and Margo Todd focus largely on the Kirk's role in regulating social behaviour following the onset of the Reformation in Scotland. See in particular M. Graham, *Uses of Reform*; M. Graham, 'Equality before the Kirk? Church Discipline and the Elite in Reformation-era Scotland', *Archiv für Reformationsgeschichte*, 84 (1993), pp. 289–310. Graham does address the secular aspect from a largely theoretical perspective in Graham, 'The Civil Sword and the Scottish Kirk in the Late Sixteenth Century', pp. 237–48; M. Todd, *Culture of Protestantism*.
56. See ch. 3, pp. 75–84.
57. E. Ewan, 'Tongue you lied'.
58. On this see DesBrisay, Ewan and Diack, 'Life in the two towns', p. 52; M. Todd, *Culture of Protestantism*, pp. 133–37.
59. NAS CH2/448/1, 100 (14 October 1576).
60. NAS CH2/448/1, 84 (29 December 1575).
61. This could take place in the kirk, at the market cross or in the tolbooth. Occasionally, it took place where the incident occurred.
62. NAS CH2/448/1, 110 (7 March 1575/6).
63. NAS CH2/448/1, 1–10; M. Graham, *Uses of Reform*, p. 61.
64. NAS CH2/448/1, 5.
65. NAS CH2/448/1, 6–8.
66. NAS CH2/448/1, 6–7.
67. Ibid., 7.
68. ACA MSS Kirk and Bridge Works, 1571–1644. These accounts note monies received at the kirk door by members of the congregation used for the kirk's upkeep and for distribution to the poor members of the parish. The accounts specifically record the 'chargis beginnand at the resait of the silver collectit at the kirk duir eich Sunday as followis'. In October 1577, Alex Malyson, for example, gave 35s at the door. ACA MSS Kirk and Bridge Works, 21/22 (numbers improperly recorded at the top of each page – the first number indicates the number as recorded, the second corresponds to the actual page number). Unfortunately, this source does not provide any information on the recipients of the 'almonis' collected. See S. Hindle, 'Dependency, Shame and Belonging: Badging the Deserving Poor, *c.* 1550–1750', *Cultural and Social History*, 1:1 (January 2004), pp. 6–35.
69. *Abdn. Counc.*, vol. 1 (18 May 1546), p. 235.
70. NAS CH2/448/1, 75 (4 October 1575).
71. While Geoffrey Elton could not see how a sinful action such as adultery could equate to criminal activity, the Kirk Session made no such distinction when articulating that Robson was guilty of the '*crym of adultery*'.
72. NAS CH2/448/1, 74 (22 September 1575).
73. NAS CH2/448/1, 78 (27 October 1575).

74. NAS CH2/448/1, 87 (9 February 1575/6).
75. NAS CH2/448/1, 97 (26 September 1576).
76. If it is the case that the Kirk required Robson to appear more than once before the session and the congregation for a single incident then it says a great deal about the difference between seeking redemption from civic authorities and spiritual authorities. In most cases brought before the burgh court, the individual, once they had paid their fine or performed their penance for the council or baillies, was free to resume his or her daily activities without expecting to appear before the court again unless convicted of further wrongdoings. On the comparisons between burgh courts and the Kirk see S. J. Davies, 'The Courts and the Scottish Legal System 1600–1747: The Case of Stirlingshire', in Gattrell, Lenman and Parker (eds), *Crime and the Law,* pp. 120–55.
77. For example see B. McLennan, 'The Reformation in the Burgh of Aberdeen'; White, 'The Impact of the Reformation on a Burgh Community'.
78. This argument stands out in both McLennan, 'The Reformation in the Burgh of Aberdeen' and M. Graham, *Uses of Reform,* esp. pp. 49–64, 114–25.
79. ACA, CR, xx, 372 (Ultimo February 1549/50).
80. ACA, CR, xxiv, 551 (26 November 1562).
81. ACA, CR, xxiv, 546 (16 November 1562).
82. Ibid.
83. ACA, CR, xxviii, 714 (9 April 1576).
84. Ibid.
85. ACA MSS Baillie Court Book 1 (26 October 1581).
86. ACA MSS Baillie Court Book 1 (14 April 1581).
87. The percentage may have been greater, but the lack of details in a number of the conviction accounts make it difficult to determine whether more individuals convicted of such crimes were required to ask forgiveness of their victims.
88. See Ewan, 'Tongue you lied'.
89. ACA, CR, xxv, 489 (11 February 1564/5).
90. ACA, CR, xxv, 491 (11 February 1564/5). It is likely that the court did not intend his banishment to be perpetual.
91. According to Lythe, throughout the last half of the sixteenth century 'the supply of daily bread remained the insistent daily concern' for the majority of the population. See, S. G. E. Lythe, *The Economy of Scotland in its European Setting, 1550–1625* (Edinburgh: Oliver & Boyd, 1960), p.15.
92. Ibid., p. 15
93. Ibid., p. 16; *Register of the Privy Council of Scotland*, vol. 1 (Scotland: General Register House 1887) , p. 201. (Hereafter *RPCS*)
94. NAS, CH2/448/1, 37 (6 May 1574).
95. NAS CH2/448/1, 91 (10 May 1576).
96. ACA, CR, xxx, 194 (1 October 1580).
97. See ch. 3, pp. 75–84.
98. NAS CH2/448/1, 35, (29 April 1574); two days earlier Philipson had been accused of blaspheming the deacons and minister of the Kirk 'for the quhilk the bailze was desired to put him fast', CH2/448/1, 35, (27 April 1574) (my emphasis).
99. For a brief introduction to this subject see Walker, *A Legal History of Scotland. vol. 3,* p. 717.
100. For a similar discussion see M. R. Boes, 'Dishonourable Youth, Guilds, and the changed World view of Sex, Illegitimacy and Women in Late Sixteenth-century Germany' *Continuity and Change*, 18:3 (2003), pp. 345–72.

101. Ian Whyte argues that in the sixteenth century blood feuds gave way to 'pursuing one's neighbour at law', I. Whyte, *Scotland Before the Industrial Revolution*, p. 201. Unproven charges, unreported instances of wrongdoing, and problems with record-keeping make it impossible to identify the exact frequency with which individuals misbehaved within the community. However, the figures in Table 3.1 (p. 94) reveal that over five decades instances of misbehaviour waxed and waned at different rates.

102. D. M. Walker, *The Institutions of the Law of Scotland. Deduced from its Originals, and Collated with the Civil, Canon and Feudal Laws, and with the Customs of Neighbouring Nations. In IV Books by James, Viscount of Stair* (Edinburgh and Glasgow: University Press, 1981), p. 193.

103. G. B. Clarke, *The Remedy of Lawborrowis in Scots Law* (LLM dissertation, University of Edinburgh, 1984), p. 26.

104. ACA, CR, xxi, 656 (16 April 1554).

105. ACA, Baillie Court Book, 1 (23 September 1575).

106. Walker reports of an incident in the Fife Sheriff court in which a cautioner was refused because he 'wes nocht a landit man'. Walker, *Legal History of Scotland*. vol. 3, p. 717.

107. ACA CR, xxi, 200 (8 August 1551).

108. ACA, CR, xxvi, 191 (31 July 1566). David Mar was put in amercement of court because he had become suretie that Thomas Mar would not trouble the town in time to come, but had been recently convicted of the strublens of Maister Robert Chalmer. D. M. Walker, *The Institutions of the Law of Scotland*, pp. 193–4, 1046–47.

109. The *Dict. Of Scots. Lang.* defines lawborrow as a 'legal security given by one person that he will keep the peace towards another who can show reason for apprehending violence or mischief at his hands', surety as 'a bond or obligation entered into between parties that they will keep the peace and not assault or molest one another' and caution as 'security or bail'.

110. ACA CR, xxi, 451 (7 July 1553).

111. On the history of the Kirk sessions in Aberdeen see M. Graham, *Uses of Reform*, pp. 114–15.

112. NAS CH2/448/1, 5–6.

113. NAS CH2/448/1, 78 (27 October 1575).

114. Ibid.

115. ACA, CR, xx, 381 (10 March 1549/50).

116. NAS CH2/448/1, 78 (3 November 1575).

117. ACA, CR, xxvi, 213 (6 September 1566).

118. ACA, CR, xvii, 607 (8 October 1543).

119. Ibid.

120. As E. P. Torrie argued, there were a number of factors involved in creating a sense of community within the burgh: the taking of the burgess oath, payment of burgess fees, the burgh seal authenticating burghal documents, but most important was the presence of the tolbooth within the urban centre. 'It was here that the burgh court met, tolls or market dues were collected, and, most importantly....[it was] the place for public proc-lamations.' Torrie also singled out 'the market as the hub of the burgh; the location of the tron, the tolbooth, the mercat cross as the secular focal points of burghal life'. Torrie, *Medieval Dundee*, pp. 35–6.

121. ACA, CR, xxi, 288 (1 January 1552/3). The court scribe recorded Ferguson's offence as disturbing the town and kirk by disrupting the 'godly service thereuntill in stryking of John Dwne with his hand on the face within the kirk upon new yeirz day in tym of the hiemas'.

122. ACA, CR, xxi, 499 (7 September 1553).
123. Ibid. The baillies informed them that if they 'beis found in doing siclyk in tym cuming to pay 40*s* to sanct nicholas wark unforgiven'.

3 Property

1. Falconer, 'Surveying Scotland's Urban Past'; Gibson and Smout, *Prices, Food and Wages in Scotland*, p. 19.
2. On this subject see K. Wrightson and D. Levine, *Poverty and Piety in an English Village*, p. 110.
3. ACA, CR, xxi, 363 (20 March 1552/3); ACA, CR, xxi., 366 (23 March 1552/3). There is no record of what happened to Andrew Lyon.
4. ACA, CR, xvii, 20 (27 October 1541).
5. This is the heart of the matter in accounts depicting tensions between merchants who dominated burgh government and craftsmen seeking enfranchisement. See E. Bain, *Merchant and Craft Guilds: A History of the Aberdeen Incorporated Trades* (Aberdeen: J. & J.P. Edmond & Spark, 1887); M. Lynch, *Edinburgh and the Reformation*; M. Verschuur, 'Merchants and Craftsmen'.
6. ACA, xxxi, 189 (5 August 1583).
7. While there is no record of the modification of Litster's unlaw in either the Council Register or the Guildry Accounts, it is likely that the council levied a fine.
8. On this subject see E. P. D. Torrie, 'The Guild in Fifteenth-Century Dunfermline', in M. Lynch, M. Spearman and G. Stell (eds), *The Scottish Medieval Town*, p. 245–60.
9. *Statuta Gilde*, c. xvi. 'if any [of] our brethren pass away from the guild negligently, none of the brethren shall administer to him council nor help in word nor in deed within the burgh nor outwith. Although he be impeded and in peril of life and member or in any other earthly charge, he shall have no help of them.'
10. See Ewan, *Townlife in Fourteenth-Century Scotland*, pp. 62–3; E. P. D. Torrie, 'The Guild in Fifteenth-Century Dunfermline'. Torrie argued that 'the guild merchant was a fraternity whose functions were social, religious & mercantile', p. 246.
11. ACA, CR, xxxi, 317 (10 February 1583/4).
12. On this see Bain, *Merchants and Craftsmen*, pp. 36–7; The *Leges Burgorum* c. 94 states that 'nothir lytstar na fleschwar na soutar may be wythin the fredome of the gylde bot gif he sal forsuer to do that craft wyth his awne propit handis bot wyth servandis undir hym.'
13. Ewan, *Townlife in Fourteenth-Century Scotland*, pp. 59–60.
14. ACA, CR, xxxi, 305 (24 January 1583/4).
15. Ibid. (my emphasis).
16. Lynch, 'Introduction: Scottish Towns 1500–1700', in M. Lynch (ed.), *The Early Modern Town*, pp. 1–36, on p. 15–16.
17. ACA, MSS Guildry Accounts, (27 April 1582) no folio numbers.
18. ACA, MSS Guildry Accounts, (23 September 1594).
19. See M. Lynch, 'Elite Society in Town and Country', p. 186. Here Lynch argues that 'the increasing size of the taxable population [in Aberdeen] and the rising numbers in the merchant guild had little to do with either population increase or increasing social mobility; both were devices for raising revenue.'
20. ACA, MSS Guildry Accounts, (25 September 1594).
21. David Walker has argued that, for the most part, the guild was not always distinct from the body of burgesses. D. Walker, *Legal History of Scotland*, vol. 3, p. 321.

22. Isabel Grant argued long ago that the link between 'burghal privileges and burghal payments' or responsibilities was clearly articulated in burgh charters. I. F. Grant, *The Social and Economic Development of Scotland before 1600* (Edinburgh: Oliver & Boyd, 1930), p. 130.
23. *Leges Burgorum*, c. 2.
24. Balfour, *Practicks*, c. xvi.
25. ACA, CR, xxviii, 730 (25 May 1576).
26. ACA, CR, xxiv, 271 (13 October 1561).
27. He may have appeared a total of eight times if the Gavane Wishert, cordiner convicted of breaking statutes in November 1541 is the same individual. ACA, CR, xvii, 42 (28 November 1541).
28. ACA, CR, xxii, 293 (27 March 1556). Wishert was convicted alongside his wife and his daughter for the 'strublens, striking and bla making' of Agnes Colle for which they were ordered to ask the injured party forgiveness and pay a fine of 7s.8d.
29. ACA, CR, xxxi, 74–5 (8 February 1582). If *modus operandi* can be used to determine identity, it is likely that the Gavin Wishert convicted in 1541 was the same Gavin Wishert convicted again in 1556, 1561, 1576, 1581, 1582, February and April 1583. In six of the eight cases, Wishert was involved in the buying/barking of raw hides or leather against town statutes.
30. ACA, CR, xxxi, 119 (9 April 1583).
31. ACA, CR, xxix, 50 (27 November 1576).
32. ACA, CR, xxxi, 119 (9 April 1583).
33. ACA MSS Guildry Accounts, Michaelmas 1582–86.
34. ACA, CR, xxiii, 103 (17 February 1558/9).
35. ACA, CR, xxiii, 146 (27 April 1559).
36. ACA, CR, xxvii, 553 (30 July 1571).
37. ACA, CR, xxvii, 697 (12 May 1572).
38. ACA, CR, xxix, 17 (19 October 1576).
39. Ibid.
40. For discussion of technical and operative definitions of the law see Introduction, pp. 6–7.
41. ACA, CR, xviii, 149 (22 April 1544).
42. Ibid. The emphasis is mine.
43. ACA, CR, xviii, 167 (30 April 1544).
44. E. P. Dennison, 'Recreating the Urban Past'.
45. A. A. M. Duncan, *Scotland: The Making of the Kingdom* (Edinburgh, 1973); Whyte, *Scotland before the Industrial Revolution*; Ewan, *Townlife*; E. P. Dennison, 'Power to the People?'.
46. Steve Hindle has argued that 'while the fundamental realities of economic differentiation might provoke those conspicuous episodes of domination and resistance with which historians of popular protests have been preoccupied, the negotiation of inequality in the civil parish was characterized by more delicate political tensions and by more fluid social alignments.' In Braddick and Walter (eds), *Negotiating Power in Early Modern* Society, p. 104.
47. This is most obviously noted in the statutes and ordinances made in the Gild Court each Michaelmas electing officials, designating quarters to each of the four officers and baillies, regulating prices of bread, beef, ale and ratifying old statutes. Blanchard, Gemmill, Mayhew and Whyte have argued that 'the basis of many regulations published by the provost, baillies and council were the rules and conventions set out in early collections of laws relating to burgh government.' See I. Blanchard, E. Gemmill, N. Mayhew and I. D.

Whyte, 'The Economy: Town and Country', in Dennison, Ditchburn and Lynch (eds), *Aberdeen before 1800*, pp. 129–158, on p. 138.

48. On this subject see Whyte, *Scotland before the Industrial Revolution*, pp. 192–3.
49. Gibson and Smout, *Prices, Food and Wages in Scotland*, p. 19.
50. See for example, ACA, CR, xxvii, 26 (7 November 1541); ACA, CR, xviii, 177 (19 May 1544); ACA, CR , xviii, 367 (7 February 1544/5); ACA, CR, xix, 150 (2 July 1546); ACA, CR, xx, 325 (16 December 1549); ACA, CR, xxiv, 17 (7 October 1560); ACA, CR , xxv, 489 (11 February 1564/5); ACA, CR, xxvi, 468 (2 December 1567); ACA, CR, xxvii, 263 (16 March 1569/70); ACA, CR, xxviii,125 (20 November 1573); ACA, CR, xxix, 242 (2 September 1577); ACA, CR, xxxii, 91 (15 August 1586).
51. Gibson and Smout, *Prices, Food and Wages*, p. 23.
52. See for example, Whyte, *Scotland before the Industrial Revolution*; Gibson and Smout, *Prices, Food and Wages*; E. Gemmill and N. Mayhew, *Changing Values in Medieval Scotland*; Blanchard, Gemmill, Mayhew and Whyte, 'The Economy: Town and Country', pp. 129–58.
53. ACA, CR, xvii, 480, (4 May 1543).
54. ACA, CR, xxix, 96 (22 January 1577).
55. Gibson and Smout, *Prices, Food and Wages*, p. 23.
56. Ibid., p. 22; Torrie, 'Power to the People', p. 104; Blanchard, Gemmill, Mayhew and Whyte, 'The Economy: Town and Country,' pp. 150–1.
57. *Abdn. Counc.*, vol. 2, pp. 167–8.
58. *APS*, 2, p. 347. By 1540 another Act under James V had the goods split evenly, half for the king and the other half for the burgh. *APS*, 2, p. 376. Acts passed in 1567 and 1579 ratified the acts of James V (*APS*, 3, p. 41, 146).
59. *APS*, 3, p. 452.
60. *APS*, 3, pp. 576–7.
61. ACA, CR, xxiv, 551 (26 November 1562); ACA MSS Baillie Court Books 1 (14 August 1581); ACA, CR, xix, 150 (2 July 1546); ACA, CR, xxvii, 47 (19 May 1569); ACA, CR, xxx, 498 (23 August 1581).
62. On this subject see Gemmill and Mayhew, *Changing Values in Medieval Scotland*, pp. 38–41.
63. ACA, CR, xxvi, 270 (19 November 1566).
64. ACA, CR, xxvii, 476 (22 February 1570/1).
65. For further discussion of John Deuchar's wrongdoings see ch. 5, pp. 131–5
66. ACA, CR, xxviii, 188 (31 March 1574).
67. ACA, CR, xxvii, 604 (8 October 1571).
68. T. C. Smout, 'Coping with Plague In Sixteenth and Seventeenth-Century Scotland', *Scotia*, 2:1 (1978), pp. 19–33; Tyson, 'People in the Two Towns,' pp. 111–28.
69. ACA, CR, xx, 314 (28 October 1549), 316 (4 November 1549).
70. Ibid., p. 231 (21 March 1546).
71. *Abdn. Counc.*, vol. 1 (17 December 1546), p. 246.
72. Ibid., 10 September 1545, p. 222; 6 August 1546, p. 240; 17 October 1549, p. 273; vol. 2, 28 September 1584, p. 52–4; 21 May 1585, p. 56; 27 May 1585, p. 57.
73. *Abdn. Counc.*, vol. 2, p. 57.
74. ACA, CR, xviii, 519 (6 August 1545).
75. The court convicted Robert Benat and James Manser of breaking statutes in selling 'measurable guids' at prices higher than those established by the town council. They were put in amercement of court and warned that if they were ever convicted for a similar

offence they were 'to be banesit of this guid town perpetually in all tyme cuming.' ACA, CR, xxiv, 505 (11 September 1562).

76. ACA MSS Baillie Court Book 1 (8 April 1595).
77. ACA, CR, xix, 150 (2 July 1546).
78. ACA CR, xviii, 177 (19 May 1544), ACA CR, xviii, 367 (7 February 1544/5), ACA, CR, xix, 150 (2 July 1546).
79. ACA, CR, xxvii, 47 (19 May 1569).
80. ACA, CR, xxx, 498 (23 August 1581).
81. Gordon DesBrisay explored this idea in 'Twisted by Definition: Women Under Godly Discipline in Seventeenth-Century Scottish Towns', in Brown and Ferguson, *Twisted Sisters*, pp. 137–56, on pp. 141–4.
82. ACA, CR, xxvi, 377 (15 May 1567).
83. For a general discussion on prices, weights and measures in medieval Aberdeen, as well as the motivations behind baxters, fleshers and brewsters for contravening ordinances, see Gemmill and Mayhew, *Changing Values in Medieval Scotland*, pp. 25–80.
84. Herrup, 'Law and Morality in Seventeenth-Century England', pp. 110–11.
85. ACA, CR, xvii, 185 (21 May 1542).
86. ACA, CR, xxvi, 142–3 (6 May 1566).
87. ACA, CR, xvii, 225 (26 June 1542); ACA, CR, xix, 252 (22 November 1546).
88. ACA, CR, xix, 57 (3 March 1546).
89. ACA, CR, xxviii, 804 (20 September 1576); ACA, CR, xxix, 122 (23 February 1576/7); ACA, CR, xxix, 365 (17 January 1577/8); ACA, CR, xxx, 528 (6 October 1581); ACA, CR, xxx, 514 (14 September 1581); ACA MSS Baillie Court Books 1 (2 January 1581/2); ACA, CR, xxx, 633 (6 April 1581/2).
90. John Duncan's troubles with the burgh magistrates forms the main part of the discussion on
91. ACA, CR, xxix, 365 (17 January 1577/78). The account states that 'the provost and consell having consideration of the obstinate disobedience of John Duncan tailzeour being thrice warnit to haff comperit befor the saidis provest ballies and consell dischargit the said Johne of his fredome of this burt and ordainit his buyth dur to be closet vp in all tyme cuming.'
92. ACA, CR, xxix, 158 (22 April 1577); ACA, CR, xxix, 560 (15 November 1578); ACA, CR, xxix, 591 (19 December 1578); ACA, CR, xxix, 679 (14 April 1578).
93. Smout and Gibson, *Prices, Food and Wages,* p. 282
94. ACA, CR, xxix, 158 (22 April 1577); ACA, CR, xxix, 560 (15 November 1578); ACA, CR, xxix, 591 (19 December 1578); ACA, CR, xxix, 679 (14 April 1578).
95. ACR, CR, xxv, 120 (17 Oct 1563); ACA, CR, xxvi, 538 (5 April 1568); ACA, CR, xxx, 399–400 (14 April 1580); ACA MSS Baillie Court Book 1 (12 May 1580).
96. ACA MSS Baillie Court Book 1 (17 February 1574/5); ACA MSS Baillie Court Book 1 (3 April 1576).
97. *RPCS*, vol. 3, p. 433. See also above, ch. 5, p. 131–5 for a fuller discussion of Deuchar's activities in the burgh.
98. As Elizabeth Ewan has suggested, the removal of parts of a house, or goods from a household, by creditors or landlords was also a means of forcing the resolution of a conflict. See E. Ewan, 'Scottish Portias: Women in the Courts in Mediaeval Scottish Towns', *Journal of the Canadian Historical Association*, 3 (1992), pp. 27–43, esp. p. 38.
99. ACA, CR, xvii, 114 (25 February 1541/2).
100. Ibid.

101. The baillies later accused William Rolland elder, William Rolland younger, David Rolland and John Sinclair of attacking Hay younger and drawing his blood. The two Williams were acquitted, but the baillies convicted David Rolland and John Sinclair for committing this crime. Interestingly enough, Nicholson did not play a part in this portion of the conflict. ACA, CR, xvii, 116 (27 February 1541/2).

102. Example given in the Introduction, p. 13; Both Amussen and Capp have argued that elites could employ violent acts, including the destruction of property, in attacks on members of lower levels of society. S. Amussen, 'Punishment, Discipline and Power', pp. 1–34; B. Capp, 'Arson, Threats of Arson and Incivility in Early Modern England', pp. 204–7.

103. ACA, CR, xxviii, 227 (21 June 1574). The same John Sanders was convicted for 'strubling the court' in March 1595 and ordered to compear 'in the presens of the haill town in the tolbuyth and grantis his offens and ask the magistrate forgiveness and to pay the unlaw of ten merks to the dein of gild and gif ever he does siclyk in tym cuming to pay unlaw of 100 poundis.' ACA MSS Baillie Court Book 1 (5 March 1594/5).

104. ACA, CR, xxviii, 404 (25 February 1574/5).

105. ACA, CR, xxviii, 559 (4 September 1575); ACA MSS Baillie Court Book 1 (5 September 1575) states that Theilgrene was ordered to pay Chalmer 30*s*.

106. ACA, CR, xxi, 485 (18 August 1553) There is no record of the modification.

107. ACA, CR, xxi, 684 (15 June 1554).

108. See the cases involving the Carmelite and Dominicans, p. 88.

109. See discussion of restorative punishments in ch. 2, pp. 58–61.

110. For a fuller discussion of Gardner's case see Falconer, '"Mony Utheris Divars Odious Crymes": Women, Petty Crime and Power in Later Sixteenth-Century Aberdeen', *Crimes and Misdemeanours*, 4:1 (2010), pp. 7–36, on pp. 15–16.

111. For discussion of a similar situation in an English village see Wrightson and Levine, *Poverty and Piety in an English Village*, pp. 121–4.

112. ACA, CR, xx, 83–4 (13 August 1548)

113. Kennedy mentions the 'public mills' within the burgh, but does not provide any further detail. Kennedy, *Annals of Aberdeen*, p. 85

114. ACA MSS Baillie Court Book 1 (30 May 1575).

115. ACA, CR, xx, 570 (29 May 1551).

116. ACA, CR, xxiii, 31 (7 October 1558).

117. ACA, CR, xxi, 228 (6 October 1552); ACA, CR, xxviii, 338 (3 December 1574).

118. ACA, CR, xx, 151 (4 September 1555).

119. ACA, CR, xviii, 109 (1 March 1543/4).

120. Herrup, 'Law and Morality in Seventeenth-Century England,' pp. 102–23.

121. ACA MSS Baillie Court Book 1 (9 April 1576).

122. ACA MSS Baillie Court Book 1 (18 August 1587).

123. ACA, CR, xx, 418 (19 May 1550).

124. ACA, CR, xxiii, 120 (17 March 1558/59). That same year a number of unnamed 'neighbours and indwellers' along with 'certane strangers' of the burgh had plundered the lodgings of the Black and White Friars of the burgh.

125. ACA, CR, xxiii, 298 (22 March 1559/60).

126. ACA, CR, xvii, 55 (13 December 1541).

127. ACA, CR, xvii, 538 (18 July 1543).

128. ACA, CR, xx, 302 (7 October 1549). I examine this case more fully in the next chapter. The victim, with the support of some of his neighbours, responded to this assault by attacking the sailors' ship during the night. Such reciprocal violence reflected an attempt

to regain the power taken from the victim by his captors and underscores the negotiation process. The court prosecuted both groups. See discussion of this incident in ch. 4, pp. 118–19.

129. ACA, CR, xxiii, 92 (26 January 1558/9).
130. ACA MSS Baillie Court Book 1 (23 April 1581), (29 April 1581).
131. For fuller details of Cruikshank's offence against Mollison see pp. 52, 129, 158–9.
132. For example, in only 1 per cent (5:473) of the total cases of physical violence brought before the burgh court was the convicted party banished from the burgh. This is a dramatic contrast to the near 37 per cent (24:65) of the cases of 'wrongous away taking' or intromission that resulted in banishment.
133. ACA, CR, xviii, 317 (21 November 1544).
134. ACA, CR, xxi, 69 (26 October 1551).
135. ACA, CR, xxvi, 352 (18 March 1567).
136. On this subject see the collection of essays edited by Braddick and Walter, *Negotiating Power in Early Modern Society*. In particular, see their 'Introduction. Grids of Power: Order, Hierarchy and Subordination in Early Modern Society', pp. 1–42; S. Hindle, 'Exhortation and Entitlement: Negotiating Inequality in English Rural Communities, 1550–1650', pp. 102–22; R. Gillespie, 'Negotiating Order in Early Seventeenth-Century Ireland', pp. 188–205.
137. Between 1550 and 1600 Scotland, as a whole, experienced twenty-four years of dearth and at least four major outbreaks of plague which contributed to a rise in the levels of poverty experienced in most parts of the realm. See Lythe, *The Economy of Scotland in its European Setting*, pp. 15–23; Smout, 'Famine and Famine Relief in Scotland', in L. M. Cullen and T. C. Smout (eds), *Comparative Aspects of Scottish and Irish Economic and Social History* (Edinburgh: John Donald, 1977), pp. 21–31; Whyte, *Scotland before the Industrial Revolution*, p. 112.
138. Gibson and Smout, *Prices, Food and Wages in Scotland*, pp. 343–4; Whyte, *Scotland Before the Industrial Revolution*, p. 112.
139. Lythe, *The Economy of Scotland in its European Setting*, p. 16.
140. See Table 3.1, p. 94.
141. Such a change can be detected for 'unspecified strublance'. See discussion of this change in ch. 4, pp. 102–3.

4 Violence

1. ACA, CR, xxiv, 479 (24 July 1562).
2. Ibid.
3. Garthine Walker has rightly argued that 'in early modern culture, verbal utterance was understood absolutely to be a form of action, not merely its weak, binary other'. G. Walker, *Crime, Gender and Social Order in Early Modern England*, p. 99.
4. See further discussion of Chalmer on, pp. 39–41.
5. This chapter utilizes two data sets: a general set that spans 1541–96 from which I utilize various examples to demonstrate types of behaviour and responses to such activities; and a second (slightly smaller) set spanning 1542–91, taken from the more general set, which I utilize for quantification purposes.
6. de Saussure, *Course in General Linguistics*.
7. The *Dict. of Scots. Lang.* defines strublance as '(The action of creating) public disorder, (causing) a breach of the peace; disturbance (of a community, gathering, etc.); moles-

tation (of an individual). Also to commit, do, mak strublance.' The *Compact Oxford English Dictionary: New Edition* defines strublance as a 'disturbance, molestation,' and 'strouble' as 'to trouble, disturb.' p. 1933; See also E. Ewan, G. DesBrisay and H. L. Diack, 'Life in the Two Towns,' p. 52.

8. ACA, CR, xvii, 413 (19 March 1542/3).
9. ACA, CR, xvii, 85 (27 January 1541/2).
10. Ibid.
11. ACA, CR, xvii, 187 (24 May 1542).
12. See above, Introduction p. 12.
13. ACA, CR, xx, 420 (13 May 1550).
14. ACA, CR, xvii, 467 (27 April 1543).
15. ACA, CR, xxxii, 6 (4 March 1585/6).
16. Example of such convictions can be found in ACA, CR, xviii, 486 (Ultimo June 1545); ACA, CR, xix, 85–6 (14 April 1546); ACA, CR, xx, 32–3 (22 May 1548); ACA, CR, xxi, 288 (1 January 1552/3); ACA, CR, xxvi, 163 (10 June 1566); ACA MSS Baillie Court Books 1 (21 January 1575/6); ACA, CR, xxviii,774 (21 July 1576); ACA, CR, xix, 280 (3 October 1577); ACA, CR, xxxi, 119 (9 April 1583); ACA, CR, xxxii, 131 (26 October 1586).
17. ACA, CR, xxxi, 119 (9 April 1583).
18. ACA, CR, xxxi, 560 (6 February 1584/5).
19. This does not include individual cases of verbal or physical violence committed against the town authorities. For fuller discussion of this, and other forms of disobedience directed at authority figures in the burgh, see ch. 5, pp. 144–8.
20. ACA MSS Baillie Court Book 1 (5 August 1587).
21. Ibid.
22. For discussion of similar attacks on authority members constituting attacks on the entire community see E. Ewan, 'There was nae justice to be got in this tolbooth'.
23. ACA, CR, xvii, 16 (24 October 1541); ACA, CR, xvii, 24 (4 November 1541).
24. Although there is no indication in the records, it is possible that Make was Blak's servant.
25. The number of cases of property crime, breaking statutes, regrating and wrongful away taking remained relatively constant. See above, Table 3.1, p. 94.
26. ACA MSS Baillie Court Books 1 (14 April 1594).
27. See for example, ACA, CR, xvii, 181 (12 May 1542). Although the convicted party, Alex Rob, was found guilty of strubling and mispersoning Nanis Gray, the clerk recorded that he was to ask 'the said nanis forgifnes for the said strublens'. It is unlikely that the mispersoning was to remained unanswered, rather that the 'strublens' summed up the entire offence committed.
28. ACA, CR, 22, 571 (28 June 1557).
29. Incidents where authority figures were victims of verbal or physical assault are included under those crimes. Disobedience/disorder refers specifically to cases of deforcement, breaking of arrestments, 'disobedience' and willful behaviour.
30. S. Hindle, *State and Social Change*, p. 59
31. K. Wrightson, 'Mutualities and Obligations: Changing Social Relationships in Early Modern England (The Raleigh Lecture, 2005)', p. 3.
32. ACA, CR, xxviii, 5 (10 April 1573).
33. C. Muldrew, *The Economy of Obligation: The Culture of Credit and Social Relations in Early Modern England* (Basingstoke: Macmillan, 1998), p. 151.
34. Ibid.

35. ACA, CR, xxiv, 271 (13 October 1561).
36. The account mentions Leslie's husband, William Coughton, but gives no further indication of her status within the burgh. Coughton does not appear in any of the other records, nor does the account mention his place in Aberdonian society.
37. ACA, CR, xxiv, 273 (13 October 1561).
38. ACA, CR, xxvii, 702 (26 May 1572); ACA MSS Baillie Court Book 1 (26 May 1572).
39. E. Ewan, 'Many Injurious Words'; G. Walker, *Crime, Gender and Social Order in Early Modern England*; L. Gowing, *Domestic Dangers: Women, Words and Sex in Early Modern London* (Oxford: Oxford University Press, 1996); J. R. D. Falconer, 'A Family Affair: Households, Misbehaving and the Community in Sixteenth-Century Aberdeen', in J. Nugent and E. Ewan (eds), *Finding the Family in Medieval and Early Modern Scotland* (Ashgate, 2008), pp. 139–50.
40. ACA, CR, xxiv, 271 (13 October 1561).
41. This is a case where the husband and the household are synonymous. The *Leges Burgorum* states that baillies were unable to brew or bake within their household during their term of office. *Leges Burgorum*, c. 59.
42. This idea has been explored in Falconer 'A Family Affair', pp. 146–8. ACA, CR, xvii, 470 (30 April 1543); See modification of Myll's unlaw in ACA, CR, xvii, 478 (4 May 1543).
43. ACA, CA, xxii, 653 (15 October 1557).
44. ACA MSS Baillie Court Book 1 (22 June 1585)
45. See above, ch. 2, p. 59.
46. ACA, MSS Baillie Court Book 1 (26 October 1581).
47. ACA, CR, xvii, 133 (17 March 1542).
48. Garthine Walker has argued that in England 'slander alleging criminal behavior ... was properly the business of the secular criminal courts'. Walker further argues that slander that alleged immoral behaviour was tried in the church courts, whereas libel cases were brought before higher criminal courts. See G. Walker, *Crime, Gender and Social Order in Early Modern England*, p. 100.
49. ACA, CR, xxx, 592 (14 January 1581/2).
50. ACA, CR, xxxi, 151 (4 June 1583).
51. ACA, CR, xxiii, 43 (21 October 1558). Mr James Burnett appears again twice in later accounts as a regrater and forestaller. ACA, CR, xxxi–1, 482 (13 Jan 1589/90); ACA MSS Guildry Accounts (23 January 1593).
52. ACA, CR, xxviii, 404 (25 February 1574/5).
53. ACA MSS Baillie Court Book 1 (10 May 1595). According to Kennedy, a John Ewyn, burgess, was convicted, hanged and beheaded in 1574 for coining. Kennedy, *Annals of Aberdeen*, p. 139.
54. ACA, CR, xvii, 485 (11 May 1543).
55. ACA, CR, xviii, 296 (7 November 1544).
56. ACA, CR, xx, 193 (1 March 1548/9).
57. ACA, CR, xx, 222 (14 April 1549).
58. ACA, CR, xxi, 539 (27 October 1553). The baillies ordered that if she was convicted for a similar fault in the future she was to pay 5 merks to St Nicholas wark unforgiven because she had 'bene divers tymes convikit for siclyk faults obefor'. The baillies modified her unlaw a few days later, raising the deterrent to a fine of 10 merks. ACA, CR, xxi, 542 (30 October 1553).
59. ACA, CR, xxiv, 275 (24 October 1561).

60. We recall that Patrick Stewart was convicted eight years later for similar charges and banished perpetually from the town. See above ch. 1, pp. 36–8.

61. See Falconer, 'Mony Utheris Divars Odious Crymes', pp. 26–7.

62. In May 1556, the baillies and provost convicted John Turner for the strublens and striking of Besse Walcar. For his crime, the baillies ordered Turner to 'sit down ane his kneis and ask hir forgifness'. However, by this time Walcar had been accused six times and convicted on five different occasions for a variety of crimes. Nonetheless, the court determined that Turner had wronged her and should seek her forgiveness. Three months later Walcar appeared before the same baillies and provost accused of defaming and mispersoning Turner and put in amercement of court. ACA, CR, xxii, 314 (5 May 1556); ACA, CR, xxii, 402 (21 August 1556). Walcar's case can be found in ACA, CR, xxii, 620 (20 August 1557).

63. ACA, CR, xxiii, 210 (25 August 1559).

64. ACA, CR, xviii, 296 (7 November 1544).

65. Ibid.

66. ACA, CR, xxvi, 613 (2 August 1568).

67. The fact that the Earl and his family were still dealing with the fallout from their rebellion in 1562 may also provide some context to this incident. On this subject see A. White, 'Religion, Politics and Society in Aberdeen 1543–1593' (PhD disseration, University of Edinburgh, 1985); A. Murray, 'Huntly's Rebellion and the Administration of Justice in North-East Scotland, 1570–1573' *Northern Scotland*, 4:1 (1981), pp. 1–6

68. ACA, CR, xx, 15 (26 April 1548).

69. E. Ewan, 'There was nae justice to be got in this tolbooth'.

70. See above, ch. 3, p. 89; ACA MSS Baillie Court Books 1 (28 April 1581).

71. See above, ch. 3, p. 89.

72. ACA, CR, xxxiii–1, 959–60 (18 January 1590/1).

73. ACA, CR, xxxi, 100 (8 March 1582).

74. ACA, CR, xxvi, 620 (16 August 1568).

75. It is difficult to determine Fynny's status in Aberdeen society. In 1564, the baillies convicted 'the wyf of maister thomas fynny' for regrating and forestalling. ACA, CR, xxv, 411 (21 October 1564). His name appears in two other accounts, the account of Donaldson's conviction and in an account of John Banderman's conviction for the 'wrongous intromission of xi dealis (planks)' that belonged to Fynny. ACA, CR, xxvi, 516 (30 April 1571).

76. Of the 390 accounts of verbal assault collected for this period only 60 provide details of the occupation or social standing of the individual accused of committing the offence. Similarly, there are 111 accounts where the clerk detailed the victim's social status. In both cases, where the convicted or injured party was female and only her marital status was recorded, this was taken to indicate her standing within the burgh.

77. On the receiving end of insults and slanders we find at least seven baxters, two cordiners, two fleshers, two litsters, two masons, two tailors, three mariners and eight websters.

78. The ideas expressed in this section have been explored elsewhere, see Falconer, 'Mony Utheris Divars Odious Crymes', pp. 28–33.

79. Michael Graham's study of reform discipline in Scotland is the only other study that offers a statistical analysis from which to compare the occurrence of verbal crimes along gender lines. However, his examination of misbehaviour utilized ecclesiastical records alone and therefore does not entirely mirror the findings in this study. The following comparison is based on what is found in chapter three of Graham's book, *Uses of Reform*, pp. 73–124.

80. M. Graham, *Uses of Reform*, p. 87.

81. Ibid., p. 100.
82. E. Ewan, 'Many Injurious Words', p. 177.
83. Ibid., p. 176.
84. An example of the tendency to view verbal crimes as a particularly female pursuit can be found in L. Gowing, 'Language, Power and the Law: Women's Slander Litigation in Early Modern London', in J. Kermode and G. Walker (eds), *Women, Crime and the Courts in early Modern England*, pp. 26–48. In the same edited volume we find Martin Ingram's response to David Underdown's study of the 'scold'. Ingram underscores the need to refine our understanding of the term and its relationship to gender studies. However, he still finds that verbal aggression was more likely a female activity. M. Ingram, '"Scolding Women Cucked or Washed": A Crisis in Gender Relations in Early Modern England?', pp. 48–80, esp. pp. 54–5. John Addy, in his *Sin and Society in the Seventeenth Century* (London: Routledge, 1989) wades carefully into the gender debate avoiding discussion of gender, but demonstrating that both men and women participated in defamation of their neighbours.
85. G. Walker, *Crime, Gender and Social Order*, p. 102. See also the introduction to K. Jones, *Gender and Petty* Crime, pp. 1–31.
86. D. Underdown, 'The Taming of the Scold: The Enforcement of Patriarchal Authority in Early Modern England', in Fletcher and Stevenson, *Order and Disorder in Early Modern England*, pp. 116–36; M. Ingram, *Church Courts, Sex and Marriage, 1570–1640*; M. Graham, *Uses of Reform*; J. Harrison, 'Women and the Branks in Stirling, *c.* 1600 to *c.*1730', *Scottish Economic and Social History*, 18:2 (1998), pp. 114–31.
87. In some instances individuals were the recipient of offences committed by more than one person. As such, they are included here as victim to each transgressor even when occurring in a single incident. Even though there is only 'one' individual on the receiving end of the physical or verbal assault, that individual was a 'multiple' victim of the crime committed.
88. This average is based on number of cases rather than individual victims. The cases where there was more than one victim count for a single case, as such the number of actual victims may be slightly higher. That said, the difference is negligible and does not undermine the overall analysis.
89. Marjorie McIntosh in her grand study of misbehaviour in England between 1370 and 1600 demonstrates that incidents of 'scolding' in the sixteenth century followed a similar pattern to that seen for Aberdeen. By 1570 there was a sharp decline in incidents of verbal abuse brought before the courts in England, dropping from anywhere from 8 to 28 per cent around 1540 and, depending on the court, to between 0 and 8 per cent between 1580 and 1599. See M. McIntosh, *Controlling Misbehaviour in England*, Appendix 7.1a, p. 253.
90. On this subject see E. Ewan, 'Many Injurious Words', pp. 166–9; L. Gowing, 'Language, Power and the Law', pp. 26–47.
91. ACA, CR, xxxiii–1, 309 (1 September 1589).
92. ACA, CR, xxxiii–1, 1104 (17 May 1591).
93. On the subject of masculinity and the importance of earning a respectable living see Shepard, 'Manhood, Credit and Patriarchy in Early Modern England c. 1580–1640', *Past and Present*, 167 (May 2000), pp. 75–106.
94. ACA MSS Baillie Court Book 1 (4 March 1586).
95. ACA, CR, xxxiii–1, 1052 (2 April 1591).
96. ACA MSS Baillie Court Book 1 (29 August 1596).
97. Mann argues that violence (in this case physical violence) is the 'bluntest, instrument of human power'. He sees the concentration and organization of this 'instrument' into

armies as an effective 'concentrated-coercive' means of exercising social power. See Mann, *Source of Social Power*, pp. 1–32, esp. 18–20, 26–7.

98. It is difficult to determine whether the gaps in the records in which Allan's name appears is the result of poor record keeping or legitimate good behaviour at times. Despite a later reference to frequent crimes committed by her and noted by the Kirk Session, town council and Ecclesiastical magistrates, there is no existing reference in the Kirk Session Records or Council Register except for those mentioned here.

99. ACA, CR, xxi, 469 (28 July 1553). In this account her name appears as Ellin Allend.

100. ACA MSS Baillie Court Book 1 (19 May 1587).

101. ACA MSS Baillie Court Book 1 (26 May 1587).

102. I am using a slightly smaller set spanning 1542–91, taken from the more general set, for quantification purposes.

103. ACA, CR, xxxi, 325 (13 February 1583/4).

104. ACA MSS Baillie Court Book 1 (21 April 1595). Acts passed in Parliament in 1551 and 1587 against causing a disturbance within the Church suggest the seriousness in which the authorities viewed such behaviour. *APS*, 2, 485, specifies that those who committed such acts and refuse to stop 'for na spirituall monitioun that the Kirkmen may vse' would incur a fine according to rank, starting at £10. Those too poor to pay this fine would be imprisoned for fifteen days. If you were convicted for a second fault the punishment would be doubled. For a third fault, the magistrates would impose a warding of their persons or banishment for a year and a day; *APS*, 3, 430, specifies that individuals convicted for such an offence would lose their goods and escheat them to the King. They were also to be excluded from the Kirk unless reconciled. More importantly, according to the language used in the act, individuals convicted for such behaviour were deemed 'criminal'.

105. See Janine Hurl-Eamon, *Gender and Petty Violence in London*, pp. 2–3.

106. ACA, CR, xxx–1, 713 (21 July 1590); See also Meyerson, Thiery and Falk (eds), *'A Great Effusion of Blood'?*

107. ACA, CR, xxiv, 199 (21 May 1561).

108. ACA, CR, xxvii, 577 (17 September 1571).

109. ACA, CR, xxv, 646 (13 August 1565).

110. ACA, CR, xxv, 273 (5 May 1564).

111. ACA, CR, xxv, 285 (29 May 1564).

112. ACA, CR, xx, 107 (12 October 1548).

113. ACA, CR, xx, 301–302 (7 October 1549). See also transcription of this account in *Abdn. Counc.*, vol. 1, p. 271–2. The baillies modified the unlaw to 20 merks to be paid to Portuus and £10 to the town.

114. *Abdn. Counc.*, vol. 1, p. 271.

115. ACA, CR, xx, 303 (8 October 1549).

116. ACA, CR, xx, 302 (7 October 1549).

117. ACA, CR, xx, 301–2 (7 October 1549).

118. On the subject of 'bloodwite' see D. Walker, *A Legal History of Scotland*, vol. 3 pp. 565–6.

119. ACA, CR, xxv, 3 (30 June 1563). Forbes was convicted six months later for the strublance and striking of Martin Mitchell. ACA, CR, xxvi, 65 (14 December 1565).

120. ACA, CR, xxviii, 509 (11 July 1575).

121. ACA, CR, xxviii, 516 (18 July 1575).

122. Davidson had been convicted in 1572 for the strublance and striking of another tailor in the burgh by the name of Thomas Mitchell. ACA, CR, xxvii, 701 (23 May 1572); ACA MSS Baillie Court Book 1 (23 May 1572).

123. ACA MSS Baillie Court Book 1 (25 May 1575).
124. ACA MSS Baillie Court Book 1 (9 October 1581).
125. ACA, CR, xxi, 499 (7 September 1553).
126. ACA, CR, xxxi–1, 605 (14 April 1590).
127. ACA, CR, xxxi–1, 606 (14 April 1590).
128. ACA, CR, xxxi–1, 618 (4 May 1590).
129. The most obvious indication of such a network is the frequency in which we see individuals connected to each other through crimes and misbehaviour either as victims or perpetrators of these crimes. The examples used throughout this chapter (and others) demonstrate how closely connected the members of this society were to each other.
130. ACA, CR, xxxi–1, 638 (17 May 1590).
131. ACA, CR, xxxi–1, 1004 (18 February 1590/1).
132. ACA MSS Baillie Court Book 1 (7 March 1594/5).
133. For an example of this type of ordinance passed in Aberdeen see the St Nicholas Kirk Session Records, NAS CH2/448/1, 7. As early as 1490 ordinances were passed in the town for the protection of the inhabitants from crimes being committed against them during the night. *Abdn. Coun.* vol. 1, p. 417, 'it wes statutit and ordanit be the consale present for the tyme, that gif euer William Lamyntone, or ony vtheris, wakes in the nicht and comitis ony injuris stribulance, or inquetis ony persone or personis, or the toune, sale pay fiwe merkis to Sanct Nicholess werk.' If the convicted party held goods they were to put in the govis for three to four days and banished if they committed a second offence.
134. *RPCS*, vol. 9, p. 133.
135. Ibid.
136. ACA, CR, xxiii, 92 (26 January 1558/9).
137. ACA MSS Baillie Court Book 1 (10 December 1575).
138. ACA, CR, xxviii, 653 (9 December 1575). This account is slightly different from the one found in ACA MSS Baillie Court Book 1 (10 December 1575).
139. ACA, CR, xxviii, 493 (18 June 1575).
140. ACR Vol. 22, 392 (5 August 1556); ACA MSS Baillie Court Books 1 (20 January 1575/6).
141. ACA MSS Baillie Court Books 1 (28 August 1587).
142. Ibid.
143. Falconer, 'Mony Utheris Divars Odious Crymes', p. 31.
144. The figure shows that in the first decade there was an approximately 1 per cent rise in the number of incidents of physical violence recorded in the burgh records. This was followed by an 18 per cent decline in the next decade, a subsequent 6.6 per cent decline the following decade and an additional 10.6 per cent decline in the last decade under consideration. The most noticeable shift can be discerned in the decline in the incidents of verbal crimes. While there is a 7.6 per cent increase in incidents of verbal crime in the first decade following the Reformation, the following decade witnesses a 52 per cent decline followed by another 12 per cent decline in the last decade under consideration. See Table 4.1 above, p. 102.
145. NAS CH2/448/1, 35 (24 Apr 1574).
146. In 1542 Alex Downye stood accused of mispersoning Andrew Crawford and his wife calling her a 'clappand bordale huir [syphilitic brothel whore]'. Interestingly enough, Downye alleged that he committed this offence 'being after drynk'. The burgh court prosecuted Downye for these offences and put him in amercement of court, ordering him to find suretie for his amends. ACA CR, xvii, 254 (28 July 1542).

147. The Kirk Session minutes that survive for the sixteenth century begin in 1562 with a gap between 1562 and 1568 and another gap between 1568 and 1573. The records are most complete between 1573 and 1576. There is another significant gap between the end of the records found in NAS CH2/448/1 (1578) and the start of the records found in NAS CH2/448/1 (1602).

148. The best authority on this subject is M. Graham, *Uses of Reform.*

149. 'Cases' reflect both single individual convictions and multiple individuals' involvement in a single incident. As such, they represent incidents as opposed to number of convictions. They are taken from all data collected for the period 3 January 1541 through 6 August 1596.

150. M. Mann, *Sources of Social Power*, pp. 6–7.

151. ACA MSS Baillie Court Book 1 (28 May 1595).

5 Disobedience and Exclusion

1.   *Abdn. Counc.,* vol. 2 (18 November 1588), pp. 62–3.

2.   Ibid., p. 63.

3.   White, 'Religion, Politics and Society in Aberdeen', pp. 304–44.

4.   See for example C. Lindberg, *Beyond Charity: Reformation Initiatives for the Poor* (Minneapolis: Fortress Press, 1993).

5.   See for example ACA MSS Baillie Court Book 1 (29 September 1581), where it states that John Duncan, deacon of the tailor craft, and John Bannerman, deacon of the baxter craft stood accused of 'casing of tumult & sedition within this burgh'. See also A. White, 'Religion, Politics and Society in Aberdeen, 1543–1593' (PhD dissertation, University of Edinburgh, 1985), p. 327, where he argues that the leadership for the tumults within the burgh came from the wealthier branches of the craft guilds.

6.   *RPCS,* vol. 3, pp. 470–1.

7.   Ewan, *Townlife in Fourteenth-Century Scotland*, pp. 136–60.

8.   Lynch and Dingwall, 'Elite Society in Town and Country', p. 185.

9.   For a good evaluation of the push for greater enfranchisement by craftsmen in a Scottish burgh see Verschuur, 'Merchants and Craftsmen in Sixteenth-Century Perth'.

10.   Falconer, 'Surveying Scotland's Urban Past'.

11.   White, 'Religion, Politics and Society in Aberdeen', pp. 327–9.

12.   Michael Lynch has shown that both the merchant and craft guilds could on the one hand be 'virtual closed shops' while on the other they could lack exclusivity. Lynch, 'Introduction: Scottish Towns 1500–1700', in *The Early Modern Town*, pp. 1–36, pp. 15–16. See also Lynch and Dingwall, 'Elite Society in Town and Country', p. 186.

13.   ACA, MSS Guildry Accounts (27 April 1582) no folio numbers. At this time a merk was roughly 2/3 of a pound Scots. By 1560, 5 pounds Scots roughly equated to 1 pound Sterling. At James VI's accession to the English throne in 1603 the rate of exchange was 12 pounds Scots to 1 pound Sterling.

14.   ACA, MSS Guildry Accounts (23 September 1594).

15.   ACA, MSS Guildry Accounts (25 September 1594).

16.   S. Hindle, 'Power, Poor Relief and Social Relations in Holland Fen', p. 68.

17.   ACA, CR, xvii, 76 (16 January 1541/2).

18.   ACA, CR, xxiii, 103 (17 February 1558/9).

19.   ACR, CR, xxvii, 553 (Pen July 1571).

20.   ACA, CR, xxviii, 730 (25 May 1576).

21. ACA, CR xxxi, 189 (5 August 1583).
22. *Statuta Gilde,* c. xvi. Loss of the liberties associated with the guild was substantial. The *Statuta Gilde* states that 'if any of our brethren leave the guild out of negligence, none of the brethren shall provide him with council nor help him in word or deed within or out-with the burgh'. Apart from losing counsel and aid from other brethren of guild, Litster put at risk the right to buy goods for sale again, the right to participate in the election of town officials, the benefit of guild assistance should he have fallen into poverty and all of the social and convivial aspects of the guildry.
23. ACA, CR, xxxi, 305 (24 January 1583/4).
24. ACA, CR, xxxi, 305 (10 February 1583/4) (my emphasis). Twenty-two years earlier Moreis had laboured as a free craftsman in the burgh when he was convicted, along with four other craftsmen, for using 'merchandyce as brether of guild thai not beand fre bot of thair craft'. Interestingly, Moreis had, on this occasion as well, asked for the case to be heard by an assise. ACA, CR, xxiv, 271 (13 October 1561).
25. ACA, CR, xxxi, 317 (10 February 1583/4). My emphasis.
26. His last name frequently appears in the records as Deuchar, Deucharis, Dugaris, Duqu-haris.
27. NAS CS96/4918. A collection of manuscripts found in the National Archives of Scot-land reveals the extent of a dossier created by the burgh council for this purpose. The description of this material is as follows: 'Relate to craftsmen of Aberdeen: acts of burgh council regulating crafts, and judgments against individual craftsmen for contravening statutes and ordinances.' Extracts dated 1581 relate mainly to dispute between burgh council and certain craftsmen who, by passing allegedly wrong information to the Privy Council, had purchased a gift of new liberties from the King, 'therethrow resing schisme and seditioun in the bowallis at this communitie'.
28. See ch. 5, p. 143.
29. ACA, CR, xxvi, 65 (14 December 1565); NAS CS96/4918, 4 (14 December 1565).
30. NAS CS96/4918, 4 (14 December 1565).
31. ACA, CR, xxvi, 377 (15 May 1567).
32. A common way individuals verbally assaulted others was to malign them as wrongdoers. For example, in January 1582 Isobel Gibson slandered Katherine Rathe, the spouse of James Menzies, calling her 'baneist theiff and resettar of greyn malt & keil [cabbage]'. ACA, CR, xxx, 592 (14 January 1581/2).
33. ACA, CR, xxvii, 621 (16 November 1571).
34. See also NAS CS96/4918 (16 November 1571) where John Deucharis was convicted of 'bying certane hydes contrare the act and statutes & prevelege of his craft'.
35. ACA, CR, xxviii, 188 (31 March 1574).
36. See Table 4.1, p. 102. During this period there were 93 convictions for breaking statutes and ordinances, 73 convictions for forestalling and regrating and 13 convictions for diso-beying the magistrates.
37. ACA, CR, xxviii, 188 (31 March 1574) (my emphasis).
38. NAS CS96/4918, 9 (19 July 1578).
39. For example NAS CS96/4918, 5 (19 Oct 1571), 7 (3 Apr 1576) where his fine is 40*s* and he is ordered to abstain under pain of £100.
40. NAS CS96/4918, 9 (1 Aug 1578).
41. NAS CS96/4918, 10 (14 Nov 1578).
42. *RPCS,* 433 (6 December 1581).
43. Ibid.

44. ACA MSS Baillie Court Book 1 (25 June 1575).
45. ACA, CR, xxxi, 30 (5 December 1582).
46. Mary Verschuur and Michael Lynch have explored this issue in their respective studies on Perth and Edinburgh. See M. Verschuur, 'Merchants and Craftsmen in Sixteenth-Century Perth', esp. pp. 44–47; M. Lynch, 'The Crown and the Burghs, 1500–1625', in Lynch, (ed.), *The Early Modern Town*, pp. 55–80. See also Lynch, *Edinburgh and the Reformation*, esp. ch. 2 'Government and Society' and D. M. Walker, *A Legal History of Scotland*, pp. 331 for discussion of the Acts of Parliament intended to regulate outside interference in the burghs.
47. For such sensitivity generally, see E. P. Dennison, 'Power to the People'.
48. NAS CS96/4918, 12 (5 Dec 1580); ACA, CR, xxx, 273–4 (5 December 1580).
49. ACA, CR, xxx, 215 (15 October 1580).
50. For example, ACA, CR, xxv, 120 (17 October 1563); NAS CS96/4918, 1 (28 October 1563), 6 (24 October 1571).
51. ACA, CR, xxviii, 263 (16 March 1569/70); ACA, CR, xxvii, 263 (16 March 1569/70); ACA, CR, xxviii, 65 (18 August 1573).
52. Dennison, 'Recreating the Urban Past'; Dennison, 'Power to the People?'; Lynch, 'What Ever Happened to the Medieval Burgh?', pp. 5–20; M. Lynch, *Edinburgh and the Reformation* (Edinburgh, 1981).
53. Lynch and Dingwall, 'Elite Society in Town and Country', p. 186.
54. See above, pp. 68–75.
55. ACA, CR, xxx, 492 (14 August 1581).
56. ACA, CR, xxx, 492–493 (14 August 1581). A similar account is in ACA MSS Baillie Court Book 1 (14 Aug 1581). Bannerman appears in a list of 'denyaris' where Leith, Rory and Duncan appear in a parallel list of 'adherentis'. On the subject of the calling of the craftsmen before the council to answer to these charges, see A. White, 'Religion, Politics and Society in Aberdeen', pp. 327–8.
57. ACA, CR, xxx, 493 (14 August 1581). In ACA MSS Baillie Court Book 1 (14 August 1581) this list has two dates: the date of the court and in the middle of the list the date 'primo marci 1564'. A subsequent list with only the court date, 'Curia Balliorum burgi de abd tanta in eiusdem decimo quarto augusti 1581' has Bannerman as absent from the proceedings, rather than a 'denyar', with Leythe, Rory and Duncan as 'adherentis'.
58. ACA, CR, xxx, 494 (15 August 1581).
59. Ibid.
60. ACA, CR, xxx, 495 (15 August 1581).
61. ACA, CR, xxx, 503 (28 August 1581); ACA MSS Baillie Court Book 1 (18 August 1581): 'The balleis ordainis the officers to warn John Duncan tailor to Monday cumis 8 dais to heir and see the declaration of the counsel given and poindit againis him for his enormiteis quhilk he is convikit for.'
62. ACA, CR, xxx, 503 (28 August 1581).
63. Ibid.
64. Ibid.; ACA MSS Baillie Court Book 1 (28 August 1581) notes that for 'his wilfull inobediens againis his ayt of obediens quhilk he maid when he was made a freeman and sua his crymes for quhilk he was convikit and deliverit to haf tynt his fredome and all privilege of the burght that myt hous thereby.'
65. ACA, CR, xxiv, 415–416 (8 May 1562).
66. Ibid, p. 416.
67. White, 'Religion, Politics and Society in Aberdeen', p. 322.

68. ACA, CR, xxiv, 423 (11 May 1562).
69. NAS CS96/4918, 2 (15 May 1565).
70. NAS CS96/4918, 2 (18 May 1565); *APS* 3, p. 543, c. 21. This Act ordained that 'nane of our Souerane Ladyis lieges presume pretend or tak vpoune hand to mak ony priuie conuentiounis nor assemblies within burgh put on armoire cleith tham selfis with wappinis or make sound of trumpet or talberone.'
71. Andrew Wysman appears in the alternative list as having been absent from the court. ACA MSS Baillie Court Book 1 (14 August 1581).
72. ACA MSS Baillie Court Book1 (29 September 1581).
73. NAS CS96/4918, 15 (2 October 1581).
74. NAS CS96/4918, 15 (2 October 1581).
75. NAS CS96/4918, 15 (2 October 1581). It is interesting that a month after having lost his freedom they still refer to Duncan as the deacon of the tailor craft. This is especially notable given that on 8 September 1581 the council had approved James Stewart to be the deacon of the tailor craft for the present year. It is unclear whether the mention of his former status was rhetorical to emphasize that he had abused his position in society or merely an attempt to paint an accurate account of the events as they had occurred.
76. ACA, CR, xxx, 492 (14 August 1581); ACA, CR, xxx, 612–613 (13 February 1581/2). See also NAS CS96/4918, 13–15; ACA, MSS Baillie Court Book 1 (7 September 1581), (29 September 1581).
77. For a discussion of this see Lynch and Dingwall, 'Elite Society in Town and Country', pp.185–7. See also ACA MSS Guildry Accounts 1581–4, 1587, 1594–1603. There are significant problems with using the Guildry Accounts to determine the changes in entrance fee for becoming either free of one's craft or becoming a free burgess of guild, not the least that the accounts are not entirely clear on when one individual was being made free of their craft, free burgess or free burgess of guild. Nonetheless, it is not difficult to see the increase in monies collected by the council for individuals being made free. For example, the 1582–83 accounts show a summa of £80.11.8, the 1585–86 accounts show a summa of £58.13.4 while the 1593–94 accounts show a summa of £462.11.1. These sums include both the 'fine' paid to be made free as well as the obligatory payment for guild wine. The fluctuation in individual costs make it difficult to determine whether the council had a standardized fee for certain crafts or other members of society. For example, in April 1582 John Ferchar became a free burgess of guild for 20 merks. Likewise, Andrew Chalmer cowper was made free burgess of guild resavit his craft for 20 merks. However, when Robert Donaldson was made free burgess of guild, his fee was only 15 merks.
78. ACA MSS Baillie Court Book 1 (7 September 1581). 'The said day the provost baillies and counsel desyrit and ordainit Alex Rutherford baillie and Wm Menzies to pas as commissionars for the brethren of guild of this burt to the hienes g and his hienes lordis of secreit consalle and complain vpoun the enormities of the craftismen of this burgh anent the striking and purchasing of the privilege of quhilk vtheris craftismen of the burghis of edinburgh, dundee and perth usit and josis.'
79. ACA MSS Baillie Court Book 1 (15 December 1581).
80. ACA, CR, xxx, 612 (13 February 1581/2); *RPC*, vol. 3, p. 483.
81. ACA, CR, xxx, 612 (13 February 1581/2).
82. NAS CS96/4918.
83. *RPCS*, vol. 3, p. 470.
84. Ibid., p. 471.
85. Ibid., p. 471.

86. Ibid., p. 481.
87. White argued that it had become apparent to the craftsmen that in order for them to attain the rights they were pursuing they would need to remove the powerful oligarchy controlling burgh politics. See White, 'Religion, Politics and Society in Aberdeen', p. 328.
88. *RPCS*, vol. 3, p. 482.
89. Ibid., p. 470.
90. Ibid., p. 482.
91. Ibid., p. 483.
92. Ibid., p. 484. According to the Court of Session records the case between the craftsmen and the bailies of Aberdeen had been 'continuit' in May of 1582 and ultimately 'suspendit' the following February (CS10/1).
93. ACA, CR, xxx, 722 (1 October 1582).
94. On this subject see E. Bain, *Merchants and Craftsmen*, pp. 82–9; A. White, 'The Menzies Era', pp. 235–6; White, 'Religion, Politics and Society in Aberdeen', pp. 329–30.
95. White, 'The Menzies Era', p. 236.
96. *RPCS*, p. 533.
97. Ibid. p. 533.
98. Ibid., p. 534.
99. ACA MSS Baillie Court Book 1 (5 August 1587).
100. Ibid.
101. ACA CR, 484 (21 September 1584). The account of this offence follows the accounts of the conviction of John Adamson for mispersoning a flesher by the name of Richard Gow who was also convicted for striking Adamson.
102. ACA, CR, xxv, 491 (11 February 1564/5).
103. ACA, CR, xxvi, 459 (21 November 1567).
104. ACA, CR, xxv, 489 (11 February 1564/5).
105. ACA, CR, xxv, 491 (11 February 1564/5).
106. ACA, CR, xxvi, 459 (21 November 1567). The account states that both Leith and his wife were in amercement of court for the strublens and striking of Reidfurd and his wife 'and the said William alsua convikit for the missaying of the Baillies behind thaur bakis'.
107. ACA, CR, xxvii, 85 (27 January 1541/2); ACA, CR, xvii, 96 (6 February 1541/2); ACA, CR, xvii, 552 (3 August 1543); ACA, CR, xvii, 552 (3 August 1543); ACA, CR, xviii, 296 (7 November 1544); ACA, CR, xix, 358–9 (22 June 1547); ACA, CR, xxii, 190 (6 November 1555); ACA, CR, xxii, 275 (9 March 1555/6); ACA, CR, xxii, 400 (17 August 1556); ACA, CR, xxiii, 216 (11 September 1559); ACA, CR, xxvii, 522 (7 May 1571); ACA, CR, xxvii, 804 (Pen December 1572); ACA, CR, xxxi, 11 (9 November 1582); ACA MSS Baillie Court Book 1–3 (1 July 1587); ACA MSS Baillie Court Book 1 (1 July 1587); ACA MSS Baillie Court Book 1 (6 August 1596). This list does not include cases of strublens, disobedience, deforcing, disturbing or perturbation where verbal assaults may have occurred but were not recorded in the accounts of the court proceedings. As such, it is very likely that more cases of verbal abuse occurred than were recorded.
108. 'The said day Alexander Snalbye wobster was convikit be the depositions of divers famous witness sworne and admittit for the slandering iniuring and mispersoning of the persons of the assise above wretin infarming off thame in callinh thame common learis and mensworne persons [liars and perjured] wherefore he was in am of court to forbear in tyme cuming and to amend as law will and that was gevin for dome be the mowthe of John Smyt dempster quhais mendis the provost and Baillies instantlie modifeit as fol-

lowis to wit ordainit the said Alexander snalbie to compear on Sunday nixt the elevent of this instant within the parish kirk off this bur and in tyme off preaching or prayeris eftir the same befoir the haill congregation revoik oppinlie the said blasphemous wordis as fals & untrew spoken be him rashelie promisand nevir to do nor comit the lyk in tym cuming under the pane of banishing of this towne and discharging of his fredome.' ACA, CR, xxxi, 10–11 (9 November 1582). The account of the conviction of the regraters and forestallers occurs on page 10 while the account of the conviction of Snalby is on page 11.

109. ACA MSS Baillie Court Book 1 (11 February 1585); the Council Register records the crime as striking and not strubling. ACA CR, xxxi, 734 (11 February 1585/6).

110. ACA, CR, xix, 85–6 (14 April 1546); ACA, CR, xix, 395 (28 September 1547); ACA, CR, xx, 301 (7 October 1549); ACA, CR, xx, 302 (7 October 1549); ACA, CR, xxiv, 215 (28 June 1561); ACA, CR, xxviii, 555 (1 September 1575); ACA, CR, xxxi, 119 (9 April 1582); ACA, CR, xxxi, 734 (11 February 1585/6). There are two cases where the crime committed has been recorded as strublens that could be either a physical or verbal attack. ACA, CR, xxii, 790 (24 June 1558); ACA MSS Baillie Court Book 1 (16 August 1586).

111. NAS CH2/448/1, 52 (30 September 1574).

112. NAS CH2/448/1, 67 (31 March 1575).

113. NAS CH2/448/1, 105 (20 December 1576).

114. ACA, CR, xxviii, 665 (10 January 1575/6); ACA MSS Baillie Court Book 1 (10 January 1575/6).

115. ACA MSS Baillie Court Book 1 (23 and 29 April 1581).

116. ACA MSS Baillie Court Book 1 (2 September 1581).

117. ACA MSS Baillie Court Book 1 (4 September 1581).

118. ACA Baillie Court Books 1 (7 September 1581).

119. ACA Baillie Court Books 1 (16 August 1587).

Conclusion

1. NAS CH2/448/1, 36 (4 May 1574).

2. On this subject see K. Wrightson and D. Levine, *Poverty and Piety in an English Village*, p. 110.

3. Muldrew, *The Economy of Obligation*, p. 151.

4. ACA, CR, xxxiii–1, 959–60 (18 January 1590/1). See discussion above, pp. 145–6.

5. ACA, CR, xxvii, 47 (19 May 1569).

6. See K. Wrightson and D. Levine, *Poverty and Piety in an English Village*, p. 197–211; Spufford, 'Puritanism and Social Control?', p. 43; See also M. McIntosh, *Autonomy and Community;* McIntosh, *Controlling Misbehaviour in England*.

7. Graham, *Uses of Reform*, pp. 114–24.

8. *Abdn. Counc.* vol. 2, p. 73.

9. Ibid., p. 71.

10. *APS*, 3, p. 212. Fines given out according to rank; poor to be locked in stocks, joggis or imprisoned for 4 hours for 1st fault; (women conform to their blood or husband); banishment for 3rd fault for a year and a day; all pecunial panes to go to the poor.

11. ACA, CR, xxxiv, 4 (1 October 1593).

12. ACA, CR, xxxiv, 5 (1 October 1593).

13. ACA, CR, xxxiv, 5 (1 October 1593).

14. ACA, CR, xxxiv, 4–8 (1 October 1593).

15. *APS*, 2, p. 485. Parliament believed that blasphemy brought 'the Ire and wraith of God vpone the pepill heirfoir'. Fines were to be established according to rank, with the 'puir folk to be put in the stokis or preson'.
16. Ibid. Fines were according to rank starting at £10. Poor folk were to be imprisoned for 15 days, the second fault resulted in the doubling of the punishment and the third fault led to warding of their persons or banishment for a year and a day.
17. ACA, CR, xxxi, 325 (13 February 1583/4).
18. ACA, CR, xxi, 288 (1 January 1552/3). The modification of his unlaw appears in ACA, CR, xxi, 302 (16 January 1552/3) where the council cites his misbehaviour as being 'strublens of this gud town and Kirk and stopping of godly service'.
19. ACA, CR, xxx, 16–17 (8 October 1593).
20. Torrie, 'The Guild in Fifteenth–Century Dunfermline'; Dennison, 'Power to the People?'; Lynch and Dingwall, 'Elite Society in Town and Country'.
21. G. R. DesBrisay, 'Authority and Discipline in Aberdeen: 1650–1700', (PhD dissertation, University of St Andrews, 1989); G. Desbrisay, 'City Limits: Female Philanthropists and Wet Nurses in Seventeenth–Century Scottish Towns', *Journal of the Canadian Historical Association* 8 (1997), pp. 39–60.
22. This is best exemplified in the creation of the 'extracts of the baillie court books anent the craftsmen 1553–1582', which highlights the activities surrounding the pursuit of 'newer liberties and privileges.' NAS CS96/4918.
23. Shoemaker, *Prosecution and Punishment*, p. 6.

.

WORKS CITED

Primary Sources, Manuscript

Aberdeen

Aberdeen City Archives (ACA)

ACA, MSS Baillie Court Books, vols i–v

ACA, Council Register, vols xvii–xxxiii–1

ACA, Guildry Accounts, 1581–4, 1587, 1594–1603

ACA, Kirk and Bridge Works Accounts, 1571–1664

ACA, Register of Mortifications, vol. i

ACA, Treasury Accounts, vols i–ii

Edinburgh

National Archives of Scotland (NAS)

NAS, CH2/448/1 (Aberdeen St Nicholas Kirk Session)

NAS, CS96/4918 (Burgh of Aberdeen, Extracts from Baillie Court Book)

Primary Sources, Printed

Charters and Other Writs Illustrating the History of the Royal Burgh of Aberdeen, ed. P. J. Anderson (Aberdeen: Printed by Order of the Lord Provost, Magistrates and Town Council, 1890).

Abredoniae vtrivsque descriptio: A description of both touns of Aberdeen, ed. C. Innes and J. Gordon (Edinburgh: Spalding Club, 1842).

Ancient Laws and Customs of the Burghs of Scotland, 1124–1424 and 1424–1707, ed. C. Innes, 2 vols (Edinburgh: SBRS, 1868–1910).

Annals of Aberdeen From the Reign of King William the Lion to the End of the Year 1818; With an Account of the City, Cathedral, and University of Old Aberdeen, ed. W. Kennedy (London: A. Brown & Co., 1818).

The Practicks of Sir James Balfour of Pittendreich, ed. P. G. B. McNeill, 2 vols (Edinburgh: Stair Society, 1962).

Cartularium Ecclesiae Sancti Nicholai Aberdonensis, ed. J. Cooper, 2 vols (Aberdeen: New Spalding Club, 1888–92).

Early Records of the Burgh of Aberdeen, 1317, 1398–1407, ed. W. C. Dickinson (Edinburgh: T. and A. Constable for the Scottish History Society, 1957).

Extracts from the Council Register of the Burgh of Aberdeen, ed. J. Stuart, 4 vols (Aberdeen: Spalding Club & SBRS, 1844–72).

Memorials of the Alderman, Provosts, and Lord Provosts of Aberdeen, 1357–1895, ed. A. M. Munro (Aberdeen: Free Press Printing Work, 1897).

Mortifications under the Charge of the Provost, Magistrates, and Town Council of Aberdeen (Aberdeen: D. Chalmers and Company 1849).

Register of the Privy Council of Scotland, ed. J. H. Burton *et al.*, 38 vols (Edinburgh: General Record Office for Scotland, 1877).

Selections from the Records of the Kirk Session, Presbytery and Synod of Aberdeen (Spalding Club, 1846).

The Acts of the Parliaments of Scotland, ed. T. Thomson and C. Innes, 12 vols (Edinburgh, 1814–75).

The First Book of Discipline, ed. J. K. Cameron (Edinburgh: St Andrew Press, 1972).

William Hay's Lectures on Marriage, ed. J. C. Barry (Edinburgh: Stair Society, 1967).

Secondary Sources

Addy, J., *Sin and Society in the Seventeenth Century* (London: Routledge, 1989).

Amussen, S., *An Ordered Society: Gender and Class in Early Modern England* (Oxford: Basil Blackwell, 1988).

—, 'Punishment, Discipline and Power: The Social Meanings of Violence in Early Modern England', *Journal of British Studies* 34 (January 1995), pp. 1–34.

Bain, E., *Merchant and Craft Guilds: A History of the Aberdeen Incorporated Trades* (Aberdeen: J. & J. P. Edmond & Spark, 1887).

Black, A., *Political Thought in Europe 1250–1450* (Cambridge: Cambridge University Press, 1993).

Blanchard, I., E. Gemmill, N. Mayhew and I. D. Whyte, 'The Economy: Town and Country', in E. P. Dennison, D. Ditchburn and M. Lynch (eds), *Aberdeen before 1800: A New History* (East Linton, Tuckwell Press, 2002), pp. 129–58.

Boes, M. R., 'Public Appearance and Criminal Judicial Practices in Early Modern Germany', *Social Science History*, 20:2 (1996), pp. 259–79.

—, 'Dishonourable Youth, Guilds, and the Changed World View of Sex, Illegitimacy and Women in Late Sixteenth–Century Germany', *Continuity and Change*, 18:3, (2003), pp. 345–72.

Booton, H., 'Economic and Social Change in Later Medieval Aberdeen', in Smith (ed.), *New Light on Medieval Aberdeen* (Aberdeen: Aberdeen University Press, 1985), pp. 46–55.

Braddick, M. and J. Walter (eds), *Negotiating Power in Early Modern Society: Order, Hierarchy and Subordination in Britain and Ireland* (Cambridge: Cambridge University Press, 2001).

Brotherstone, T. and D. Ditchburn (eds), *Freedom and Authority, Scotland* c. *1050– c. 1650: Historical and Historiographical Essays presented to Grant G. Simpson.* (East Linton: Tuckwell, 2000).

Brown, K., *Bloodfeud in Scotland, 1573–1625* (Edinburgh: John Donald, 1986).

—, 'In Search of the Godly Magistrate in Reformation Scotland', *Journal of Ecclesiastical History*, 40 (1989), pp. 553–81.

Brown, Y. G. and R. Ferguson, *Twisted Sisters: Women, Crime and Deviance in Scotland since 1400* (East Linton: Tuckwell Press, 2002).

Brundage, J., 'Sin, Crime and the Pleasures of the Flesh: The Medieval Church Judges Sexual Offences', in P. Linehan and J. L. Nelson (eds), *The Medieval World* (London & New York: Routledge, 2001), pp. 294–307.

Burke, P., *The Historical Anthropology of Early Modern Italy* (Cambridge: Cambridge University Press, 1987).

Capp, B., 'Arson, Threats of Arson and Incivility in Early Modern England', in P. Burke, B. Harrison and P. Slack (eds), *Civil Histories: Essays in Honour of Sir Keith Thomas* (Oxford, 2000), pp.197–213.

—, *When Gossips Meet: Women, Family and Neighbourhood in Early Modern England* (Oxford: Oxford University Press, 2003).

Carlyle, R. W. and A. J. Carlyle, *A History of Mediaeval Political Theory in the West*, vol. 4 (Edinburgh: William Blackwood & Sons, Ltd., 1922).

Cockburn, J. S., *Crime in England, 1550–1800* (Princeton: Princeton University Press, 1977).

— (ed.), 'Twelve Silly Men? The Trial Jury at Assizes, 1560–1670', in Cockburn and Green (eds), *Twelve Good Men and True: The Criminal Jury in England, 1200–1800* (Princeton: Princeton University Press, 1988), pp. 158–81.

Cogswell, T., 'Underground Verse and the Transformation of Early Stuart Political Culture', in S. Amussen and M. A. Kishlansky (eds), *Political Culture and Cultural Politics in Early Modern Europe* (Manchester: Manchester University Press, 1995), pp. 277–300.

Collinson, P., *Godly People: Essays on English Protestantism and Puritanism* (London: The Hambledon Press, 1983).

—, 'From Iconoclasm to Iconophobia: The Cultural Impact of the Second English Reformation', The Stenton Lectures (Reading: Department of History, 1986).

—, *The Birthpangs of Protestant England: Religious and Cultural Change in the Sixteenth and Seventeenth Centuries* (New York: St Martin's Press, 1988).

—, *The Sixteenth Century, 1485–1603* (Oxford: Oxford University Press, 2002).

Connors, R. and J. R. D. Falconer, 'Cornering the Cheshire Cat: Reflections on the "New British History" and studies in Early Modern British Identities', *Canadian Journal of History*, 36 (April 2001), pp. 85–108.

Corfield, P. J., 'East Anglia', in P. Clark (ed.), *The Cambridge Urban History of Britain* (Cambridge: Cambridge University Press, 2000), pp. 31–48.

Curtis, T. and J. A. Sharpe, 'Crime in Tudor and Stuart England', *History Today*, 38 (1988), pp. 23–9.

Davies, S. J., 'The Courts and the Scottish Legal System 1600–1747: The Case of Stirlingshire', in Gattrell, Lenman and Parker (eds), *Crime and the Law: The Social History of Crime in Western Europe Since 1500* (London: Europa, 1980), pp. 120–55.

Dawson, J. '"The Face of Ane Perfyt Reformed Kyrk": St Andrews and the Early Scottish Reformation', in J. Kirk (ed.), *Humanism and Reform: The Church in Europe, England and Scotland, 1400–1643* (Oxford: Blackwell, 1991), pp. 413–36.

de Saussure, F., *Course in General Linguistics*, ed. C. Bally and A. Sechehaye, (Toronto: McGraw-Hill, 1966).

Dean, T., *Crime in Medieval Europe, 1200–1550* (New York: Longman, 2001).

Dennison, E. P., 'Power to the People? The Myth of the Medieval Burgh Community', in S. Foster, A. Macinnes and R. Macinnes (eds), *Scottish Power Centres: From the Early Middle Ages to the Twentieth Century* (Glasgow: Cruithne Press, 1998), pp. 100–31.

—, 'Recreating the Urban Past', in T. Brotherstone and D. Ditchburn, (eds), *Freedom and Authority, Scotland c. 1050–c. 1650: Historical and Historiographical Essays presented to Grant G. Simpson* (East Linton: Tuckwell Press, 2000), pp. 275–84.

—, D. Ditchburn and M. Lynch (eds), *Aberdeen Before 1800: A New History* (East Linton, Tuckwell Press, 2002).

DesBrisay, G., 'City Limits: Female Philanthropists and Wet Nurses in Seventeenth–Century Scottish Towns', *Journal of the Canadian Historical Association*, 8 (1997), pp. 39–60.

—, 'Twisted by Definition: Women Under Godly Discipline in Seventeenth-Century Scottish Towns' in Y. G. Brown and R. Ferguson (eds), *Twisted Sisters: Women, Crime and Deviance in Scotland Since 1400* (East Linton, 2002), pp. 137–56.

Diefendorf, B., *Beneath the Cross: Catholics and Huguenots in Sixteenth-Century Paris* (Oxford: Oxford University Press, 1991).

Duncan, A. A. M., *Scotland: The Making of the Kingdom* (Edinburgh: Edinburgh University Press, 1973).

Durkheim, E., *The Elementary Forms of the Religious Life,* trans. J. W. Swain (London: George Allen & Unwin Ltd., 1976).

Elton, G. R., 'Introduction: Crime and the Historian', in J. S. Cockburn (ed.), *Crime in England 1550–1800* (Princeton, NJ: Princeton University Press, 1977).

Ewan, E., 'The Community of the Burgh in the Fourteenth Century', in M. Lynch, M. Spearman and G. Stell (eds), *The Scottish Medieval Town* (Edinburgh: John Donald, 1988), pp. 32–45.

—, *Townlife in Fourteenth-Century Scotland* (Edinburgh: Edinburgh University Press, 1990).

—, 'Scottish Portias: Women in the Courts in Mediaeval Scottish Towns', *Journal of the Canadian Historical Association* 3 (1992), pp. 27–43.

— and M. Meikle (eds), *Women in Scotland: c. 1100 – c. 1750* (East Linton: Tuckwell Press, 1999).

—, '"Many Injurious Words": Defamation and Gender in Late Medieval Scotland', in R. A. McDonald (ed.), *History, Literature, and Music in Scotland, 700–1560* (Toronto, 2002), pp. 163–86.

—, '"Tongue you lied": The Role of the Tongue in Rituals of Public Penance in Late Medieval Scotland', in E. D. Craun (ed.), *The Hands of the Tongue: Essays on Deviant Speech* (Kalamazoo: Medieval Institute Publications, 2007), pp. 115–36.

Falconer, J. R. D., 'A Family Affair: Households, Misbehaving and the Community in Sixteenth-Century Aberdeen', in J. Nugent and E. Ewan (eds), *Finding the Family in Medieval and Early Modern Scotland,* (Aldershot: Ashgate, 2008), pp. 139–50.

—, '"Mony Utheris Divars Odious Crymes": Women, Petty Crime and Power in Later Sixteenth-Century Aberdeen', *Crimes and Misdemeanours: Deviance and the Law in Historical Perspective*, 4:1 (March, 2010), pp. 7–36.

—, 'Surveying Scotland's Urban Past: The Pre-Modern Burgh', *History Compass*, 9:1 (2011), pp. 34–44.

Finch, A. J., 'The Nature of Violence in the Middle Ages: An Alternative Perspective', *Historical Research*, 70 (1997), pp. 249–68.

Finlay, J., *Men of Law in Pre-Reformation Scotland* (East Linton: Tuckwell Press, 2000).

Fletcher, A. and J. Stevenson (eds), *Order and Disorder in Early Modern England* (Cambridge: Cambridge University Press, 1985).

Flett, I., and J. Cripps, 'Documentary Sources', in M. Lynch, M. Spearman and G. Stell (eds), *The Scottish Medieval Town* (Edinburgh: John Donald Publishers Ltd., 1988), p. 18–41.

Foucault, M., *Discipline and Punish: The Birth of the Prison* (New York: Random House, 1978).

Foucault, M., 'The Subject and the Power', *Critical Inquiry*, 8:4 (1982), pp. 777–95.

Gaskill, M., *Crime and Mentalities in Early Modern England* (Cambridge: Cambridge University Press, 2000).

Gatrell, V. A. C., B. Lenman and G. Parker (eds), *Crime and the Law: The Social History of Crime in Western Europe Since 1500* (London: Europa, 1980).

Gemmill, E. and N. Mayhew, *Changing Values in Medieval Scotland: A Study of Prices, Money, and Weights and Measures* (Cambridge: Cambridge University Press, 1995).

Gibson, A. J. and T. C. Smout, *Prices, Food and Wages in Scotland, 1550–1780* (Cambridge: Cambridge University Press, 1995).

Gillespie, R., 'Negotiating Order in Early Seventeenth-Century Ireland', in M. Braddick and J. Walter (eds), *Negotiating Power in Early Modern Society: Order, Hierarchy and Subordination in Britain and Ireland* (Cambridge: Cambridge University Press, 2001), pp. 188–205.

Goodare, J., *State and Society in Early Modern Scotland* (Oxford: Oxford University Press, 1999).

Gowing, L., 'Language, Power and the Law: Women's Slander Litigation in Early Modern London', in J. Kermode and G. Walker (eds), *Women, Crime and the Courts in Early Modern England* (London: London University College, 1994), pp. 26–48.

—, *Domestic Dangers: Women, Words and Sex in Early Modern London* (Oxford: Oxford University Press, 1996).

Graham, M. 'Equality before the Kirk? Church Discipline and the Elite in Reformation-era Scotland', *Archiv für Reformationsgeschichte* 84 (1993), pp. 289–310.

—, 'The Civil Sword and the Scottish Kirk in the Late Sixteenth Century', in W. F. Graham (ed.), *Later Calvinism: International Perspectives* (Kirksville: Sixteenth Century Publishers, 1994), pp. 237–48.

—, *The Uses of Reform: Godly Discipline and Popular Behaviour in Scotland and Beyond, 1560–1610* (Leiden: E. J. Brill, 1996).

Grant, I. F., *The Social and Economic Development of Scotland before 1600* (Edinburgh: Oliver & Boyd, 1930).

Gramsci, A., *Selections From the Prison Notebooks,* ed. Q. Hoare and G. N. Smith. (New York: International Publishers, 1971).

Greenshields, M., *An Economy of Violence in Early Modern France: Crime and Justice in the Haute Auvergne, 1587–1664* (Pennsylvania: Penn State University Press, 1994).

Griffiths, P., *Youth and Authority: Formative Experiences in England, 1560–1640* (Oxford: Oxford University Press, 1996).

—, 'Meanings of Nightwalking in Early Modern England', *The Seventeenth Century* 13:2 (Autumn 1998), pp. 212–38.

—, 'Bodies and Souls in Norwich: Punishing Petty Crime, 1540–1700,' in S. Devereaux and P. Griffiths (eds), *Penal Practice and Culture, 1500–1900* (New York, NY: Palgrave, 2004), pp. 85–120.

—, *Lost Londons: Change, Crime, and Control in the Capital City, 1550–1660* (Cambridge: Cambridge University Press, 2008).

—, A. Fox and S. Hindle (eds), *The Experience of Authority in Early Modern England* (New York, NY: St Martin's Press, 1996).

Gunn, S., 'From Hegemony to Governmentality: Changing Conceptions of Power in Social History', *Journal of Social History*, 39:3 (2006), pp. 705–20.

Hanawalt, B. '"Good Governance" in the Medieval and Early Modern Context', *JBS*, 37:3 (July 1998), pp. 245–57.

— and D. Wallace (eds), *Medieval Crime and Social Control* (Minneapolis, MN: University of Minnesota Press, 1999).

Harris, T. (ed.), *The Politics of the Excluded, c. 1500–1850* (Basingstoke: Palgrave, 2001).

Harrison, J., 'Women and the Branks in Stirling, *c.* 1600 to *c.* 1730', *Scottish Economic and Social History* 18:2 (1998), pp. 114–31.

Herrup, C. B., 'New Shoes and Mutton Pies: Investigative Responses to Theft in Seventeenth-Century East Sussex', *Historical Journal*, 27 (1984), pp. 811–30.

—, 'Crime, Law and Society: A Review Article', *Society for Comparative Study of Society and History* 27:1 (January 1985), pp. 159–70.

—, 'The Law and Morality in Seventeenth-Century England', *Past and Present*, 106 (1985), pp. 102–23.

—, *The Common Peace: Participation and the Criminal Law in Seventeenth-Century England* (Cambridge: Cambridge University Press, 1987).

Hindle, S. 'The Shaming of Margaret Knowsley: Gossip, Gender and the Experience of Authority in Early Modern England', *Continuity and Change,* 9:3 (1994), pp. 391–419.

—, 'Custom, Festival and Protest in Early Modern England: The Little Budworth Wakes, St Peter's Day, 1596', *Rural History,* 6:2 (1995), pp. 155–78.

—, 'The Keeping of the Public Peace', in P. Griffiths, A. Fox and S. Hindle (eds), *The Experience of Authority in Early Modern England* (Basingstoke: Macmillan Press, 1996), pp. 213–48.

—, 'Power, Poor Relief, and Social Relations in Holland Fen, *c.* 1600–1800', *Historical Journal,* 41:1 (1998), pp. 67–96.

—, 'A Sense of Place? Becoming and Belonging in the Rural Parish, 1550–1650', in Shepard and Withington (eds), *Communities in Early Modern England: Networks, Place, Rhetoric* (Manchester: Manchester University Press, 2000), pp. 96–114.

—, *The State and Social Change in Early Modern England, 1550–1640* (Basingstoke: Palgrave, 2000).

—, 'Exhortation and Entitlement: Negotiating Social Inequality in English Rural Communities, 1550–1650', in M. Braddick and J. Walter (eds), *Negotiating Power in Early Modern Society: Order, Hierarchy and Subordination in Britain and Ireland* (Cambridge: Cambridge University Press, 2001), pp. 102–22.

— , 'Dependency, Shame and Belonging: Badging the Deserving Poor, *c.* 1550–1750', *Cultural and Social History,* 1:1 (January 2004), pp. 6–35.

—, *On the Parish? – The Micro-Politics of Poor Relief in Rural England c. 1550–1750* (Oxford: Oxford University Press, 2004).

Houlbrooke, R., *Church Courts and the People During the English Reformation, 1520–1570* (Oxford: Oxford University Press, 1979).

Hsia, R. P., *Social Discipline in the Reformation: Central Europe 1550–1750* (London: Routledge, 1989).

Hurl-Eamon, J., *Gender and Petty Violence in London, 1680–1720* (Ohio: Ohio State University Press, 2005).

Ingram, M., 'Communities and Courts: Law and Disorder in Early-Seventeenth-Century Wiltshire', in J. S. Cockburn (ed.), *Crime in England, 1550–1800* (Princeton, NJ: Princeton University Press, 1977), pp. 110–34.

—, 'Religion, Communities and Moral Discipline in Late Sixteenth- and Early-Seventeenth-Century England: Case Studies', in K. von Greyerz (ed.), *Religion and Society in Early Modern Europe* (Boston, MA: Allen & Unwin, 1984), pp. 177–93.

—, *Church Courts, Sex and Marriage, 1570–1640* (Cambridge: Cambridge University Press, 1987).

—, '"Scolding Women Cucked or Washed": A Crisis in Gender Relations in Early Modern England?', in J. Kermode and G. Walker (eds), *Women, Crime and the Courts in Early Modern England* (London: London University College, 1994), pp. 48–80.

—, 'Law, Litigants and the Construction of "Honour": Slander Suits in Early Modern England', in P. Coss (ed.), *The Moral World of the Law* (Cambridge: Cambridge University Press, 2000), pp. 134–60.

James, M., 'At the Crossroads of the Political Culture: The Essex Revolt, 1601', in M. James (ed.), *Society, Politics and Culture: Studies in Early Modern England* (Cambridge: Cambridge University Press, 1986), pp.416–66.

Jones, K., *Gender and Petty Crime in Late Medieval England: The Local Courts in Kent, 1460–1560* (Woodbridge: Boydell, 2006).

Jutte, R., *Poverty and Deviance in Early Modern Europe* (Cambridge: Cambridge University Press, 1994).

Keith, A., *A Thousand Years of Aberdeen* (Aberdeen: Aberdeen University Press, 1972).

Kermode, J. and G. Walker (eds), *Women, Crime and the Courts in Early Modern England* (London: London University College, 1994).

King, P. 'Legal Change, Customary Right, and Social Conflict in Late Eighteenth-Century England: The Origins of the Great Gleaning Case of 1788', *Law and History Review*, 10:1 (1992), pp. 1–31.

—, 'Punishing Assault: The Transformation of Attitudes in the English Courts', in *Journal of Interdisciplinary History*, 27:1 (1996), pp. 43–74.

—, *Crime, Justice and Discretion in England, 1740–1820* (Oxford: Oxford University Press, 2000).

Kishlansky, M. A. and S. D. Amussen (eds), *Political Culture and Cultural Politics in Early Modern England: Essays Presented to David Underdown* (Manchester: Manchester University Press, 1995).

Lake, P., 'Periodization, Politics and "the Social"', *Journal of British Studies*, 37:3 (July 1998), pp. 279–90.

Laqueur, T., 'Crowds, Carnival and the State in English Executions, 1604–1868', in A. L. Beier, D. Cannadine and J. M. Rosenheim (eds), *The First Modern Society: Essays in English History in Honour of Lawrence Stone* (Cambridge: Cambridge University Press, 1989), pp. 305–56.

Lawson, P. G., 'Property Crime and Hard Times in England, 1559–1624', *Law & History Review,* 4 (1986), pp. 95–127.

—, 'Patriarchy, Crime and the Courts: The Criminality of Women in Late Tudor and Early Stuart England', in G. T. Smith, A. N. May and S. Deveraux (eds), *Criminal Justice in the Old World and the New: Essays in Honour of J.M. Beattie* (Toronto: University of Toronto Press, 1998), pp.16–57.

Lenman, B. 'The Limits of Godly Discipline in the Early Modern Period with particular reference to England and Scotland', in K. von Greyerz (ed.), *Religion and Society in Early Modern Europe* (Boston, MA: Allen & Unwin, 1984), pp. 124–45.

Lenman, B. and G. Parker, 'Crime and Control in Scotland, 1500–1800', *History Today*, (January 1980), pp. 13–17.

Levack, B. P., 'The Great Scottish Witch Hunt of 1661–1662', *Journal of British Studies,* 20:1 (1980), pp. 90–108.

Lindberg, C., *Beyond Charity: Reformation Initiatives for the Poor* (Minneapolis, MN: Fortress Press, 1993).

Lynch, M., *Edinburgh and the Reformation* (Edinburgh: John Donald Publishers, 1981).

—, 'Whatever Happened to the Medieval Burgh? Some Guidelines for Sixteenth and Seventeenth Century Historians', *Scottish Economic and Social History*, vol. 4 (1984), pp. 5–20

— (ed.), *The Early Modern Town in Scotland* (London: Croom Helm, 1987).

— (ed.), *The Scottish Medieval Town* (Edinburgh: John Donald Publishers, 1988).

—, 'Urbanisation and Urban Networks in Seventeenth Century Scotland: Some Further Thoughts', *Scottish Economic and Social History*, 12 (1992), pp. 24–41.

— and H. Dingwall, 'Elite Society in Town and Country' in E. P. Dennison, D. Ditchburn and M. Lynch (eds), *Aberdeen Before 1800: A New History* (East Linton, Tuckwell Press, 2002), pp. 181–200.

—, G. DesBrisay and M. Pittock, 'The Faith of the People', in E. P. Dennison, D. Ditchburn and M. Lynch (eds), *Aberdeen before 1800: A New History* (East Linton, Tuckwell Press, 2002), p. 289–308.

Lythe, S. G. E., *The Economy of Scotland in its European Setting, 1550–1625* (Edinburgh: Oliver & Boyd, 1960).

MacDougall, N. (ed.), *Church, Politics and Society: Scotland 1408–1929* (Edinburgh: John Donald, 1983).

Mann, M., *The Sources of Social Power: vol. 1, A History of Power from the Beginning to AD 1760* (Cambridge: Cambridge University Press, 1986).

Marsh, C., 'Order and Place in England, 1580–1640: The View from the Pew', *Journal of British Studies*, 44:1 (January 2005), pp. 3–26.

Mason, R. A., *Kingship and the Commonweal: Political Thought in Renaissance and Reformation Scotland* (East Linton: Tuckwell Press, 1998).

McIntosh, M., *Autonomy and Community: The Royal Manner of Havering, 1200–1500* (Cambridge: Cambridge University Press, 1986).

—, *Controlling Misbehaviour in England, 1370–1600* (Cambridge: Cambridge University Press, 1998).

McLennan, B., 'The Reformation in the Burgh of Aberdeen', *Northern Scotland*, 2:2 (1976–7), pp. 119–44.

McNeill, P. G. B. (ed.), *The Practicks of Sir James Balfour of Pittendreich*, vol. 1 (Brussels, 1962).

Meyerson, M. D., D. Thiery and O. Falk (eds), *'A Great Effusion of Blood'?: Interpreting Medieval Violence* (Toronto: University of Toronto Press, 2004).

Muldrew, C., 'The Culture of Reconciliation: Community and the Settlement of Economic Disputes in Early Modern England', *Historical Journal*, 39:4 (1996), pp. 915–42.

—, *The Economy of Obligation: The Culture of Credit and Social Relations in Early Modern England* (Basingstoke: Macmillan, 1998).

Murray, A., 'Huntly's Rebellion and the Administration of Justice in North-East Scotland, 1570–1573', *Northern Scotland*, 4:1 (1981), pp. 1–6.

Myeroff, B., 'Rites of Passage: Process and Paradox', in V. Turner (ed.), *Celebration: Studies in Festivity and Ritual* (Washington, DC: Smithsonian Institution Press, 1982), pp. 109–35.

Parker, D., *La Rochelle and the French Monarch: Conflict and Order in 17th Century France* (London: Royal Historical Society, 1980).

Parsons, T., *Structure and Process in Modern Societies* (New York: Free Press, 1960).

Pickett, J. P. (ed.), *The American Heritage Dictionary of the English Language*, 4th edn (Boston, MA: Houghton Mifflin, 2000).

Robbins, K., *City on the Ocean Sea: La Rochelle, 1530–1650: Urban Society, Religion, and Politics on the French Atlantic Frontier* (New York, NY: E. J. Brill, 1997).

Roberts, P., *City in Conflict: Troyes during the French Wars of Religion* (Manchester: Manchester University Press, 1996).

Rollison, D., *The Local Origins of Modern Society: Gloucestershire 1500–1800* (London: Routledge, 1992).

—, 'Discourse and Class Struggle: The Politics of Industry in Early Modern England', *Social History*, 26:2 (May 2001), pp. 166–89.

Ruff, J. R., *Violence in Early Modern Europe, 1500–1800* (Cambridge: Cambridge University Press, 2001).

Sanderson, M. H. B., *Scottish Rural Society in the Sixteenth Century* (Edinburgh: J. Donald, 1982).

—, *Ayrshire and the Reformation: People and Change, 1490–1600* (East Linton: Tuckwell Press, 1996).

—, *A Kindly Place? Living in Sixteenth Century Scotland* (East Linton: Tuckwell Press, 2002).

Schilling, H., '"History of Crime" or "History of Sin"? Some Reflections on the Social History of Early Modern Church Discipline', in E. Kouri and T. Scott (eds), *Politics and Society in Reformation Europe* (New York, NY: St Martin's Press, 1987) pp. 289–310.

Scott, J., *The Moral Economy of the Peasant: Rebellion and Subsistence in Southeast Asia* (New Haven, CT: Yale University Press, 1976).

Sharpe, J. A. 'The History of Crime in Late Medieval and Early Modern England: A Review of the Field', *Social History*, 7:2 (1981), pp. 187–203.

—, '"Such Disagreement betwyx Neighbours": Litigation and Human Relations in Early Modern England', in J. Bossy (ed.), *Disputes and Settlements: Law and Human Relations in the West* (Cambridge: Cambridge University Press, 1983), pp.167–87.

—, '"Last Dying Speeches": Religion, Ideology and Public Execution in Seventeenth-Century England', *Past and Present*, 107 (1985), pp. 144–67.

—, 'The People and the Law', in Barry Reay (ed.), *Popular Culture in Seventeenth-Century England* (New York, NY: St Martin's Press, 1985), pp. 244–70.

—, *Crime in Early Modern England, 1550–175*, 2nd edn (London: Longman, 1999).

Shepard, A., 'Manhood, Credit and Patriarchy in Early Modern England c. 1580–1640', *Past and Present*, 167 (May 2000), pp. 75–106.

Shepard, A. and P. Withington (eds), *Communities in Early Modern England: Networks, Place, Rhetoric* (Manchester: Manchester University Press, 2000).

Shoemaker, R., *Prosecution and Punishment: Petty Crime and the Law in London and Rural Middlesex, c. 1660–1725* (Cambridge: Cambridge University Press, 1991).

Slack, P., *Poverty and Policy in Tudor and Stuart England* (New York: Longman, 1988).

—, *From Reformation to Improvement: Public Welfare in Early Modern England* (Oxford: Clarendon Press, 1999).

Smith, J. (ed.), *New Light on Medieval Aberdeen* (Aberdeen: Aberdeen University Press, 1985).

Smout, T. C., 'Famine and Famine Relief in Scotland', in L. M. Cullen and T. C. Smout (eds), *Comparative Aspects of Scottish and Irish Economic and Social History* (Edinburgh: John Donald, 1977), pp. 21–31.

—, 'Coping with Plague in Sixteenth and Seventeenth-Century Scotland', *Scotia*, 2:1 (1978), pp. 19–33.

Spufford, M., 'Puritanism and Social Control?', in A. Fletcher and J. Stevenson (eds), *Order and Disorder in Early Modern England* (Cambridge: Cambridge University Press, 1985), pp. 41–57.

Thomas, J., 'The Craftsmen of Elgin, 1540–1660', in T. Brotherstone and D. Ditchburn (eds), *Freedom and Authority, Scotland c. 1050– c. 1650: Historical and Historiographical Essays presented to Grant G. Simpson* (East Linton: Tuckwell, 2000), pp. 143–54.

Thompson, E. P., *The Making of the English Working Class* (London, 1963).

Tilly, C. 'War Making and State Making as Organized Crime', in P. Evans *et al.* (eds), *Bringing the State Back In* (Cambridge: Cambridge University Press, 1985), pp. 169–85.

—, *Coercion, Capital, and European States, AD 990–1990* (Cambridge, MA: Blackwell Publishing, 1992).

— and W. Blockmans (eds), *Cities and the Rise of States in Europe, A.D. 1000 to 1800* (Boulder, CO: Westview Press, 1994).

Todd, M. 'Profane Pastimes and the Reformed Community: The Persistence of Popular Festivities in Early Modern Scotland', *Journal of British Studies,* 39:2 (2000), pp. 123–56.

—, *Culture of Protestantism in Early Modern Scotland* (New Haven, CT: Yale University Press, 2002).

Torrie, E. P. D., 'The Guild in Fifteenth-Century Dunfermline', in M. Lynch, M. Spearman and G. Stell (eds), *The Scottish Medieval Town* (Edinburgh: John Donald, 1988), pp. 245–60.

—, *Medieval Dundee: A Town and its People* (Dundee: Abertay Historical Society, 1990).

Tyson, R., 'People in the Two Towns', in E. P. Dennison, D. Ditchburn and M. Lynch (eds), *Aberdeen Before 1800: A New History* (East Linton, Tuckwell Press, 2002), pp. 111–28.

Underdown, D., 'The Taming of the Scold: The Enforcement of Patriarchal Authority in Early Modern England', in A. Fletcher and J. Stevenson, *Order and Disorder in Early Modern England* (Cambridge: Cambridge University Press, 1985), pp. 116–36.

Verschuur, M., 'Merchants and Craftsmen in Sixteenth-Century Perth', in M. Lynch (ed.), *The Early Modern Town in Scotland*, pp. 36–54.

Walker, D. M., *The Institutions of the Law of Scotland. Deduced from its originals, and Collated with the Civil, Canon and Feudal Laws, and with the Customs of Neighbouring Nations. In*

IV Books by James, Viscount of Stair (1965) (Edinburgh and Glasgow: University Press, 1981).

—, *The Scottish Jurists* (Edinburgh: W. Green, 1985).

—, *A Legal History of Scotland. vol. 3, The Sixteenth Century* (Edinburgh: T & T Clarke Ltd., 1995).

Walker, G., 'Women, Theft and the World of Stolen Goods', in J. Kermode and G. Walker (eds), *Women, Crime and the Courts in Early Modern England* (London: University College London, 1994), pp. 81–105.

—, *Crime, Gender and Social Order in Early Modern England* (Cambridge: Cambridge University Press, 2003).

Walter, J., *Understanding Popular Violence in the English Revolution: The Colchester Plunderers* (Cambridge: Cambridge University Press, 1999).

Warrack, A. (ed.), *Chambers Scots Dictionary* (Edinburgh: W & R Chambers Ltd, 1977).

Weisser, M., *Crime and Punishment in Early Modern Europe* (New Jersey: Humanities Press, 1979).

White, A., 'The Reformation in Aberdeen', in J. Smith (ed.), *New Light on Medieval Aberdeen* (Aberdeen: Aberdeen University Press, 1985), pp. 58–66.

White, A., 'The Impact of the Reformation on a Burgh Community: The Case of Aberdeen', in M. Lynch (ed.), *The Early Modern Town in Scotland* (London: Croom Helm, 1987), pp. 81–101.

White, A., 'Queen Mary's Northern Province', in M. Lynch (ed.), *Mary Stewart Queen in Three Kingdoms* (Oxford: B. Blackwell, 1988), pp. 53–70.

White, A., 'The Menzies Era: Sixteenth-Century Politics', in E. P. Dennison, D. Ditchburn and M. Lynch (eds), *Aberdeen Before 1800: A New History* (East Linton, Tuckwell Press, 2002), p. 224–37.

Whyte, I. D. 'Urbanisation in Early-Modern Scotland: A Preliminary Analysis', *Scottish Economic and Social History*, 9 (1989), pp. 21–37.

—, *Scotland Before the Industrial Revolution: An Economic and Social History, c. 1050–c. 1750* (Harlow, Essex: Longman, 1995).

Wood, A. 'Social Conflict and Change in the Mining Communities of North-West Derbyshire, c. 1600–1700', *International Review of Social History*, 38 (1993), pp. 31–58.

—, '"Poor Men Woll Speke One Day": Plebeian Languages of Deference and Defiance in England, c. 1520–1640', in T. Harris (ed.), *The Politics of the Excluded, 1500–1850* (Basingstoke, 2001), pp. 67–98.

—, *Riot, Rebellion and Popular Politics in Early Modern England* (London and New York: Palgrave, 2002).

Wormald, J., *Mary Queen of Scots: Politics, Passion and a Kingdom Lost* (London: Tauris, 2001).

Wrightson, K., 'Alehouses, Order and Reformation in Rural England, 1590–1660', in E. and S. Yeo (eds), *Popular Culture and Class Conflict, 1590–1914: Explorations in the History of Labour and Leisure* (Sussex: Harvester Press, 1981), pp. 1–27.

—, *English Society, 1580–1680* (London: Hutchinson, 1982).

—, 'The Politics of the Parish in Early Modern England', in P. Griffiths, A. Fox and S. Hindle (eds), *The Experience of Authority in Early Modern England* (Basingstoke: Macmillan Press, 1996).

—, 'Mutualities and Obligations: Changing Social Relationships in Early Modern England', in Proceedings of the British Academy, 2005 Lectures, vol. 139 (Oxford: Oxford University Press, 2006), pp. 1–37.

— and D. Levine, *Poverty and Piety in an English Village, 1525–1700*, 2nd edn (Oxford: Oxford University Press, 1995).

Unpublished Theses and Papers

Booton, H., 'Burgesses and Landed Men in North-East Scotland in the Later Middle Ages: A Study in Social Interaction' (PhD dissertation, University of Aberdeen, 1987).

Clarke, G. B., 'The Remedy of Lawborrowis in Scots Law' (LLM dissertation, University of Edinburgh, 1984).

DesBrisay, G. R., 'Authority and Discipline in Aberdeen: 1650–1700' (PhD dissertation, University of St Andrews, 1989).

Ewan, E., "There was nae justice to be got in this tolbooth': Insults against Officials in Sixteenth-Century Scottish Towns' (Paper presented at the Sixteenth-Century Studies Conference, Toronto, Ontario, 29–31 October 2004).

White, A., 'Religion, Politics and Society in Aberdeen, 1543–1593' (PhD dissertation, University of Edinburgh, 1985).

INDEX

For Product Safety Concerns and Information please contact our EU
representative GPSR@taylorandfrancis.com
Taylor & Francis Verlag GmbH, Kaufingerstraße 24, 80331 München, Germany

www.ingramcontent.com/pod-product-compliance
Ingram Content Group UK Ltd.
Pitfield, Milton Keynes, MK11 3LW, UK
UKHW021613240425
457818UK00018B/532